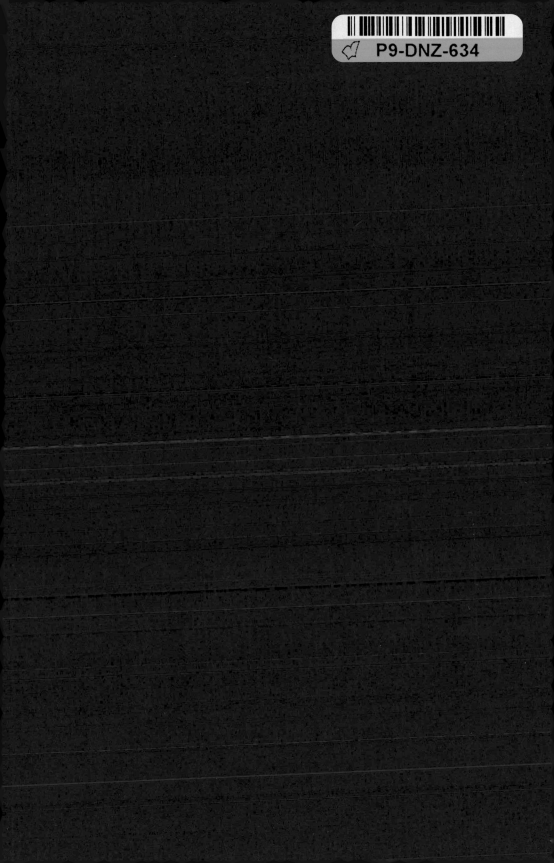
P9-DNZ-634

Intercollegiate Athletics
and the American University

John,

Still tilting with windmills . . .
All the best!

Jim Diotenda

Intercollegiate Athletics and the American University

A University President's Perspective

James J. Duderstadt

Ann Arbor

THE UNIVERSITY OF MICHIGAN PRESS

Copyright © by the University of Michigan 2000
All rights reserved
Published in the United States of America by
The University of Michigan Press
Manufactured in the United States of America
⊗ Printed on acid-free paper

2003   2002   2001   2000   4   3   2   1

A CIP catalog record for this book is available from the British Library.

Library of Congress Cataloging-in-Publication Data

Duderstadt, James J., 1942–
    Intercollegiate athletics and the American university : a university
president's perspective / James J. Duderstadt.
        p.   cm.
    Includes bibliographical references and index.
    ISBN 0-472-11156-6 (cloth : alk. paper)
    1. College sports—Corrupt practices—United States.   2. College
sports—United States—Management.   3. College sports—Social
aspects—United States.   4. College sports—Moral and ethical
aspects—United States.   I. Title.
    GV351.D83   2000   00-08203

To all of those Michigan coaches
and student-athletes who strive so
hard to achieve an appropriate balance
between athletics and academics

Preface

There is an old saying among college presidents that the modern university might be viewed as a fragile academic enterprise, delicately balanced between the medical center at one end of the campus and the athletic department at the other. The former can threaten the institution financially; the latter puts at risk the university's integrity, reputation, and academic priorities.

But I remember another saying even more appropriate, at least for the University of Michigan. One of my predecessors imparted these words of wisdom, which apparently have been passed along from one Michigan president to the next: The best way to keep from being consumed by athletics is to hope that the football team wins most of its games each year; but pray that Michigan never, *ever,* wins its last game. If the football team wins consistently, the alumni, students, and fans remain interested and supportive. But if it loses its last game, Michigan will never end the season ranked so high that folks take athletics too seriously.

Earlier presidents, apparently, had their prayers granted, at least in modern times. While Michigan was always highly competitive on the football field and frequently won the Big Ten championship, it had great difficulty in winning the last game of the season, which not infrequently occurred in the Rose Bowl. Unfortunately, my presidency got off to a rocky start in my first year with not only a Big Ten football championship and Rose Bowl win, but an NCAA basketball championship as well. It was all downhill from there. (My successor faces an even greater challenge. He began with both a national football championship and a national ice hockey championship in his first year, 1997!)

One of the frequent complaints heard from college coaches and athletic department staff is that university administrators rarely understand the nature, complexity, and pressures of today's inter-collegiate athletics. To some degree this is natural, since many academic leaders view college sports as a distraction from their primary responsibilities in areas such academic quality, faculty hiring, and private fund-raising. However the vast gulf separating the university administration and the athletic department on most campuses is also due to an intense desire for autonomy on the part of most athletic directors and coaches.

As I was to learn quickly when I became president, such independence of the athletic department, while perhaps a convenient tradition in years past, is a prescription for disaster in the complex political environment of the contemporary university. While it is tempting for academic administrators to regard intercollegiate athletics as merely a peripheral activity, far removed from the mainstream mission of the university, it is also clear that the unusual public visibility of big-time sports programs can place the university at considerable risk.

This book is intended to provide one former university president's evolving perspective on the fundamental issues that swirl about intercollegiate athletics today. Of course there have been many excellent books and articles written about this subject from an array of perspectives over the years. Historians such as Murray Sperber have placed today's concerns within the context of the historical origins. Distinguished columnists such as George Will and David Broder have seen in the problems of college sports broader issues facing our society. Even an occasional sports writer experiences an epiphany and trades in the customary promotional approach of sports journalism for a more hard-nosed investigative analysis. But the voices of university leaders have been strangely silent on these issues. Perhaps it is appropriate that the former president of a university long identified with "big-time college sports" weigh in on these matters.

While many of my conclusions echo those expressed by many others, my own views have been formed and shaped through thirty years of experiences as a faculty member, academic administrator, and president of the University of Michigan. Throughout its history

Michigan has been not only a flagship of public higher education in America, but also a leader in intercollegiate athletics. Yet the very scale and complexity of the institution sometimes magnifies issues to levels far beyond those experienced by most other institutions. Money, for example, tends to be measured in hundreds of millions of dollars. A typical student demonstration can involve thousands of participants, while attendance at football games in Michigan Stadium averages over 110,000. Controversies involving the university—in athletics or academics or faculty/student behavior—tend to appear in the national news media, not just the local papers. Partnerships with the private sector, whether with industrial corporations or athletic equipment manufacturers, tend to be approached as strategic alliances between organizations of comparable size, global scope, and, unfortunately, legal complexity. The political environment is both intense and unforgiving, whether at the national, state, local, or campus level.

Fortunately, the very complexity and comprehensive nature of the University of Michigan make it likely that many of the issues considered in this book will have relevance to other colleges and universities. Yet it should also be stated at the outset that this book is primarily concerned with the challenges faced by those institutions grouped into NCAA's Division I-A.

Let me warn the reader at the outset about another bias: my belief that intercollegiate athletics are and can continue to be an important part of higher education. College sports can provide an important educational opportunity to the student-athlete. They can act as a unifying force for the university community and beyond. Played with integrity and in line with the educational mission of our schools, college sports can serve both as entertainment and even as educational lessons for our broader society.

In fact, for most of college athletics the current models seem to achieve these objectives. Although the participants in sports programs such as swimming, gymnastics, softball, and crew may be remarkably talented athletes, they are first and foremost students, with their first priority being a college education. For most, academic priorities dominate athletic ambitions. While coaches of these sports are highly motivated to build winning programs, they also understand and support the academic goals of their student-athletes.

Yet two sports stand apart: football and basketball. These sports have become captured by the entertainment industry, commercialized and professionalized to the extreme. They now threaten not only the academic welfare of their participants but the integrity and reputation of the very institutions that conduct them, our colleges and universities. Driven by the insatiable public demand for entertainment, the commercial nature of the news, broadcasting, and entertainment industry, and the feverish hype of the sports press, our two most prominent college sports, football and basketball, have been transformed into big-time show business. Players and coaches have become celebrities. Athletic events have become media products. The objectives of these college sports activities have become market share and commercial value, and the welfare of their players as students has been largely ignored. Any educational mission—indeed, relevance of these programs to the rest of the university—has been subverted if not destroyed entirely.

Although the commercialization—and, on occasion, the corruption—of big-time college sports has been well recognized, there has been no slowing the mad dash toward even more professionalization. To be sure, the faculties of our universities have never been comfortable with big-time college sports and have been frequent critics, particularly during times of scandal. They have been joined in their concerns by some elements of the press—although rarely by the sports press, which all too frequently has assumed the role of promoter and apologist for the excesses of college sports. Even elected public leaders have raised concerns at times. But time after time college sports has deflected these criticisms and avoided any serious effort to de-emphasize the commercialism of the enterprise. The public's love of intercollegiate athletics, the media's influence, and the commercial power of the marketplace have overwhelmed attempts at reform.

Perhaps part of the reason is that we fail to recognize—or at least acknowledge—where the real problems lie. All too frequently we seek scapegoats rather than solutions. For example, it is customary and convenient to blame external forces such as the television networks, the sports apparel manufacturers, the sporting press, and alumni boosters and fans for the appalling state of big-time college sports. To be sure, these groups can be predators, exploiting college sports, their participants and their universities, for profit, fame, or personal enjoyment. So too, these media- and market-driven organizations are characterized by a culture alien to the university, with little understanding or sympathy for our academic mission. But their practices are only symptoms, not causes. Instead we should look within our institutions for both the source of the illness and the remedy.

Here, we might be tempted to blame those coaches who have been driven to excess by competitive ambition or who exploit the university for their personal gain. Sometimes we blame those athletes who see the university as no more than a convenient way station, a place to polish their athletic skills en route to a professional career. Or perhaps we single out those athletic directors who focus myopically on the financial bottom line or their personal visibility and power, willing to sell the integrity and reputation of their university to the highest bidder. But to use coaches, players, or athletic administrators as scapegoats is to ignore the fact that most in intercollegiate athletics are people of integrity, trying to do their best to succeed in a manner that falls within the rules and benefits their institutions, at least in the way they understand them.

Instead, it is my belief that the blame for the current corruption of college sports lies at the academic heart of the university itself, with its faculty, its governing boards, and, perhaps most of all, with its presidents. The faculty has largely abdicated its responsibility for student activities beyond the classroom, with intercollegiate athletics usually far removed from faculty interest or influence. University governing boards are all too often influenced by athletics boosters, sports media, or perhaps the personal interest and inappropriate involvement of some board members with intercollegiate athletics. And university presidents succumb to timidity and procrastination, unwilling to face up to the pressures and risks associated with reforming college sports.

To address these issues, this book has been organized in the following way. It begins with a personal perspective on college sports, very much formed from my experiences as a faculty member and then president of the University of Michigan. The second part of the book looks more closely at the reality of college sports today, its evolution over the years, its place within the university, and its governance and financing. The third part focuses on the fundamental flaws in the conduct of big-time college sports: its commercialization, the impact on the student-athlete, the occasional lapses in integrity, and the difficulty in controlling the enterprise. Finally, the book introduces a series of proposals designed to reform college sports to better protect the fundamental purpose and values of the university.

This book will argue that it is time for universities to reassert control over intercollegiate athletics and to realign them with the academic priorities of higher education. Key in this effort will be the difficult but essential task of resisting the pressure—whether from the media or politicians, trustees or alumni, fans or the public at large, or even some of our coaches, athletic directors, and university presidents—to transform college sports into an entertainment industry. This will certainly require us to de-emphasize many of our varsity sports programs. It may even require us to spin off those programs that have moved too far down the road as commercial enterprises—football and basketball—allowing them to become truly independent and professional activities.

Clearly such a restructuring of intercollegiate athletics will meet the fierce resistance of the sports establishment, those who profit most directly from the excesses in big-time college sports. University presidents must lead the way into this battle, even if it means that some will become casualties in the war to restore integrity to college sports and to higher education in America. In the end, the academy must recapture control of college sports by breaking it free from the grasp of the media, the entertainment industry, and the sports fans and reconnecting it with the educational mission of the university.

Put another way, it is my belief that it is time for universities to reestablish their own principles, objectives, and priorities for college sports. Our faculties, university leaders, and governing boards must then commit themselves to holding fast to these principles and objectives in the face of the enormous pressure that will be exerted by those who benefit from the commercial and professional nature of big-time college sports. In the end, intercollegiate athletics must reflect the fundamental academic values of the university. There is no other alternative acceptable to higher education.

Acknowledgments

Although the author accepts fully the responsibility for the content of this book, particularly its weaknesses and flaws, it is also important to acknowledge the impact that many people of considerable wisdom and experience have had on this project. As president, I had the privilege to work with three exceptional individuals who served as Michigan's athletic director: Bo Schembechler, Jack Weidenbach, and Joe Roberson. Although each brought quite different experiences and talents to the position, each taught me a great deal about college athletics, albeit from considerably different perspectives.

So too, the coaches and staff of the Michigan Department of Intercollegiate Athletics were important in shaping my views of intercollegiate athletics. They were dedicated professionals of great ability and integrity, loyal to the university, and deeply committed to the welfare of our student-athletes. As such, they frequently shared and shaped my own concerns about the growing commercialization of college sports.

My colleagues among Michigan's leadership team, particularly the executive officers of the university during my presidency, provided both important insight and key leadership. So too did many other members of the Michigan faculty, staff, and governance, including in particular Dee Eddington, Ed Wojtys, Don Brown, Jeff Long, Percy Bates, and Paul Brown. It is important to acknowledge as well the influence of many other university leaders, particularly those presidents and chancellors who served with me on the governing board of the Big Ten Conference, as well as Commissioner Jim Delany and the staff of the Big Ten Conference office. I should also acknowledge the considerable efforts of those who assisted in the preparation of the manuscript for this book: Liene Karels for design, Mary Miles and Clara Haggerty for clerical assistance, and Julie Steiff, Ann Curzon, and Elise Fraser for editing assistance.

Finally, let me acknowledge the impact of the other half of the presidential team, Anne Duderstadt, who through her role as First Lady of the University became a particularly important member of the Michigan athletics family. Her involvement with the families of coaches, staff, and students provided a strong sense of university support for the dedication and sacrifices required to build and sustain leading athletics programs of high integrity. Her perceptiveness and wisdom were critical in shaping my own views of both the importance and the challenges of college sports today. She was then and remains today one of Michigan athletics' most loyal fans.

Contents

PART I
Hail to the Victors

Chapter 1   Introduction

Mention Michigan to a sports fan, and the image that probably comes to mind is that of the university's football team storming onto the field wearing those ferocious maize-and-blue striped helmets. Fans think of our great rivalries with Ohio State and Notre Dame. They recall the names of such legendary Michigan sports figures as Yost, Crisler, Harmon, and Schembechler. Some may even remember one of our most famous alumni, Gerald R. Ford, as the Michigan football player who became president of the United States! Indeed, much of armchair America thinks of us first and foremost as a football school, even though the University of Michigan is widely regarded as one of the finest academic institutions in the world.

College sports are woven deeply into people's lives in university towns like Ann Arbor. Men (almost always men) sit for hours in bars or golf clubhouse locker rooms debating the wisdom of certain offensive formations or defensive strategies. They remember critical moments of critical games better than they remember events from their own lives: Michigan's great upset of Ohio State in 1969, or the catch by Desmond Howard that beat Notre Dame in 1992 and won him the Heisman Trophy, or Brian Griese leading an undefeated Michigan team to a Rose Bowl victory and a national championship in 1997, while his proud father Bob Griese called the television play-by-play. More broadly, college sports permeate these university communities as their culture revolves around these events, season by season: football in the fall, basketball and hockey in the winter, the NCAA tournaments in the spring. Merchants, restaurants, and hotels depend on football crowds. Alumni are bound to their institution by the common experience of returning each year for a football weekend or attending a bowl game or an NCAA tournament.

The Michigan football tradition

But our university communities feel the repercussions of athletics programs at an even deeper level. College sports can affect the morale, the psychological state, of our entire population. When Michigan is winning, on track for the Rose Bowl, life is upbeat in the university, in Ann Arbor, and across the state. But when Michigan is losing, clouds gather, people become depressed, and New Year's Day looks like a grim experience. Pity the poor Michigan coach—or president—who actually has a losing football season, subjecting all those Wolverine fans to a barren holiday season in the frigid Michigan winter.

For many, whether as athletes or spectators, intercollegiate athletics provide some of the very special moments in their lives. Athletic competition can teach both the athlete and the spectator some of the most enduring lessons of life: the importance of discipline, perseverance, and teamwork. Through sports we learn that

"The Catch": Desmond Howard's game-winning touchdown catch against Notre Dame in 1991. (UM Photo Services.)

the most important goals are achieved only through effort and sacrifice—and, sometimes, even these are not enough. They provide a sense of excitement, pride, and involvement for the entire, extended university community. They even help *make* that community by providing an important emotional bond among the diverse constituencies that identify with these ever-more complex social institutions we call universities.

The Dark Side of the Force

Yet today there is another, darker side of intercollegiate athletics, one that should give us all cause for serious concern. Many question whether the quasi-professional nature of college sports is consistent with our academic purpose. Some universities take advantage of student-athletes, exploiting their athletic talents for financial gain and public visibility, and tolerating low graduation rates and meaningless degrees in majors like general studies or recreational life. The perceived pressure to win at all costs can lead to cheating and scandal. We are occasionally embarrassed by misbehavior in college sports: players taunting one another, coaches engaging in tirades against officials, athletes getting into trouble with crime or drugs.

Of less public concern but of great concern to the academy is the gross overcommercialization of sports: the pressure to schedule events every night of the week to fill the schedule of the broadcasting networks, the hype and sensationalism generated by the sports press, the predatory behavior of sports agents, the advertising plastered over competitive venues and institutional images. The pressures generated by the commercialization of college sports can be seen all around us. Perhaps the most extreme example continues to be the NCAA basketball tournaments (now both men's *and* women's)—appropriately labeled March Madness—as frenzied broadcasters and writers chronicle each step to the Final Four—the "Sweet Sixteen," the "Elite Eight"—almost as if they were counting down to Armageddon. (Ironically enough, the count always seems to stop at four, almost as if the last step, the championship game, were an afterthought.) Both the public and the sports media continue to clamor for a national football championship playoff for NCAA Division I-A schools, despite university presidents' resistance because of the playoff's potential impact on academic schedules and university reputations. The desire to enhance the commercial appeal of sporting events has led to the realignment and dismantling of athletic conferences, sacrificing decades-long athletic rivalries for television market share. And then, of course, Nike's urging to "Just do it!" has led universities to accept the most extreme forms of offensive marketing to generate more licensing income.

The excessive commercialization of college sports threatens the academic priorities of the universities that host these programs. Our athletics programs have evolved far beyond their stated missions of providing an important learning and recreational experience for students and a unifying, community-building opportunity for spectators. Instead they have become entertainment businesses, competing as much for public exposure and commercial revenue as for victory on the playing field. The majority of the public believes that intercollegiate athletics are out of control and shows a widespread negative perception of sports programs. As former NCAA executive director Dick Schultz put it, "If you ask the average person what his perception of colleges athletics is, he'll tell you four things: Colleges make millions of dollars at the expense of the college athlete; all coaches cheat; athletes never graduate; and all athletes are drug addicts."[1] With over one-half of all Division I-A institutions receiving sanctions for violating NCAA regulations over the last decade, it is easy to understand the public's concerns.

Almost monthly a new book on the scandals of intercollegiate athletics appears. Many influential columnists, like David Broder and George Will, have taken a crack at intercollegiate athletics. Congressmen and legislators have repeatedly attempted to introduce legislation that would regulate programs.

Many agencies and organizations, ranging from the Carnegie Commission of the 1920s to the American Council on Education in the 1950s to the Knight Commission of the 1980s, have called for reform and made recommendations for change. The range of proposals runs the gamut. At one extreme are calls for returning to the so-called Ivy model—no athletic scholarships, no spring practice, no bowls—although the Ivy League itself acknowledges its institutions face many of the problems plaguing intercollegiate athletics nationwide. At the other extreme, some—including many members of the media—call for the complete professionalization of college sports with payment to players (so-called pay-for-play proposals).

Even within the NCAA itself, there have been fierce internal battles between reform-minded presidents and faculty and status quo–defending coaches and athletic directors. As a consequence of this division of opinion, the NCAA has largely avoided systemic reform and instead implemented wave after wave of rules and regulations governing the conduct of sports, resulting in a complex, hard to understand, unusable code of conduct. As the Knight Commission noted in 1993, "The NCAA manual more nearly resembles the IRS Code than it does a guide to action."[2] Unfortunately, but not surprisingly, this complex maze of regulations focuses almost entirely on the "athletic" side of the student-athlete, ignoring that these individuals are—or at least should be—first and foremost students. Also not surprisingly, since these rules generally ignore the primary purpose of a college education, the reform agendas have largely failed to constrain the commercial forces pulling sports farther and farther away from the university.

Michigan Athletics

Intercollegiate athletics programs have long been an important tradition of the University of Michigan. College sports attract more public visibility than any other university activity, with hundreds of thousands of spectators attending our athletic events and millions more watching on television across the nation. Although it is perhaps understandable that a large, successful intercollegiate athletics program such as Michigan's would dominate the local media, it also has farther-reaching visibility. Michigan receives far more ink in the national media for its activities on the field that it ever does for its classroom or laboratory activities. This media exposure is due in part to the university's long tradition of successful athletics programs of high integrity. It also stems from the increasingly celebrity character of college sports: successful and quotable coaches such as Bo Schembechler, flamboyant teams such as the Fab Five, and the extraordinary scale of Michigan athletics, with a football stadium now averaging 110,000 spectators a game.

When viewed from another perspective, however, intercollegiate athletics is really not a very large player in the university. After all, only about seven hundred of our thirty-seven thousand students are involved in varsity competition. While the $45 million budget of our athletic department is large relative to its peer programs at other universities, it is minuscule relative to the $3 billion budget of the university as a whole. And while many firmly believe that athletic competition can be a valuable educational experience for undergraduate students, so too can a vast array of other extracurricular opportunities such as the student newspaper, political organizations, or the Michigan Marching Band.

The Michigan athletics campus. (UM Photo Services.)

Yet, as any leader of an NCAA Division I-A institution will tell you, a university president ignores intercollegiate athletics only at great peril—both institutional and personal. The popularity of Michigan athletics is a double-edged sword. While it certainly creates great visibility for the university—after each Rose Bowl or Final Four appearance, the number of applications for admission surges—it also poses a significant threat to the institution. Every athletic department, no matter how committed and vigilant its leadership, can expect the occasional misstep that draws damaging bad press, and so it has been at Michigan. After all, we have many real and serious liabilities—most student-athletes are still in their teens and relatively immature; the great popularity of college sports attracts all manner of hangers-on to key programs, some well intentioned, some predatory; there is intense pressure from the sports media; unintentional rule violations are common.

Equally serious is the extraordinary emotional attachment that ordinarily rational people can develop toward college sports. We have all seen how many fans behave at sporting events, not simply cheering on the favored team, but taunting the opposition, berating officials, and even occasionally booing their own players and coaches. For many, this emotional involvement extends long after the moment of athletic competition, with misbehavior and even sports-driven riots spilling beyond the campuses into surrounding communities. After a series of disappointing seasons, boosters and alumni are not only likely to call for the firing of the coach, but will go after the athletic director and the president as well. One-dimensional views of the university through sports binoculars are easily conveyed to other fans, and to legislators and trustees as well—folks who have the power and sometimes the inclination to do serious damage to the institution in their desire to associate with winning programs.

For What Purpose? For Whose Benefit?

As a former student-athlete, as a faculty member, as an academic administrator, and, quite frankly, as a fan at the University of Michigan, I have long held the view that sports can contribute to the educational mission of the university. Competitive sports, whether at the intramural, club, or varsity level, can provide important educational experiences for students. Even big-time intercollegiate athletics, when kept in balance with academic life, can contribute in a positive way to a college education. Varsity sports can provide unifying events that pull together the extraordinary complex and diverse communities that make up the contemporary university. When they are conducted with integrity and in accord with our educational mission, college sports can provide students with opportunities to develop important traits such as dedication, sacrifice, and teamwork. Yet, as a university president, I also became convinced that intercollegiate athletics, as it is currently conducted and perceived, has the potential to do great harm to the university. The pressures it brings to bear upon the host institution threaten the far broader purpose and significance of higher education in America.

To be sure, big-time college sports has entertained the American public, but it has all too frequently done so at the expense of our colleges and universities, their students, faculty, and staff, and the communities they were created to serve. They have infected our academic culture with the commercial values of the entertainment industry. They have distorted our priorities through the disproportionate resources and attention given to intercollegiate athletics. They have distracted and in some cases destabilized the leadership of our academic institutions. They have exploited and, on occasion, even victimized players and coaches while creating a sense of cynicism on the part of the faculty and broader student body. Most significantly, big-time college sports have threatened the integrity and reputation of our universities, exposing us to the hypocrisy, corruption, and scandal that all too frequently accompany activities driven primarily by commercial value and public visibility.

What is at the heart of the problem? Is it simply the usual human frailties? Greed? Arrogance? Ignorance? While all of these are certainly contributing factors, the real problem lies not in any failure of human character but rather in the very nature of intercollegiate athletics today, with its very purpose. Big-time college athletics has little to do with the nature or objectives of the contemporary university. Instead, it is a commercial venture, aimed primarily at providing public entertainment for those beyond the campus and at generating rewards for those who stage it. The public, driven by the sports media and commercial interests, seeks from our universities entertainment through football and basketball, staged at a commercial level in every way comparable to professional leagues—except with the fiction that this can be provided through the use of young, "amateur," athletes who also happen to be college students.

As a result, college sports have become a major source of public entertainment. Coaches and players have become media celebrities. Dollars from television and licensing coupled with the escalating costs of mounting entertainment-quality athletic events have warped institutional priorities, forcing athletic directors to focus more on the bottom line than on student welfare, educational objectives, or integrity. And the media have created a feeding frenzy in which sports columnists and broadcasters have imitated gossip columnists in their efforts to pander to public curiosity and build personal reputation, market ratings, and advertising income. The importance of intercollegiate athletics has become distorted as it has changed from an extracurricular activity into a form of show business.

Let me hasten to add that for most of college athletics, in "nonrevenue" sports such as swimming and volleyball, soccer and cross-country, my concerns are minor. For the most part, athletes who participate in these sports are students, coaches are teachers, and academic priorities dominate athletic ambitions. Football and basketball are real exceptions in this regard—ironically the only two that trace their origins to the college campus itself rather than to broader society. These two sports have become so entangled with the efforts to provide mass entertainment for our society that they now threaten not only the viability of college sports, but more sweepingly the very institutions that host and sustain them, our colleges and universities.

The most fundamental question is why this particular form of public entertainment should be the responsibility of the university. Certainly the contemporary university engages in many forms of public service, such as the health care provided by our medical centers, the technology that is transferred from our research laboratories to industry, and the concerts provided by our music schools. But each of these activities has firm roots within the academic mission of the university. They are conducted by faculty and by students as a component of their educational mission. Big-time athletics is quite different, conducted largely as an independent, highly commercial entertainment business, administered by professionals with little relationship to the academic programs of the university, and increasingly performed by participants who are allowed to benefit educationally in only marginal ways from the academic programs of the university, and financially not at all from the commercial success of the college sports business.

Unfortunately, the traditional organizations that are supposed to guard the academic and amateur goals and values of college sports, the NCAA and the athletic conferences, have been largely ineffective. In part this is because these organizations are unwieldy and cumbersome. But more significantly, these organizations' efforts are unsuccessful precisely because they view their primary mission as promoting and marketing sports and protecting the enterprise from those who would threaten it with reform or de-emphasis. Even the powerful national associations of universities (including the American Council of Education and the Association of American Universities) that oversee the academic mission of the university system, have tended to keep their distance, assuming that the situation is simply intractable and that the national addiction to college sports is too strong.[3]

Most significantly, those people charged with the responsibility for the academic integrity of the university have largely looked away from intercollegiate athletics. Although the faculty played important roles in the evolution and governance of intercollegiate athletics in its early years, today most faculty members have become detached from sports, aside from their role as spectators, just as they have abandoned any substantive role in student extracurricular activities. Few faculty members even come into contact with the student-athletes involved in big-time sports programs, since these students are frequently channeled into specially designed academic programs such as physical education or sports management.

Governing-board members have more direct involvement with intercollegiate athletics, since they are sometimes held accountable for both the competitive success and the integrity of their university's programs. However, many trustees are strongly influenced by athletics boosters—whether alumni, politicians, or influential fans—as well as by the sports media and perhaps their own personal interest and involvement in college sports. They, too, tend to resist proposals for major reform.

Perhaps the most serious concern, however, is the laissez-faire attitude of most university presidents toward intercollegiate athletics. Though most recognize the downside of big-time college sports, many are also unwilling to take on the challenge, to face the risks, associated with serious reform of football and basketball. After all, they argue, there are many other battles to fight on behalf of their institution. Why should they risk their presidencies on such a dangerous and thankless quest as recapturing control of intercollegiate athletics from the powerful forces of the entertainment industry, the sports media, and the public at large?

A Time of Change, a Time of Opportunity

Concerns about intercollegiate athletics are not new. Each generation calls for reform; strong public demand and media and commercial pressure doom each of these reform efforts. Little wonder that most universities have chosen the path of benign neglect, tolerating this perverse commercial aberration in the university's portfolio and hoping that it causes little lasting harm.

But our social institutions are now changing more rapidly than ever, and we can no longer afford such passivity. Corporations have been restructured, governments have been streamlined, and even venerable institutions such as the university are being asked to transform themselves to better serve a changing society. We are challenged to reemphasize the centrality and quality of our educational mission, to provide the broader educational opportunities needed by a knowledge-intensive society, to provide the new knowledge and innovation required for economic competitiveness, and to do all of this while controlling expenditures—to do more with less.

We face a broad consensus, both among leaders of American higher education and in our various external constituencies, that we must see our universities through a period of transformation if they are to meet the challenges, opportunities, and responsibilities before them. We can take some comfort in the idea that change has always been key to the survival and vitality of the university, even as it sought to preserve and propagate our intellectual achievements. The university has endured as an important social institution for a millennium precisely because it has evolved in profound ways to serve the changing world around it.

This pivotal moment in higher education provides the context for this discussion of intercollegiate athletics. As we question all other aspects of the university, from undergraduate education to professional training, from basic research to technology transfer, from civic responsibilities to individual benefit, is it not also appropriate to examine peripheral activities such as intercollegiate athletics? While change can be a challenge, it can also be an opportunity. Given all of these pressures, it is clearly time to take this opportunity to reevaluate the character and the conduct of intercollegiate athletics. It is also time to examine its very relevance to the changing mission of the university.

Chapter 2   Go Blue

It doesn't take long for newcomers to the University of Michigan campus to discover the centrality of intercollegiate athletics in the life of the institution. The local newspapers and television broadcasts are saturated with news about Michigan teams, coaches, and players. Michigan insignia are plastered on sweatshirts and T-shirts, caps and scarves, coffee cups and car bumpers, billboards and street signs. Anything and everything is a potential advertisement for Michigan athletics—and a source of licensing income for the athletic department. It is very hard to avoid Michigan athletics if you work at the university or live in Ann Arbor, since both communities come largely to a standstill—rather, a gridlock—during major sporting events. Of course, intercollegiate athletics has also been a long-standing tradition at the university. Michigan has been both fortunate and envied for its unusual ability to combine world-class academic programs with nationally competitive programs in college sports. Beyond that, Michigan has always played a leadership role in intercollegiate athletics through the success and integrity of its programs and its influence within the Big Ten Athletic Conference and the NCAA.

Therefore it seems both appropriate and instructive to begin a discussion of intercollegiate athletics by selecting the University of Michigan as a case study. By focusing on a single institution, we can better understand the nature of college sports, its organization and financing, its culture, and its relationship to the university and the rest of society. This chapter has been constructed primarily as a series of vignettes, impressions of college sports at a major university, as seen from the perspective of the president. These are intended to illustrate both the character and complexity of college

The Michigan Wolverines take the field. (UM Photo Services.)

sports and to lay the foundation for a more thorough analysis of the many issues swirling about them.

First, Some History

Far more histories have been written about Michigan athletics than have been written about the university itself. The names of Michigan's sports heroes—Yost, Crisler, Harmon—are better known than any members of Michigan's distinguished faculty or its presidents. Tellingly, most of these histories have been written by sportswriters, former athletic directors, coaches, or fans. Hence it seems both appropriate and amusing to provide a brief historical corrective from the perspective of a longtime faculty member (me).

Although the legends of the good old days of Michigan athletics make enjoyable reading, my purpose is better served by beginning somewhat later, in the mid-1960s, when Michigan athletics, and college sports more generally, began their mad dash toward the cliff of commercialization.[1] During today's heady times of national championships and lucrative television and licensing contracts, Michigan fans sometimes forget that the university's athletics programs have not always been dominant. During the 1960s, the Michigan football program had fallen on hard times, with typical stadium attendance averaging sixty to seventy thousand per game (about two-thirds the capacity of Michigan Stadium). Michigan State University, just up the road, drew most of the attention with its powerful football teams—actually, this was part of its president's strategy to transform what had once been Michigan Agricultural College into a major university. Furthermore, student interest on activist campuses such as Michigan's had shifted during the 1960s from athletics to political activism, with great causes such as racial discrimination and an unpopular war in Vietnam to protest.

There were, nevertheless, a few bright spots in Michigan's athletic fortunes. Michigan's basketball team had enjoyed considerable success in the mid-1960s, with Cazzie Russell leading the team to the NCAA championship game, only to lose to an upstart UCLA team (which would then dominate the sport for the next decade). Largely as a consequence of this success, the university used student-fee-financed bonds[2] to build a new basketball arena, Crisler Arena, named after former football coach and athletic director Fritz Crisler.[3] This facility was known to many as "the house that Cazzie built."

Some of the other athletics programs were also successful. The ice hockey team won the national championship in 1964. Swimming began what was to become a three-decade-long domination of the Big Ten Conference. There were considerable accomplishments in other sports such as wrestling, track, and gymnastics. But at Michigan, football was king, and when the football fortunes were down, students and fans were apathetic about Michigan athletics.

Former UM president Harlan Hatcher congratulates Michigan basketball great Cazzie Russell during the retirement of his basketball number. (UM Photo Services.)

This began to change in the late 1960s. Although many attribute Michigan's turnaround to a new athletic director, Don Canham, reputed to be the shrewd marketing genius who transformed Michigan athletics into a commercial juggernaut, most of us on the faculty saw the situation differently. Following the advice of the former athletic director, Fritz Crisler, Canham recruited a talented young football coach, Bo Schembechler, who revitalized the Michigan program in his first year, beating Ohio State and going to the Rose Bowl.[4] The sports scene in southeastern Michigan strongly supports winners, and within a couple of years, Michigan Stadium began to sell out on a regular basis. It does not take a rocket scientist—or a Michigan faculty member, for that matter—to realize that if one can regularly fill the largest football stadium in the country with paying customers, prosperity soon follows. And indeed it did, since year after year Michigan fielded nationally ranked football teams.

The annual matchup between Michigan and Ohio State, often personified as a battle between Bo Schembechler and Woody Hayes, soon grew to mythical proportions. Fans experienced some initial frustration because of a Big Ten Conference rule that allowed only the conference champion to compete in a bowl game, the Rose Bowl. However the quality of the Michigan and Ohio State teams during the early 1970s soon forced the Big Ten to relax this rule, and Michigan began to add a bowl game to its schedule every year.

To be sure, Canham was inventive. He began to market Michigan football in sophisticated ways. He arranged for planes to pull banners advertising Michigan football over Detroit's Tiger Stadium

Former athletic director Don Canham. (UM Photo Services.)

during the 1968 World Series. He launched the practice of mass-mailed advertising and catalogs of souvenir items. Michigan athletics began to function like a business, complete with marketing, advertising, and promotion, along with the development of new commercial activities. To many, Canham became the prototype of the athletic director–CEO who would drive college sports into a commercial entertainment industry.

During the 1970s and 1980s, for all intents and purposes, Michigan athletics was a one-sport program. Football ruled the roost, and other sports were secondary priorities. Taking a more objective look at this era, one cannot help but note that while several of the men's programs competed effectively within the Big Ten Conference, none were regarded as national leaders. In fact, Michigan went twenty-five years without a national championship in any sport, from 1964, when Al Renfrew's hockey team won the NCAA tournament, until 1989, when Steve Fisher's basketball team won the Final Four. Even the football team, generally nationally ranked during the season, always fell short by season's end, either losing to Ohio State in the season finale or in its annual bowl appearance.

While Michigan paved the way in commercializing college sports and generated new revenues, this leadership was not beneficial to the university's image and reputation, at least in the faculty's view. The athletic department's increasing autonomy largely eliminated any substantive role of the faculty in governing intercollegiate athletics. While other universities moved rapidly to introduce varsity programs for women, Michigan remained largely fossilized in a prehistoric state of football-dominated men's sports. In fact, in the 1970s Michigan became the focus of one of the early federal investigations of gender discrimination in intercollegiate athletics under Title IX of the Higher Education Act.

Although in theory the athletic director reported directly to the president, Canham resented any higher authority, bolstering the perception of the athletic department as an independent entity. Canham was also autocratic, both in his management of the athletic department and in his efforts to keep the faculty and the university administration far away from influence or control. But financial and structural factors also led to this separation. The financial independence of the athletic department, due almost entirely to Schembechler's success in filling Michigan Stadium on football weekends, led the department to believe that it was administratively separate from the rest of the university and therefore not subject to the rules and policies governing other units. Although criticized from time to time for the increasing independence and commercialism of Michigan athletics, Canham usually shrugged it off, pointing to Schembechler's winning football teams and the department's financial health.[5]

The athletic department routinely ignored university regulations and policies concerning personnel, financial accountability, and conflict of interest. And, most significantly, the vast gulf between the athletic department and the university isolated student-athletes from academic life and coaches and staff from the rest of the university community. This unusual degree of independence led to scandal in the 1980s. The university experienced the most serious rules violation in its modern history, with a major scandal in the baseball program involving slush funds, illegal payments to players, and recruiting violations.

When I became president of the university in 1988, it was clear that steps needed to be taken to address these problems. The high degree of public exposure of the university's athletics programs was a double-edged sword that both advanced and damaged the institution. As a former college football player, I had some understanding of both the challenges and the opportunities of intercollegiate athletics, including the difficulty in balancing the values and culture of academics with the values and culture of competitive athletics. Apart from my own personal experience with college sports, changes at the conference and NCAA level required presidents to play a far more active role in intercollegiate athletics. The NCAA had adopted a fundamental principle that institutional control and accountability of athletics rested with the presidents. Furthermore, in the late 1980s, the Big Ten Conference filed legal papers to become a nonprofit corporation, with the university presidents serving as its board of directors. This new conference structure demanded both policy and financial oversight by the presidents.

I was not alone in my belief that the athletic department needed to be brought back into the mainstream of university life. Working closely with the athletic directors who succeeded Canham—Bo Schembechler, Jack Weidenbach, and Joe Roberson—my administration took a series of actions in the late 1980s and 1990s to better align athletics with the academic priorities of the university. We tried to ensure that student-athletes received the same educational and extracurricular opportunities as other Michigan students. Coaches were encouraged in their roles as teachers and provided with more employment security as staff members. We developed clear policies in admissions, academic standing, substance abuse, and student behavior that were consistent with the rest of the university. While an active presidential role helped restore and maintain the integrity of Michigan athletics, it was sometimes not well understood or accepted by the old guard.

At the same time, we took steps to secure the financial integrity of Michigan athletics. The athletic department began to apply cost-containment methods to its operations, and a major fund-raising program was launched. The department developed more sophisticated strategies for licensing. A sizeable reserve fund was built to serve as a hedge against a downturn in revenue. Finally, the university invested in major improvements in the athletics facilities, including rebuilding Michigan Stadium (returning to natural grass and repairing the stadium's infrastructure), new facilities for swimming, gymnastics, ice hockey, tennis, and track, and new fields for women's soccer, field hockey, and softball.

During this period the university finally began to take women's athletics seriously by providing women with the same opportunities for varsity competition as men. Major investments were made in existing women's programs as well as in new programs (soccer and rowing). In fact, despite earlier decades of neglect of women's athletics, Michigan became one of the first major universities in the nation to make a public commitment to achieving full gender equity in intercollegiate athletics by the late 1990s.

Michigan also provided leadership at the conference and national level. It played a key role in restructuring revenue-sharing agreements within the Big Ten, by helping to better position the conference with respect to television agreements, and by building a stronger alliance with the Pac-10 Conference. At the national level, Michigan strongly supported the effort to gain presidential control over intercollegiate athletics and to restructure the NCAA.

We also began to see improvements in Michigan's overall competitiveness. While once Michigan had been content to be successful primarily in a single sport, football, during the 1990s it began to compete at the national level across its full array of twenty-three varsity programs. It began to rank each year among the top institutions for the national all-sports championship (the Sears Trophy). During the decade from 1988 to 1998, Michigan went to five Rose Bowls and won a national championship (1997) in football; three Final Fours and a national championship (1989) in men's basketball; and four Frozen Fours and two championships in ice hockey (1996 and 1998). Michigan teams won over fifty Big Ten championships during this period, dominating the Big Ten in men's and women's swimming (winning the NCAA championship in men's swimming), men's and women's cross-country, women's gymnastics, men's and women's track, and women's softball. The decade saw some of the most exciting moments in Michigan's long sports tradition, including two Heisman trophies (Desmond Howard and Charles Woodson) and a number of Olympians.

On one hand, Michigan athletics had never been more successful. The success and integrity of its athletics programs, coupled with their extraordinary popularity in both the electronic and print media, positioned Michigan as the model for college sports. The Michigan insignia dominated the sales of athletic apparel worldwide and led to a controversial marketing agreement with Nike, the sporting-goods company, that set the model for similar agreements with other leading universities.

On the other hand, Michigan's public profile was causing serious strains. The heightened visibility of Michigan athletics, particularly in the marquee sports of football and men's basketball, accompanied by the ever-escalating expectations on the part of fans, put great pressure on both coaches and players alike. After five Big Ten championships in a row and the entrance of Penn State into the conference, the football team experienced a series of mediocre seasons ("mediocre" for Michigan meant winning eight or nine games a season and appearing in a second-tier holiday bowl). In basketball, Steve Fisher continued to recruit top talent after the Fab Five,[6] but his teams never were able to win the Big Ten championship or return to the Final Four. Each misstep by a student-athlete or coach, the inevitable defeats that characterize every leading program in off years, or the loss of a key recruit resulted in a torrent of adverse media coverage. The sports media, which had been strong Michigan boosters during the championship years, were now viciously critical of these same programs and coaches as they struggled through occasionally mediocre seasons. The unrealistic expectations of fans, coupled with the ruthless criticism of the sports media, soon pushed both Michigan football and basketball to a crisis.

Football was the first target. Media pressure brought Michigan's football coach, Gary Moeller, to the breaking point, leading to his controversial resignation in 1995. Steve Fisher was the second casualty when the Detroit papers published a series of articles based on anonymous allegations that, unknown to Fisher, a local booster had been slipping cash to Michigan basketball players. Although an investigation was unable to substantiate any more than very minor infractions (e.g., giving a birthday cake to a player and providing a parent with a ride to a game), the pressure became so intense that a new athletic director decided to fire Fisher, much to the consternation of Michigan fans and players. Both instances illustrate the hazards of leading highly visible college sports programs, particularly in an intensely competitive and unforgiving sports media environment.

Season by Season

In preparation for our later discussions, it is useful to consider in more detail the diverse nature of the varsity sports programs conducted on college campuses today. College sports follow the seasons, influenced not only by the weather but by the university calendar. One of the best ways to understand the nature and diversity of intercollegiate athletics is therefore to trace college sports through the various seasons of the academic calendar.

Fall is a time of new beginnings for university life. College towns and campuses fill once again with returning students and faculty after the summer doldrums, bringing with them excitement and enthusiasm. Michigan falls are joyful, with clear blue skies and brilliant fall foliage. As winter approaches, university life moves into more serious academic activities, into the classrooms, libraries, laboratories, and concert halls. Although the days get shorter, the academic pace quickens and the workload intensifies. The holiday season brings examinations and, usually, a trip to a football bowl game. January, February, and March are bitterly cold; the sun disappears and activities move indoors, except for the occasional student demonstration. April brings spring, hope, an occasional NCAA basketball or hockey tournament, and in early May, commencement.

Fall Sports

A college football weekend has become a tradition of the fall, in a sense, an American holiday for its participants. It is a community experience, drawing tens of thousands of fans together in a festival, in many ways designed as much to celebrate the joys of a fall weekend as to focus on athletic competition. In fact, while some spectators do come primarily to see the game, many others come to enjoy the spectacle, the tailgate parties, the bands, and the crowds.

Much of life in Ann Arbor and the university during the fall—social, economic, and even political—revolves around football weekends, and Ann Arbor's population doubles on a football Saturday. Most of the university's "development" events (a university code word for fund-raising) occur around football weekends. Alumni reunions, visiting committees, major fund-raising events, cultivation of politicians, and other forms of university advancement activities all occur on the Thursday through Saturday of football weekends. The reason is simple: many people appreciate the opportunity to visit Ann Arbor and experience the pageantry and excitement of a Michigan football game.

Although most armchair fans see such an event as simply another televised football game, it is much, much more to those who come to Ann Arbor to experience the event in person. The town is alive with activity, student pep rallies, fraternity and sorority parties, concerts, plays, and much more, during the days leading up to the weekend. The "game" itself generally starts early in the morning as thousands of cars, vans, and mobile homes gather about the stadium for tailgate parties. In fact, there are certain areas set aside, such as the Victors Club parking area adjacent to the stadium, where those who are sufficiently supportive of Michigan football (in a financial sense) have reserved parking to set up their tents, tables and chairs, barbecue grills, and the other necessities of tailgating life. Many groups have special tents set up around the stadium, some in parking areas, others on the Michigan golf course. Others arrive in specially designed vehicles, mobile homes and the like, all equipped for the tailgate experience.

Ironically, this festival atmosphere saps from Michigan football much of the intensity of other sports. To be sure, there are moments of high drama, but in part because of the way in which the game flows, with one team or the other on offense far from the goal line, the crowd can become detached. Many other amusements vie for the fans' attention: the band, the cheerleaders, and the antics of the students. In fact, if the game is rather uninteresting, which can happen if Michigan gets a big lead, the crowd frequently begins to entertain itself by starting "the wave."

Michigan's gigantic football stadium itself plays a critical role in sports at the university. Michigan Stadium, named the "Big House" by sportscaster Keith Jackson, has long been the largest football stadium in the nation, averaging well over one hundred thousand in attendance per game for the past three decades. Although most major NCAA Division I-A universities have large football stadiums—indeed, this is one of the requirements for belonging to the division—few approach the megasize of the Big House. This gigantic stadium itself creates the sense of spectacle, a feeling of excitement, that animates Michigan football.

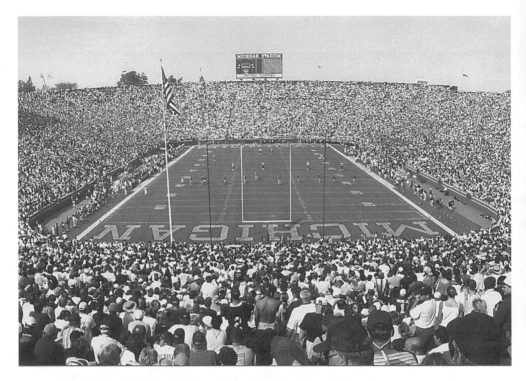

The "Big House": Michigan Football Stadium. (UM Photo Services.)

The stadium was the creation of the legendary Michigan football coach and athletic director Fielding Yost. It was built in the 1920s by hollowing out a huge bowl south of the campus, and then building stadium seating for 70,000 fans—then the largest in the nation. Yost was a visionary who had the stadium designed with conduits for wires, in the event that radio would someday be used to broadcast the games. He also made certain that footings were poured that could support the addition of a deck for more seating. Over the years, a steel superstructure was built to allow the addition of another 30,000 seats, and a large press box was added.

Although Michigan Stadium has been the largest athletic facility in the nation, from time to time it is challenged by other universities (most recently, the University of Tennessee, which expanded its stadium to 107,000 in 1997). Usually an ambitious athletic director then responds by enlarging Michigan Stadium yet again to regain the attendance record, most recently expanding the stadium from 105,000 to 111,000 in the euphoria following Michigan's national football championship in 1997.

The other fall sports stand in sharp contrast to the spectacle of football. To be sure, a sport like soccer may someday rival college football in popularity, drawing the sort of interest it has in the rest of the world. Even today, soccer is far more popular than football as a participatory sport at the grade school and high school level. Yet it is still at an early stage at most universities. Michigan elevated its women's soccer team from club to varsity status in 1994, as one of its steps to achieve gender equity in sports.[7] In 1998 it announced plans to do the same for men's soccer.

Women's soccer and field hockey are becoming increasingly popular as fall sports. The university built new fields for each sport—natural turf for soccer and artificial turf for field hockey. But at this early stage, while the fields, equipment, and team facil-

The women's soccer team. (UM Photo Services.)

ities are of very high quality, there is little provision made for spectators. The games are usually played on weekends or in the late afternoon, and typically a few hundred fans will show up. Many of them are local parents and grade school players learning the sport. While these crowds are small, they are loyal and enthusiastic. And they represent the future.

Volleyball can be livelier, since it is played in a special arena designed for that purpose, with seating for one thousand or so around the court. (Actually, the arena was once our competition swimming pool, which was redesigned when a new swimming natatorium was constructed.) It seems unfortunate that volleyball is played in the fall, since it is an indoor sport at a time when most folks want to be outside, fall being our best season weather-wise. Although the sport is rather new at Michigan, it does attract good crowds, and the action can be intense.

The ultimate fall sport is cross-country. At Michigan, cross-country meets are held on our golf course, which is beautiful in the fall colors. The problem, of course, is that the length and hilly terrain of the course make it a very difficult sport for a spectator to follow. You can see the runners start off together and then disappear over a hill. Twenty minutes or so later, they reappear one by one to cross the finish. That is about it for the spectator—the beginning and the end. Hence, although Michigan always has some outstanding athletes participating in the sport, the crowds are generally very small. Yet the sport has become an important tradition.

Winter Sports

As the days grow shorter and the leaves disappear, the university braces itself for winter, and for work, since November through March is the heart of the academic calendar. Winters in Michigan can be rugged. The temperature usually drops below freezing by Thanksgiving and sometimes does not thaw out again until March. The Arctic clipper sweeping across the Great Lakes can be ferocious. Even when Michigan is not in the deep freeze, winters are wet and overcast. The phrase "good, gray Michigan" is apt. Winter is just the kind of season when one wants to stay home, curled up in front of a warm fire.

In the cold and wet gloom of a midwestern winter, college

The women's cross-country team. (UM Photo Services.)

sports give one an excuse to get out and see others—albeit protected from the elements in sports arenas. Since there are no indoor facilities that can accommodate the huge crowds drawn to football, college sports in winter take on the feel of a three-ring circus, since so many competitive events occur simultaneously. Basketball, ice hockey, swimming, gymnastics, wrestling—each draws its own fans and has developed its unique culture.

Perhaps it is this need for shelter from the elements that contributes to the character of winter sports. Yet, ironically, winter is probably Michigan's best season in terms of team performance, with programs such as men's basketball, ice hockey, men's and women's swimming, and women's gymnastics generally being nationally ranked.

Perhaps most visible among the winter sports is men's basketball. Although the sport is played in Crisler Arena, which seats over twelve thousand, there is a certain intimacy and a decided inten-

Good, gray Michigan.
(UM Photo Services.)

sity to the sport. Unlike football, basketball fans can see the faces of the players. The crowd identifies with the team members as individuals. The action is fast-paced, with sharp swings in momentum. No matter how much of a lead one team has, there is a chance the other team will come back to create an exciting finish.

Because of this visibility of players and fans, basketball crowds have a different character. Sometimes it seems as if many fans come to be seen, to be a part of the spectacle themselves. Fans' dress is a lot more upscale—even in the worst weather. The particular style of Michigan basketball has also contributed to this theatrical approach. Michigan has long played a free-wheeling, improvisational style of basketball, perhaps best epitomized by the

Basketball in Crisler Arena. (UM Photo Services.)

Fab Five. While such a style can be nerve-wracking to watch, it is nevertheless very entertaining.

Despite having one of the most successful and entertaining basketball programs in the nation for the past decade, the team almost never plays to a full house, even though most games are announced as sellouts. In part, this is because for the past several years essentially all Michigan basketball games have been televised. On cold winter nights, it is very tempting to stay in and watch the game on television. But the real reason for the muted frenzy surrounding Michigan basketball, unlike other high-profile schools such as Indiana, Duke, and North Carolina, is that Michigan remains a football school in the minds of most fans. Basketball is the winter diversion, but never their prime interest.

There is one exception to the supremacy of football: ice hockey. No sport has a more loyal or fanatic following in Ann Arbor. Michigan plays its games in Yost Arena, a onetime basketball field house that has been renovated to accommodate hockey and the six thousand fans who turn out for every game to cheer on the team. And cheer they do, with their own humorous and occasionally bawdy style. When the visiting team is introduced, the student fans hold newspapers in front of their faces, yelling after each name is announced, "Who cares?!!!" When Michigan scores, they yell at the opposing goalie, "Sieve, sieve, sieve! It's all your fault! It's all your fault!"—sometimes tossing kitchen sieves onto the ice. The repertoire of highly specific cheers occurs perfectly in sync with the action on the ice, and it seems that everybody is an expert on the game. This enthusiasm is stimulated not just by the team's remarkable success. It reflects both the enjoyment fans take in this fast and sometimes violent game, and a certain esprit de corps that has long been part of college hockey.

The team itself is fascinating in its international diversity. American colleges have long recruited large numbers of Canadian players, many from small towns, who benefit greatly from the educational opportunities at universities like Michigan. Increasingly there are international students from Sweden, Russia, and the Eastern European countries that have built strong hockey programs.

A strong international flavor also characterizes men's and women's swimming. Michigan has long had a reputation as a

Ice hockey in Yost Arena. (UM Photo Services.)

The women's swimming team. (UM Photo Services.)

national leader in swimming and diving, and its coaches have been active in the Olympic Games. As a result, they are able to attract outstanding swimmers from all over the world, many of whom later swim for their own countries in the Olympics. In fact, the coaches will occasionally take the Michigan teams to train in exotic locations such as Hawaii or Australia, to provide an unusual opportunity for their student-athletes and to build their visibility for recruiting. The opening of a new Olympic-class swimming facility for competition and training in 1989 contributed to the attractiveness of the program.

Despite the success of men's and women's swimming in dominating the Big Ten for many years and competing every year for the national championship against the leading teams in the nation, they are not big draws in Ann Arbor. There are many parents in attendance, along with student friends, but rarely a crowd of more than a few hundred, even for major events such as the Women's NCAA Championship, hosted by Michigan in 1995. Perhaps the most excitement occurs in an Olympic year, when the coaches groom their best swimmers for the Olympic Games, usually giving preparation for the conference and national championships a lower priority.

Another Olympic sport of increasing popularity at Michigan is women's gymnastics. During the early 1990s, Michigan hired a talented coach who rebuilt the gymnastics program, recruiting top gymnasts from North America, and developing a program that now competes year after year for the national championship. While women's gymnastics is an Olympic sport, like swimming and diving, at the college level it does not have the direct link to the Olympics that characterizes swimming. The scoring in Olympic gymnastics places a high premium on acrobatics rather than grace and style, making it more suitable for very young and small gymnasts. While women college gymnasts are not large, their size and physical development makes it very difficult for them to compete under current Olympic standards. Gymnastics crowds are also quite unusual. Since it is such a popular sport for young girls, the meets are generally packed with school-age gymnasts and their parents. But there are also other students, including a number of gigantic football players who seem to love to watch gymnastics.

What about men's gymnastics? Although Michigan's team had been highly successful at the conference and national level, in 1994 the athletic department made the controversial recommendation that the varsity program be discontinued and men's gymnastics be converted into a club sport. This was viewed by some as an effort to improve the gender balance among varsity sports by reducing the number of male athletes. However, the real motivation was the declining status of men's gymnastics at the college level, and Michigan was following the lead of many colleges and universities that had eliminated their programs or converted them into club sports. The reason was simple: the physical difficulty of the events performed in the men's programs put adolescent boys at considerable risk, so most high schools had eliminated their programs. As a result, only about thirty-five colleges still had men's gymnastics programs.

However, as is generally the case whenever a program is proposed for downgrading or elimination, there was considerable resistance to the athletic department's recommendation. After a few years of compromise in which the program retained its varsity classification, but without athletic scholarships, the athletic department recanted and restored the sport to full varsity status. The men's gymnastics team went on to win the NCAA championship in 1999.

Wrestling has also traditionally been quite strong at Michigan and within the Big Ten, but without high visibility. The new Keen Arena provides an outstanding venue for the team, but in the face of so many other competing programs, it is difficult to generate a large following. Wrestling ran into serious problems in 1998 when a young wrestler died after a strenuous workout trying to make the weight required for a match the next day.

Women's basketball was singled out for major focus as an important element of the university's commitment to achieving gender equity. Michigan had long had a women's program, but it had never been given high priority or visibility. There was a small cadre of extremely loyal fans, but the women's team had never enjoyed major success. Injuries and dropouts decimated the early teams. The strong competition within the Big Ten made it even more difficult to climb the steep hill toward success, and throughout the 1990s the team generally finished at or near the bottom of the conference. Yet hopes for success and the fans' interest continued to build. Many of the coaches would bring their families to the women's games, creating an athletic department community to cheer the program on. Finally, in 1996, a coaching change was made, the team began to improve, and the crowds began to build to several thousand per game. However, in sharp contrast to the men's game, which had acquired an upscale, theatrical character, the women's events were still a family affair, with lots of school-age children in attendance.

Spring Sports

A university approaches spring with mixed enthusiasm. The end of winter and the transition from gray slush to green growth is welcome. Yet spring also signals the approaching end of the academic calendar, commencement, and the departure of students and faculty. Spring is a strange time for sports at northern schools like

The women's basketball team. (UM Photo Services.)

Michigan. The spring sports are among the most popular in America—baseball and softball, track and field, golf, tennis, and crew—yet university interest in these programs always remains quite low.

This lack of support is due in part to the fact that these are outdoor sports. In the Big Ten universities' northern climate, nature remains quite severe until April, in sharp contrast to southern or western schools, which can effectively practice year-round and compete outdoors from the beginning of the season. As a result, northern teams must travel south for games and meets during the early months of the season, and then suffer from unpredictable weather when they finally return to compete at home. By the time it becomes warm enough in Michigan, the academic year is almost over. Students and faculty are turning their attention to finals and commencement, and fans are absorbed in championship playoffs in professional basketball and ice hockey.

Hence, while Michigan's spring sports are highly competitive and involve some of its most talented student-athletes, they are almost invisible. There are community members who love to wander out on a sunny spring day to see a baseball game or a track meet. But this is probably more serendipity than loyalty.

This is not to say that Michigan de-emphasizes its spring sports. During the 1990s, the university built a new women's softball stadium, rebuilt its golf course and its indoor and outdoor varsity tracks, and constructed a world-class tennis center. Furthermore, many of the spring sports programs have been quite successful.

During the 1990s, the women's softball program began to dominate the Big Ten Conference and compete each year in the College World Series. Like other spring sports, the softball program would reach its stride each season just about the time the academic term was ending and students were leaving the campus. Yet it had a loyal following of local fans.

The Tisch-Ford Tennis Center

Women's softball. (UM Photo Services.)

Baseball has had a long tradition at Big Ten universities such as Michigan. Yet it faces two formidable challenges. First, like other spring sports, it must contend with a season that starts in late winter, long before the weather permits outdoor play at northern institutions. As a result, college baseball is dominated by southern schools that can play year-round. Second, college baseball has been largely decimated by the professional leagues. It is common for the best college baseball players to be drafted and signed by professional clubs early in their college careers. This situation is compounded by the minor-league system, which competes for players with colleges. Although there have been attempts to negotiate an arrangement to allow baseball players to finish their amateur careers and college education, professional baseball has been largely unresponsive. Hence college baseball faces an unusual level of turnover among players.

The Michigan golf teams compete on one of the finest golf

courses in America. It was created in the 1920s by the famous Scottish golf course designer Alistair McKenzie. McKenzie designed only seven courses in America, among them the Masters at Augusta and Cypress Point in Monterey. In the 1990s, with the help of private gifts, the university completely renovated the course and restored its original design and difficulty.

Men's and women's crew have long been popular spring sports at the club level at Michigan. Students would endure incredible hardships to compete in these sports, rarely having quality equipment, almost never having the resources to respond to the great student interest. Frequently one would see members of the rowing teams selling raffle tickets outside community shopping centers or hosting car washes or bake sales to raise money.

All of this changed in 1994, when it was recognized that women's crew was one of the few sports that would have enough participants to balance the large size of the men's football team. There was also probably no other club sport at Michigan with stronger student interest. Hence, a decision was made to move women's crew to varsity status, complete with full-time coaches,

The Michigan Varsity Golf Course. (UM Photo Services.)

Men's track (NCAA Champion Kevin Sullivan). (UM Photo Services.)

quality equipment, and athletic scholarships. Once again, the university faced the frustration of not being able to elevate men's crew to varsity status as well, since to do so would imbalance gender participation. Just as it had initially in soccer, the university was forced to keep men's programs at the club level while taking the women's programs to varsity status.

What about summer sports? Summer is a strange time on university campuses. Most students and faculty are gone, many campus facilities are closed, and campus life is generally dormant. Not so the athletic department. Many student-athletes stay for the summer term, to make up the course credits they were unable to accumulate during their competitive seasons. Many others are involved in an array of informal physical training programs.

But most of the coaches are busy, conducting an array of summer camps for grade school and high school students. Not only do these camps provide a lucrative source of outside income for coaches, but they also are useful in identifying future recruiting prospects. During summertime student dormitories are crowded with youngsters attending the sports camps, with visions of Charles Woodson or Chris Webber in their heads.

Club Sports

While only about seven hundred Michigan students have the opportunity to compete in varsity athletics in any year, several thousand students compete in sports at the club or intramural level. Because of the size of the university, many of these club and intramural programs are of high quality and intensively competitive.

Club sports teams compete at the regional or national level with other colleges and universities, frequently at a highly competitive level. The Michigan rugby and ski teams, for example, regularly compete for the national championship with many other colleges that classify them as varsity sports.

Intramural sports are also highly competitive. Many of the successful walk-on varsity athletes first compete at the intramural level. In fact, when varsity coaches run into roster problems due to player injury or ineligibility, they sometimes conduct tryouts for the team from the pool of intramural players.

Michigan has developed outstanding facilities for intramural athletics for its students, faculty, and staff. Although this level of competition does not attract the visibility of varsity programs, it nevertheless provides an important recreational and educational opportunity for students.

It is always fascinating to observe that some of our most outstanding students have been intense competitors in club sports. A good example was provided by one of our Rhodes Scholars who was captain of the women's rugby team. When asked by the

Intramural sports. (UM Photo Services.)

Rhodes Scholarship interview committee why she had chosen this sport, she responded with confidence, "I like to hit people." Amen.

Concluding Remarks

The brief remarks in this chapter are not an encyclopedic treatment of each varsity sport in the contemporary university's portfolio. They are simply intended to illustrate the remarkable diversity in college sports. As much as anything, I hope to counter the belief of most fans—and, unfortunately, of most sports media—that college sports consist only of football and basketball, augmented by a few obscure sports seen only after midnight on ESPN.

In fact, most college sports—particularly Olympic sports—are conducted at very high levels of quality and competitiveness. They attract some of the very finest athletes in the world. And while the world-class swimmers, gymnasts, or cross-country runners attracted to Michigan rarely get media attention and never sign multi-million-dollar professional sports contracts, they do benefit significantly from another important characteristic of the university all too frequently ignored by the sports media. They receive an outstanding college education. In fact, the academic performance of athletes in most varsity sports ranks above that of the student body in general. Although these student-athletes will not have the opportunity for a lucrative professional contract, they are preparing themselves for careers in teaching, medicine, law, business, engineering, and so on. Furthermore, their experiences in intercollegiate athletics, though not as visible as the experiences of varsity football and basketball players, prepare them for another important role in our society: leadership.

So, too, student participation in club or intramural sports, while not at the competitive level of most of our varsity programs, is nevertheless of educational value. These sports also teach important attributes such as teamwork, sacrifice, and leadership.

In fact, the nature of college sports today might be best captured as follows: There are sports at the varsity, club, and intramural levels . . . and then there are football and basketball. The former provide valuable educational and recreational experiences for many students. The latter have become entertainment businesses, largely designed to satisfy the appetite of the spectator and television viewer, while maximizing financial returns from the commercial marketplace.

Chapter 3

A University President's Perspective

Before I became provost and then president of the University of Michigan, I was a member of its faculty. Like many members of the Michigan faculty family, my wife Anne and I were loyal but distant spectators of Michigan athletics. Joining most of the rest of Ann Arbor, we attended football games, sitting in the same seats near the end zone year after year with other members of the faculty. We had moved from California to Michigan in late 1968—arriving the same week that Bo Schembechler moved to Michigan, albeit without the same fanfare. Schembechler's first football season was also our first at Michigan. We cheered the Wolverines on as they upset Ohio State in 1969 to win a trip to the Rose Bowl. Then we agonized along with the rest of the university as Schembechler had his heart attack just before the game and Michigan was defeated by Southern California. We were enthusiastic fans, but no more closely involved with Michigan football than hundreds of thousands of others in the stands or in front of the television.

We were a little less absorbed in basketball. During the 1970s, we shared season tickets with some friends for a few years, holding seats in the upper reaches of Crisler Arena under the scoreboard. But as our children grew older and became involved in their own sporting activities—and as the trek across bitterly cold parking lots to Crisler Arena made television a more comfortable alternative—we became armchair fans.

Coming from warmer climates (California and Missouri) made it difficult for us to understand hockey, the other revenue sport at

Michigan. Although women's athletics were not yet on the athletic department radar screen, Michigan did sponsor other men's sports such as swimming, baseball, and gymnastics. But these were never given high visibility by either Michigan athletics or the media, and it was largely a case of out of sight, out of mind. This is not to say that we were uninterested. We were just not personally involved beyond the level of common fan interest.

All this changed when we suddenly found ourselves part of the university's central administration as I took on first the role of provost and then of president. Our crash course in intercollegiate athletics provided by these executive positions helped shape my evolving views concerning the challenges faced by college sports today.

Cosmic Confusion

It did not take long for me to realize just how complex Michigan athletics could be. In August 1986, during my first summer as provost, I was holding down the fort while President Harold Shapiro was off at his summer cottage on Lake Michigan. I received a phone call from the czar of the athletic department, Don Canham. "We have big problems! You know what those idiots in Admissions have done? They have refused to admit two of the best basketball players in the country! And you've got to do something about it right now!"

"Calm down. I'll look into it and see what can be done and then get back to you . . ." Well, come to find out, Canham was partially right. The Admissions Office had refused to admit two blue-chip players—none other than Rumeal Robinson and Terry Mills, who would later lead Michigan to a national basketball championship. Granted, they were Proposition 48 players who would be unable to play their first year because of their low scores on the Scholastic Aptitude Test. But our basketball coach, Bill Frieder, had recruited them with great public fanfare and offered them scholarships before their applications had even been received and processed by the Admissions Office. It was clear that there had been a major breakdown in communication, with the real victims being the students themselves.

After assessing the situation, I concluded that at this late date it would be both embarrassing and unfair to the students not to proceed with admission. They had been dealing with the university in good faith. It was not the students' fault that the basketball coach had short-circuited the admissions process. Hence, after touching base with the president, I asked the Admissions Office to admit both students.

Like many crises, this one provided not just obstacles to overcome, but an opportunity as well. I was able to get the attention of both the athletic department and the Office of Admissions and begin to develop a more rational approach to the recruitment and admission of student-athletes. Soon after the beginning of the fall term, I scheduled a meeting of the Michigan "power coaches," Bo Schembechler (football), Bill Frieder (basketball), and Red Berenson (hockey), to discuss the admission of student-athletes.

It took only a few minutes of discussion to learn that these coaches were trying their best to negotiate the complexities of both NCAA recruiting rules and Michigan's admissions policies. But the competition for the best athletes was intense, and the uncertainty and delay the coaches often experienced in getting a response from the admissions office was very frustrating, and from time to time they were tempted to cut corners. In fact, Schembechler had been pushing for some time a "wild card" approach to recruiting, in which a certain number of blue-chip prospects would be admitted each year only on the coach's word. He claimed this was necessary for Michigan to compete with other football powerhouses such as Ohio State. He had actually once met with members of the faculty senate to make the case for such wild-card admissions, with the predictable response: "No way, Bo!"

Although technically the athletic department reported to the president while the Office of Admissions reported to the provost, I viewed this as primarily an academic matter and took the lead in its resolution. I proposed a very simple agreement with the coaches that became the basis for our future admissions policies. The underlying premise was difficult to challenge: the academic welfare of the student-athlete would dominate all our decisions, policies, and procedures, subject of course to NCAA and Big Ten Conference rules. In particular, the university would agree to admit only those student-athletes who we were confident had the academic abilities—with adequate academic support—to benefit from a Michigan education and successfully complete a degree program. I acknowledged that there might be times when the student's formal academic record would not be fully indicative of their potential for success. In some of these cases, additional information about family background or extracurricular achievements could be considered. In the end, I challenged the coaches themselves, telling them that if they were absolutely convinced the student could succeed at Michigan, we would be willing to admit on a trial basis, again subject, of course, to NCAA and conference rules. But if they were wrong and the student did not make it, it would undermine the coaches' credibility for future cases.

My next task was to put into place a more effective procedure within the admissions office, including an appeals process to resolve possible differences of opinion. I made it clear to the coaches and later to the athletic director that with these policies in place, the coaches should be able to recruit student-athletes with the confidence that timely decisions on admissions would be made. But I also stated that there would be zero tolerance for end runs to the president or anybody else, such as regents. The appeals process for academic admissions ended at the level of the provost.

While it took a bit of fine-tuning, this process worked well, and it continues to be used to this day. While some other universities sometimes allow coaches a certain number of wild-card recruits, no questions asked, at Michigan we have continued the practice of admitting only those students with a reasonable probability of academic success, albeit to certain academic programs with strong support networks for athletes, such as our Department of Kinesiology. To their credit, the coaches make great effort to comply with this policy, even though it does mean from time to time they lose the opportunity to recruit some extraordinary athletes with weak academic skills.

Mainstreaming

Despite some of my best efforts to integrate the athletic department into the university at large, I still sometimes found myself face-to-face with startling examples of how far we still had to go. For instance, after I had finished negotiating our admissions policies with the coaches, I set up an appointment to explain this agreement to the athletic director, Don Canham. Since I had never visited the inner sanctum of the athletic department during my years on the faculty, I arranged to meet him at his office. I arrived a few minutes early, and his secretary waved me on into his office. When I sat down and began to talk to Canham, whom I had never formally met, he kept looking at me in a strange way. After about ten minutes, he suddenly slapped his forehead and said, "Hell, you're the provost, aren't you? I thought you were a shoe salesman or something!"

Ah, twenty years as a faculty member, dean, and chief academic officer, and the AD still doesn't know who you are. Humbling to be sure. But also symptomatic of the problem.

This story leads me to the second phase of my growing involvement with Michigan athletics. The fact that the athletic director did not know the provost—who, after all, as chief academic officer is second in command at the university—demonstrates the vast gulf that had opened between the athletic department and the rest of the university. Coaches, staff, and athletes were perceived as separate from the university. There was little understanding between the athletic department and those folks "up on the Hill," their reference to the central administration because of the campus topography that sited the athletics complex in a valley below the academic campus.

This pattern of benign neglect extended both ways. During one of his visits back to Michigan after becoming president of Princeton, Harold Shapiro made an interesting comparison of the two institutions. He noted that while he was president of Michigan, he doubted that he had received more than a dozen letters a year about Michigan athletics. But at Princeton, almost a third of his mail involved athletics. He believed this was due, in part, to the fact that a very significant fraction (about 30 percent) of the Princeton student body participated in varsity sports and hence as alumni took an intense personal interest in athletics. In contrast, at Michigan only a small fraction of the student body, roughly seven hundred out of twenty-two thousand undergraduate students, participated in varsity athletics. Hence most mail was from fans rather than former participants, and it was channeled to the athletic department rather than the Office of the President.

More serious was the considerable administrative and cultural separation that had evolved between the athletic department, its staff, coaches, and students, and the rest of the university. While some of this gap was due, no doubt, to the strong and independent personality of the athletic director, there were other factors. Michigan had long taken pride in the fact that its athletic department was prosperous enough that it required no university subsidy, largely because of the gate receipts it took in from the largest football stadium in America. This very financial independence contributed to the isolation of the department. The vast separation between Michigan athletics and the rest of the university posed a real challenge, since it deprived student-athletes of many of the important experiences that should have been part of their education. It also placed coaches in the awkward position of being cut off from the rest of the institution, their isolation aggravated by the compartmentalization of the athletic department itself, coaches and athletes in one program having little interaction with those in others.

Certain imminent changes forced me to take personal action. Since the athletic director was approaching retirement age, it was clear that building new bridges of cooperation and respect between the department and the rest of the university could help smooth the transition in leadership. My wife Anne and I decided to take on the task of "mainstreaming" Michigan athletics from the Office of the Provost. This was probably a more natural task for us than many realized. Anne and I had both been actively involved in sports. Anne had been a cheerleader in high school, the only "sport" available for girls in our small country school, and I had played football in high school and college. Furthermore, one of our daughters had been a varsity athlete in college, competing in the heptathalon and crew. Hence we had an intuitive appreciation for both the importance of sports to the education of students and the importance of athletics to the university. It also seemed to us that there was an important symbolism associated with the provost, the chief academic officer of the university, taking on this role. It made a strong statement that athletics should be aligned with the academic mission of the university.

We began by arranging a series of events where we brought together student-athletes and coaches in various academic settings—museums, concert halls, and such. We wanted to stress that student-athletes were students first, and that coaches were, in reality, teachers. In the process of arranging and hosting these events, we began to realize that the isolation of one sports program from

Old Yale Number 71

another was just as serious as the chasm between the athletic department and the rest of the university. Students and coaches enjoyed the opportunity to meet participants from other sports programs. We also began to build personal relationships with coaches and athletic department staff, both through attending events and by meeting with them individually. For example, even while I was provost, we began to attend the annual football awards banquet held to honor the team following each season, an event we would continue to attend regularly throughout my presidency.

After serving for two years as provost and occasionally as acting president, I was elected as president of the university in 1988. It didn't surprise Anne or me that we adjusted naturally to the more visible role of the presidency in athletics because of our strong involvement while I was provost and acting president. Our

Anne Duderstadt at a reception for the football team sandwiched between Joe Cocozzo and John (Jumbo) Elliot

efforts to strengthen relationships with student-athletes, coaches, and staff of the athletic department led to many friendships, among them Bo Schembechler. In fact, Schembechler made it a point to show up at my public interview for president. When the papers reported my selection by the regents the next day, whose picture should be on the front page but Schembechler's, with the quote: "He was my choice!" (a most revealing example of the clout that a football coach has with the local press).

The Buck Stops Here

One of the Michigan hockey traditions is a student chant that erupts after every Michigan goal. The fans point at the visiting goalie and chant, "It's all your fault! It's all your fault! It's all your fault!" Whenever this happened at a game I was attending, I found

Bo Schembechler:
"You're my choice!"
(UM Photo Services.)

myself instinctively slouching down in my seat, trying to hide, as if the chant were directed at me.

"It's all your fault!" This may be the most common invective tossed at a university president. The presidency of a major university is one of those rare leadership roles in which anything good that happens is generally attributable to someone else, but anything bad that happens is the president's fault. Or so students, faculty, trustees, and the media like to suggest. And particularly so in intercollegiate athletics.

When students celebrating a Michigan victory caused damage to the town, or student-athletes broke the law, or when an athletic team fell on hard times and began to lose, there was always an expectation that the president would accept responsibility. In my more paranoid moments, I sometimes wondered whether some disappointed fans blamed me for cosmic events such as "the play of the decade," when Colorado quarterback Kordell Stewart faded back and tossed a seventy-yard bomb to beat Michigan as the clock expired. I didn't call the prevent defense, but since I was at the game, I suppose it was my fault. When Chris Webber called an illegal time-out during the closing seconds of the Final Four to ice the national championship for North Carolina, whose fault was it? Our seats were so far from the action that even if I had yelled for a time-out, nobody could possibly have heard me. But I was there, so it must have been my fault. Needless to say, the administration never received any credit for successes such as Rose Bowl wins or national championships. Of course, we did not deserve any. But the logic of academic administration dictates that a president is responsible for all of the bad things that happen.

The president has many additional roles and responsibilities in intercollegiate athletics beyond serving as a convenient scapegoat. The NCAA's rule of "institutional control" requires that the president accept ultimate responsibility for the integrity of intercollegiate athletics. Hence many universities are organized so that the athletic director reports directly to the president. The extraordinary visibility of intercollegiate athletics, with its show business character, requires that the president frequently be seen "flying the flag," supporting the team and representing the university at major athletics events. As with other components of the university, the president frequently must become "defender of the faith," defending the university's athletics programs against the forces of darkness that threaten them: the media, boosters, politicians, and on occasion even trustees.

Michigan's role as a leader in intercollegiate athletics demands many of these command performances. Not only is the president expected to be present at every home football game, but for the twenty-four hours preceding these games, the president and his spouse are usually scheduled to host a wide array of events. To Anne and me, fall sometimes seemed like a never-ending flurry of receptions, tailgate luncheons, and press box events, requiring dozens of speeches, hundreds of personal greetings, and thousands of handshakes.

Winter was somewhat less intense, but we were nevertheless

Seeking advice from Michigan football great Tom Harmon. (UM Photo Services.)

expected to be present—and visible—at the majority of home basketball games, an occasional hockey game, and when possible, at
the array of other sporting events such as swimming, gymnastics,
and volleyball. Added to this range of normal activities were those
special events such as a football bowl—for Michigan, this "special"
event occurred every year—and the NCAA Final Four—a rarity for
most schools, but not infrequent for Michigan. Anne and I also felt
it important to represent the university at other key events such as
the end-of-season banquets for the football and basketball teams,
the academic honors banquet for student-athletes, and special
events for the women's athletics programs. Beyond this were the
additional responsibilities associated with the Big Ten Conference
and NCAA, frequently involving both the president and spouse.

There is yet another presidential role, even more enjoyable and
perhaps even more important but far less visible: providing a sense
of caring for and involvement with the coaches, student-athletes,
and athletics staff. Ironically, at Michigan, the athletic department
is the only major unit of the university that reports directly to the
president, through the athletic director. (Other units report through
vice presidents.) Both my wife and I felt a particular responsibility
to provide TLC for the various programs. We tried to attend as
many athletic events as our time permitted, particularly the less
visible "nonrevenue" sports such as gymnastics and swimming. We
hosted a variety of events and activities for the athletic department. We developed personal friendships with many of the coaches
and staff. We tried to be as supportive as possible, during both
good times and bad. We developed a deep appreciation for the tri-
als and tribulations of the people who guided and participated in
varsity athletics. While we always thought of student-athletes as
students first, and of coaches as teachers, we also regarded them
almost as members of our family, with a strong sense of responsibility for their welfare.

Defending against the Forces of Darkness

Unfortunately, there were other aspects of my role as president that
were not nearly as rewarding. It fell to me as president to protect

the athletic department from inappropriate intrusion by alumni and boosters, the media, politicians, and occasionally even regents. I thought it was critical to stand solidly behind Michigan's athletic directors when they were faced with difficult decisions or challenges. Actually, there were some occasions when I even had to stand solidly *in front* of them to protect them from the slings and arrows launched by others!

We needed the strong support and cooperation of the coaches in these instances. Each year I would meet with all of the coaches to stress the importance of the integrity of their programs and their role in protecting it. It was made clear that while Michigan rarely dismissed a coach simply because of a won-lost record, we would take immediate action to dismiss a coach if we had evidence that he or she had been cheating. But all too frequently, violations in intercollegiate athletics occur without the knowledge of a coach; rather, alumni or boosters or others become too close to a program or have an inadequate knowledge of the complex rules governing intercollegiate athletics. While the final responsibility falls to the coaches to keep such threats at arm's length from their programs, they clearly need our strong support in this effort.

Success can sometimes be its own challenge. The high public exposure of Michigan athletics was a particular burden. Rare was the month when a Michigan athlete or coach was not either celebrated or attacked by the media. The coaches, particularly in the more visible programs, came under intense pressure from both the media and the fans, who had developed an insatiable appetite for success.

Hence it was also occasionally necessary to take on the media in order to protect our programs. As I will discuss at length later, the sports press is all too frequently driven by the commercial value system of the entertainment industry rather than the journalistic values characterizing other areas of reporting. Some reporters are after the big investigative story, the Pulitzer Prize, and sometimes in their hunger for sensational stories, they play fast and loose with the truth. On top of this, there is also an old-guard element of the press, those who were curried and cultivated in the good old days with access, favors, or entertainment by enterprising athletic directors and coaches. The old-timers in the media try to convey a nostalgic view of a world of college sports that probably never existed. They generally resist any change, no matter how necessary. Sometimes the president was in a better position to fight the battle over misrepresentations in the sports media than the coaches or the athletic director, who needed to maintain a more cordial relationship with them.

The president also had the task of dealing with that most sensitive of all constituencies, the governing board of the university. Most regents or trustees approach athletics as they do other parts of the university, certainly interested and supportive, but also recognizing that the detailed management of programs is best left to those most directly responsible, that is, in the athletic department, coaches and the athletic director. However, a few board members are inevitably drawn to intercollegiate athletics like moths to a flame because of their interest in the program or the high visibility it provides. On rare occasions one will even encounter trustees who believe their primary role is to represent the interests of those who identify most closely with the institution through its athletics programs. It is sometimes a great challenge to protect the integrity of both the athletics programs and the board itself from inappropriate involvement.

At the level of the Big Ten Conference or the NCAA, it frequently fell to me and to presidents before me to defend the interests of the athletic department and the university. Many were the lonely, invisible battles we fought on issues such as sharing gate revenue from football, expanding the conference, and establishing gender equity. Some we won. Some we lost. Most battles were unseen, unrecognized, and certainly unappreciated.

While the defense of truth, justice, and the Michigan way in intercollegiate athletics was a necessary role for the president, it was often an unpleasant and difficult one. But this was a vitally important role, although over time, it took its toll.

The People of Michigan Athletics

As is true for most people, the memories that remain freshest for me over time are those of people. And the people associated with

Michigan athletics—the coaches, the staff, and the student-athletes—were truly among the most remarkable my wife and I met during my presidency.

Athletic Directors

Although players and coaches are the most visible participants in intercollegiate athletics, the athletic director is the key to the competitive and financial success and the integrity of a university's programs. Furthermore, most athletic departments have a highly top-down organizational structure in which the athletic director has considerable power and is responsible for hiring and firing coaches, compliance with numerous NCAA and conference rules, and the interface of the department with the university. Many athletic directors exercise this power behind the scenes, avoiding the press, and leaving the more visible role to their coaches and players. However some athletic directors prefer to assume a more visible role, as a symbol of absolute authority and even overshadowing coaches and programs.

In most universities, the athletic director reports directly to the president of the university. This relationship is not only key to the principle of institutional control of intercollegiate athletics, but it also reflects a concern for the hazards presented by the high visibility of college sports. During my tenure as president, I was fortunate to have been able to work with three outstanding individuals in this important role: Bo Schembechler, Jack Weidenbach, and Joe Roberson. Each was quite different, of course. Schembechler was almost an icon, a symbol of Michigan athletics, and his celebrity status overshadowed everybody else in the department. He had great leadership skills and a strong sense of pride both in Michigan's winning traditions and its reputation for integrity. Weidenbach was far more of a behind-the-scenes leader, with great wisdom and experience, yet choosing to work through other people rather than play a highly visible leadership role. Roberson was an educator at heart, combining a good understanding of the culture of college sports with a deep commitment to the most important academic principles of the university.

The visibility—and vulnerability—of intercollegiate athletics makes the selection and support of a strong athletic director one of a president's most important tasks. As I will note later, the high visibility of Michigan's athletics programs made these searches particularly difficult because of external interference, from boosters, politicians, and even regents. Yet, despite these challenges, we were able to attract very talented, albeit quite different, individuals. And in each case, we were fortunate that the relationship between the athletic director and the president was based on a spirit of open communication and a deep respect for, and confidence in, their ability to lead the athletic department. Although the athletic director would always touch bases with me on important issues, there was a clear understanding about areas of responsibility and authority. As athletic directors, they were responsible for the day-to-day leadership of Michigan athletics. I always took great care to give them my strong support but never to issue direct marching orders.

Although the athletic director and president were frequently paired together at major events such as bowl games or NCAA basketball tournaments, the area where we worked together most closely was conference and NCAA matters. Although there had been a long history of influence—indeed control—by athletic directors and power coaches in the governance of intercollegiate athletics, with conference incorporation the presidents began to play a more active role by the 1990s. Although in the end the president usually cast the university vote on conference or NCAA matters, the athletic director frequently had the knowledge and experience necessary to make key decisions. During my years as president, we were very fortunate to have such a close relationship when it came to tackling these matters. As a result, Michigan was able to play a significant leadership role in conference matters.

Coaches

Coaching a modern college athletic program is a demanding and intense profession. The rigors of recruiting, of coaching, of working with student-athletes, of handling the enormous public attention—particularly that from the press—and of adhering to the complex rules governing athletes and athletics are challenging.

Coaching requires extraordinary commitment, long hours of work, and demanding travel schedules. It often brings frustration and disappointment.

While the celebrity head coaches in highly visible football and basketball programs are usually paid at astronomical levels, at least at NCAA Division I-A universities, their colleagues in other sports programs receive very modest compensation. The same is true for assistant coaches, whose salaries are sometimes ten times less than the head coach's in the revenue sports. For the majority of coaches in intercollegiate athletics, the real reward lies not in the income but rather in the enjoyment of working with talented student-athletes, of seeing their progress, and of watching them succeed, both on the field and in the classroom.

While most Michigan coaches felt a strong sense of responsibility for the welfare of their student-athletes, they were also driven to build and sustain nationally competitive programs. While they made every effort to do so within the rules as they understood them, the athletic department's independence effectively isolated them from the rest of the university. Little wonder that many of our coaches had limited understanding of the academic priorities and values of the university or the academic goals and pressures on their student-athletes. And not surprisingly in view of this sep-

A history of Michigan football coaches, displayed on the 1999 Michigan football tickets

aration, coaches sometimes believed their own athletic objectives for their program, for "the team," were more important than the academic goals of a particular student-athlete.

Student-Athletes and Families

In our presidential role, Anne and I frequently attended athletics events, but we rarely had any direct interaction with players. Of course, at events such as receptions or bowl games we met their families. But the players were generally sufficiently occupied with other activities, athletics and academics, that more than a brief conversation with the president was difficult. Furthermore, we were constrained by NCAA rules that, because of the potential for abuse, limit the use of such events as receptions to bring student-athletes closer to the university.

Although I always found the time if asked to meet with prospective students and parents, I rarely became involved in recruiting student-athletes. Most often, I would simply greet them if they were brought up to the president's box during the half-time of a football game, or meet with the parents to assure them that their son or daughter would get a good education. Perhaps my relative inactivity in recruiting was due to my remarkable lack of success.

Anne's involvement with Michigan athletics deserves a note here. Although she had never been a big football or basketball fan, as she got to know the coaches, staff, and players on a personal level, she became quite emotionally invested in Michigan athletics. In part, it was probably akin to a parental attachment, since in a sense, the president and spouse of the university act as surrogate "mom and pop" to the students. Anne also developed a very deep appreciation for the wives and families of the coaches, the stresses and challenges they faced, and the importance of providing some visible support. Usually before major football and basketball games, Anne would make a point to visit briefly with the coaches wives. And, over time, she probably became as nervous as the wives during the games themselves, as excited by victories and as disappointed in defeats. It was largely at her urging that we did our best to attend at least a part of an event for each of our teams throughout the year, although our calendar sometimes made this very difficult. Anne became particularly attached to the rapidly evolving programs in women's athletics at Michigan.

Anne and I developed a deep affection and empathy for the coaches and staff of the athletic department. Perhaps it was because we, too, felt many of the public pressures and the frustrating lack of understanding of our roles by the media and the fans. We had a sympathetic understanding of the sacrifices made by the coaches and players, and their families. Beyond this, there was a refreshing simplicity of values among most of our sports programs, an absence of politics, and a deep concern for the welfare of the student-athletes, which was usually missed or ignored by those outside the athletic department.

Athletes and Coaches; Students and Teachers

We found our personal involvement with the students, coaches, and staff of our athletics programs a refreshing alternative to other presidential roles both within and external to the university. We found a remarkable absence of politics and infighting in the athletic department. Despite the great public attention and media pressure focused on Michigan athletics, within the programs themselves there was always a sense of camaraderie and support. During our latter years, as our efforts began to succeed in eliminating barriers within the athletic department and building new linkages with the rest of the university, students and coaches from various sports began to attend and cheer on their friends in other programs. This was particularly evident as more and more male athletes began to attend the athletic events for our emerging women's sports programs.

Jack Weidenbach, Michigan's athletic director during the early 1990s, once confided to me that his job was the best in the university because he had the opportunity to work with such outstanding students. Although the media tend to portray athletes as academically marginal, in reality, many of our student-athletes were outstanding students, performing at the highest level both in the classroom and on the field, on the court, or in the pool. The model of the true student-athlete is alive and well in most of college sports, in programs such as swimming, hockey, gymnastics, and cross country, where students train to world-class levels while excelling in some of our most difficult academic programs. I once asked one of our women swimmers how she managed to train for several hours a day while pursuing an intense premed academic program. She said the secret was "power napping," the ability to use odd moments of time to catch up on sleep debt. Talk about optimizing one's time!

Weidenbach was right about his job. But I would go beyond the students to highlight our coaches and athletics staff as well. We tend to think of coaches as managing highly competitive athletics programs, recruiting star athletes, developing game strategies, and dealing with the media, but their most important role is that of teacher. Even a cursory involvement with college sports soon reveals that successful coaches demonstrate a deep commitment toward their student-athletes, developing relationships that remain strong for a lifetime. I always found our coaches concern for the total welfare of their students, beyond simply their athletic performance, quite remarkable.

It is this perspective, of athletes as *students* and of coaches as *teachers,* that most clearly reveals the true goal of college sports, at least to my mind. At its best, college athletics provide an opportunity for students to learn and develop more fully the values necessary for a meaningful life, values such as determination, sacrifice, courage, and teamwork, perhaps more easily learned through athletic competition than in the classroom. It is in this sense that college sports can indeed complement and broaden the educational experiences of our students.

PART II
How Do Things Really Work?

Chapter 4   The Evolution of College Sports

A random sampling of media coverage would suggest that college sports consists primarily of big-time football and basketball programs, led by celebrity coaches, and played by soon-to-be professional athletes. In reality intercollegiate athletics is characterized by great diversity among institutions, sporting activities, and participants. This is not particularly surprising, considering the great diversity among colleges and universities themselves, ranging from small liberal arts colleges to gigantic university systems, from commuter campuses to global "cyberspace" universities. But it also reflects the diverse evolutionary paths taken by various sports.

The history of college sports in America can shed light on current challenges. One can distinguish several distinct stages in the evolution of American college sports. The first stage, which probably existed only in mythology, might be called the classical or "amateur" model. The second stage might be called the "exhibition" phase, when college sports evolved from sportsmanship to gamesmanship, with strong fan interest. The third stage, clearly characteristic of our times, might best be referred to as the "show business" phase as football and basketball have evolved into commercial entertainment products.

If we are to understand today's concerns and challenges of intercollegiate athletics, it is important to understand how these activities have evolved over the years. In this chapter, we discuss the evolution of college sports, along with the efforts to control and reform these activities. We then illustrate the multiple realities of college sports by considering three case studies: basketball, swimming, and ice hockey.

The Myth of Amateur Athletics

Sports have always been an important part of our civilization. Intercollegiate athletics continue a tradition from ancient times, in which games allowed athletes to test and develop their own ability in competitions with one another. In theory, at least, college sports provided an important opportunity for teaching people about character, motivation, endurance, loyalty, and the attainment of one's personal best—all qualities of great value in citizens. In this sense, competitive athletics were viewed as an extracurricular activity, justified by the university as part of its ideal objective of educating the whole person.

Like most ideals, this image of college sports, portraying the student as an amateur athlete and athletic competition as just one component of a college education, contrasted sharply with the reality of intercollegiate athletics even during their early years. At the turn of the century, many of our college games were already far down the road to professionalism. Many athletes were not only paid but were not even students. And coaches went to any and all extreme to produce winning teams. Rumor has it that once a Harvard coach choked a bulldog, the Yale mascot, in front of his team at the halftime of the Yale-Harvard game to motivate them. Fielding Yost once imported ten live wolverines from Alaska to motivate the Michigan football team before a big game.[1]

To be sure, some college presidents expressed their concerns about the impact of sports on their institutions. In 1873, football seemed sufficiently far removed from academic life to prompt a classic remark by President Andrew D. White of Cornell. In response to a challenge from thirty players at the University of Michigan who wanted to arrange a game in Cleveland against Cornell, President White telegraphed, "I will not permit thirty men to travel four hundred miles merely to agitate a bag of wind."[2] President White's being a former Michigan faculty member poured even more salt upon the wounds!

By the turn of the century, football had already evolved far beyond the control of the colleges. In 1906 President Theodore Roosevelt became so concerned about brutality and injuries that he called together leaders of Harvard, Yale, and Princeton to take the lead in restoring ethical conduct. Roosevelt strongly supported the principle of amateurism, and in calling for this meeting he stated the principle later adopted by the NCAA: "No student shall represent a college or university in any intercollegiate game or contest . . . who has at any time received, either directly or indirectly, money, or any other consideration."[3] As a result of his efforts, the National College Athletics Association was formed, and its constitution declared, "An amateur sportsman is one who engages in sports for the physical, mental, or social benefits he derives therefrom, and to whom the sport is an avocation. Any college athlete who takes pay for participation in athletics does not meet this definition of amateurism."[4]

At the same time, President James Angell of Michigan led the effort in the Midwest to restore a sense of integrity and discipline to football. He persuaded several fellow presidents of midwestern universities to join with Michigan to form the Western Conference, later to be known as the Big Ten, so they could jointly adopt rules to regulate athletic competition among their institutions.

Early Attempts to Control Growth

Despite these early efforts at control, college sports continued to grow in popularity, evolving from a participatory activity for students to a spectator activity for students and fans alike. Football became one of the few opportunities to bring together growing American university campuses where students, faculty, and alumni became connected by identification with major sporting events and athletic activities. This sense of community and engagement surrounding athletics extended far beyond the campus to include not simply alumni but hundreds of thousands of fans with otherwise little direct connection to the university.

The press and the film industry seized on the popularity of college football to create the myth of the football hero and the beloved coach. Frank Meriweather, Fritz Crisler, and Knute Rockne became household names. Universities built massive stadiums to accommodate the growing crowds. With the beginning of commercial radio in the early 1920s, college football gained national popularity. In fact, the first coast-to-coast broadcast was the 1927 Rose Bowl.

But many within the academy became increasingly concerned of the growing commercialism of football and the corruption and scandal it threatened to bring to the university. Although a supportive sports press continued to promote college football and its participants, abuses were plentiful. Recruiting was vicious, players and coaches were frequently on the take, and rule violations plentiful.

In 1929 a report commissioned by the Carnegie Foundation found serious fault with college football, noting its increasing commercialization and professionalization, the lack of integrity of players, coaches, and fans, and the dangers its "demoralizing and corrupt system" posed both for participants and academic institutions.[5] The report went on to note that the relationship between intercollegiate athletics and their academic hosts had long been an uneasy one and called for de-emphasis of football. And yet while the report generated debate, it did not result in significant progress to reform and control college sports.

There were some rare efforts by individual institutions or athletic conferences to de-emphasize big-time athletics. In 1946, President Robert Hutchens managed to convince the trustees of the University of Chicago to leave the Big Ten Conference, arguing, "To be successful, one must cheat. Everyone is cheating, and I refuse to cheat." He ridiculed the conference's emphasis on athletics by observing, "Whenever I feel a desire to exercise, I lie down until it goes away."[6] Similarly, the Ivy League and the service academies backed away from the growing professionalism and commercialization of football.

But for most major universities, big-time football had become an important part of the culture, soon to be joined by basketball. Although the NCAA was promoted as the guardian of amateur principles and integrity in sports, since it was dominated by coaches and athletic directors, its primary purpose increasingly became that of defending college sports against true reform. For example, in the early 1950s, the American Council on Education proposed a series of modest reforms, such as eliminating bowl games, spring training, and athletic scholarships.[7] However, the chairman of the ACE committee, Michigan State president John Hannah, undercut the effort by siding with the NCAA coaches when he realized that his efforts to build his fledgling university on the back of a successful football program might be more successful without reform.

Although this NCAA effort, known as the Sanity Code, was not approved by the membership largely because of the lobbying of football coaches, it was adopted by the Ivy League universities, along with a number of other restrictions such as a ban on post-season play, designed to de-emphasize football. And for a brief period from 1957 to 1961, the Big Ten Conference attempted to follow suit by shifting to need-based scholarship grants. However the Big Ten universities rapidly returned to full athletic grants-in-aid when it became clear that they were losing some of the best athletes to other schools that refused to go along.

This rapid growth in the competitive nature of college sports, away from extracurricular games toward intercollegiate competition with strong fan interest, may be one of its most important evolutionary stages. While the ideals of "sportsmanship" were commonly used to justify sports as a participatory activity for students, in reality, sports were more dominated by "gamesmanship," with a stress on winning rather than just competing.

Television Takes Over

In the 1960s and 1970s, these spectator events turned into public entertainment on a national scale, with television as the driving force. College sports represented a very attractive opportunity for television since most of the production costs were borne by the institutions themselves or subsidized by ticket sales. Furthermore, television networks found that by promoting and marketing college sports much as they would other commercial activities—generating great media hype, hiring sensationalistic broadcasters, urging colleges to arrange even more spectacular events—they could build major nationwide audiences. College football and basketball ceased to be simply spectator events. They became commercial products.

In the early days, television broadcasting was tightly controlled and rationed by the monopoly powers of the NCAA through its "Football Game of the Week" format. The basic idea was to balance the broadcasting of major games with a broad representation of institutions and geographic regions. While this arrangement was supported by many of the major institutions, it was strongly resisted by Notre Dame, which already benefited from its own national radio network and sought the same from exclusive rights for television broadcasting. Throughout the next two decades, Notre Dame consistently fought efforts to coordinate football broadcasting and was a major force in driving the further commercialization of college football.[8]

Several other factors contributed to the acceleration in the commercialization of college sports in the 1970s and 1980s. First was the breakup of the NCAA monopoly over broadcasting. Frustrated with NCAA control, a group of major football powers formed the Collegiate Football Association in 1981 and negotiated their own broadcasting contract with ABC. In 1984, the Supreme Court ruled that the NCAA limitation on the broadcasting of football games amounted to restraint of trade and violated federal antitrust statutes. The floodgates opened. Several conferences, including the Big Ten and Pac-10, were powerful enough to negotiate their own television contracts. The CFA continued for a few more years, but it eventually disintegrated when Notre Dame negotiated its own contract with NBC and withdrew from the CFA, albeit under considerable criticism.

The next quantum leap in commercialization came from a new direction: college basketball. For most universities, basketball had always been a minor sport, with the exception of several large cities such as New York and Philadelphia and the midwestern United States. However, basketball was popular with gamblers, particularly after the introduction of the point-spread. In many ways, basketball was a game tailor-made for television broadcasting. Compared to football, at least, it was relatively inexpensive to conduct, so that many colleges, both large and small, could mount competitive programs. By expanding the postseason NCAA tournament from two to three weeks and sixty-four teams, the NCAA created a television extravaganza that came to dominate the sporting scene every spring, a time of the year when there was relatively little interest in professional sports.

College basketball hit the big time in 1984 when CBS agreed to pay the then-staggering sum of $1 billion for exclusive rights to broadcast the NCAA basketball tournament. The broadcasting contract for the NCAA tournament took the commercial value of college sports to new heights. It also provided the NCAA with not only very considerable revenue but also very considerable clout over intercollegiate athletics, following the golden rule of college sports: whoever gets the gold makes the rules.

Major athletic conferences moved rapidly to negotiate broadcasting contracts for football and basketball. The entry of cable television and ESPN into the market bumped commercialization to new levels. In order to feed the insatiable appetite of armchair sports fans, football and basketball games were scheduled on all days of the week—and all times of the day and night. Conferences jumped at the chance for broader exposure through regional broadcasts. The values of network contracts escalated rapidly, into the hundreds of millions of dollars for a typical conference season. The broadcasting rights for the NCAA basketball tournament was negotiated in 1999 with CBS for the sum of $6 billion over eleven years—amounting to $550 million annually. Although the size of these contracts sounds very large, the sums pale in comparison to the advertising revenues generated by the broadcasting of professional sports, as evidenced by the $18 billion of broadcasting contracts negotiated by the NFL in 1998.

Show Business

Even more significant than the growth of television dollars was the way that college sporting events were increasingly viewed as public entertainment, as commercial products, rather than as competitive events. Winning coaches and players rapidly assumed celebrity status, surrounded by their own cadre of fans and subject to all of the associated temptations and pressures of fame. Although players continued to receive only pocket change—and, of course, the opportunity for a college education—celebrity coaches benefited from compensation packages that were extreme, even by professional standards, running into the millions of dollars.

Conferences began to be run more like professional leagues. To some degree, this is to be expected since many athletic conferences rivaled the professional leagues in the complexity of their governance, administration, and financial structures. For example, today the Big Ten Conference conducts and televises more sporting events than any professional league, including professional baseball, basketball, and football. But the professionalization of college athletics conferences was driven far more by the commercialization of their products, football and basketball.

In this third and current stage—the "big-time show business stage"—television, in particular, and the sports press, more generally, seriously distorted the nature of intercollegiate athletics. Media demands disrupted university schedules by demanding excessively long seasons and pressuring for postseason play and conference tournaments. In the end, this trivialized the idea of seasonal conference play. Broadcasters and advertisers repackaged athletic events, coaches, and players as entertainment products, creating a celebrity culture that sharply contrasted with the academic culture of the university. And most universities were quite willing to oblige. Some conferences agreed to completely restructure their schedules; one even agreed to start its basketball games at midnight in order to accommodate a major cable sports network. Advertising invaded athletic facilities, even for products that seemed antithetical to the objectives of higher education, beer ads for example. And the association of higher education with the crass, even offensive, nature of many advertisements for beer and athletics apparel eroded public confidence in the integrity of intercollegiate athletics even further.

Media exposure transformed coaches and players into celebrities, with their pictures on the front pages of newspapers and magazines and their film clips seen regularly on the evening news. Bobby Knight, Joe Paterno, Charles Woodson, and Peyton Man-ning are as well known to the American public as many movie stars, and certainly far better known than anyone else at their universities. But celebrity status can be a double-edged sword, because it also creates powerful expectations that these college sports heroes will continue to excel and to win. And while some will do so with talent and integrity, others succumb to the temptation to cheat. As Murray Sperber notes in *College Sports, Inc.*, intercollegiate athletics have "become a huge commercial entertainment conglomerate with extremely well-paid coaches, elite athletes, gleaming facilities, and enormous media coverage; and, in the process, the institutions, their academic programs, and the academic objectives of their students have not been well served."[9]

The media have played a mixed if not outright hypocritical role in the evolution of college sports into show business by simultaneously both promoting and condemning this commercialization. For decades magazines like *Sports Illustrated* have charged that college football and basketball are saturated with corruption, hypocrisy, and misplaced values, and that those with authority over such matters—the universities, conferences, and NCAA—were doing nothing about it. Yet, at the same time, the sports media continue to promote college sports as their bread and butter.

Commercial pressures will not only continue but intensify. The entertainment value of college football and basketball products continues to increase. There have been numerous experiments in pay-for-view for college football broadcasting. Direct satellite television broadcasting makes available hundreds of college sporting events every week. Radio narrowcasting of college sports over the Internet has already become common (e.g., using Internet-based services such as RealPlayer), and video narrowcasting is being tried on an experimental basis. It will soon be possible for the avid fan to click to a website that contains any sporting event of interest.[10] Furthermore we are beginning to see the early emergence of multimedia, in which the viewer can actually control part of the experience by choosing camera angles or background statistics. Imagine when virtual reality becomes available, providing not simply all of the sensations of being physically present at an event, but possibly also those of being a competitor!

Three Case Studies

The University of Michigan not only followed but sometimes led college sports down this evolutionary path, from the mythical amateur phase to spectator sports to the big-time show business of today's college football and basketball. However, while most major universities marched along the road toward the commercialization and professionalization of college sports together, not all sports programs on our campuses evolved into commercial carnivores. Some, such as the Olympic sports of swimming and gymnastics, actually managed to avoid commercialization and remain aligned with the academic purpose of a university, involving real students as participants, and stressing their benefit as an athletic *and* educational extracurricular experience.

The great diversity in the evolutionary path taken by different college sports can best be illustrated by three case studies drawn from experiences at the University of Michigan.

Case Study 1: Men's Basketball (Big-Time Show Biz)

Men's basketball undoubtedly provides the most extreme example of the corrosive influence of the sports media and entertainment industry. Long before the season begins, the media hype is in high gear, with a continual buzz about who will make it to the Final Four months down the road. At midnight before the first day that the NCAA allows basketball practice in October, many teams stage "Midnight Madness" events, drawing both sellout crowds and national television.

Today most teams carefully tailor their schedules to give them the best possible won-lost record in the hopes of being selected for the NCAA tournament at season's end. Hence the early games of the season are usually blowouts, pitting powerhouse Division I-A teams against weak lower-division teams. The exceptions are special promotional events, such as the Great Eight Tournament, featuring the eight quarterfinalist teams of the preceding year, or the National Invitational Tournament, which now occurs both at the start and the end of the season. While some teams such as Indiana, Kansas, and Duke do schedule tough preconference schedules, many others (including Michigan) pad their schedules with cup-cake opponents so that by the time the conference season gets under way after the first of the year, they may already have won ten or more games.

Since competition within the conference is frequently more intense than that from nonconference opponents, many coaches would probably prefer to eliminate conference games altogether. Besides, with the media hype and commercial dollars focused on the NCAA tournament, the conference championship no longer amounts to very much. Most conferences ignore the conference season and pick their champion in a weekend tournament at the end of the season. About the only consequences of conference play these days are losses.

Yet conference play is necessary because it helps feed the television monster, which needs game fodder every hour of the day, every day of the week. While some major conferences have been able to resist the media pressure, most have agreed to schedule their games at the whim of the networks. Imagine the impact on the academic schedule of students, both basketball players and fans, when late evening games are scheduled randomly throughout the week. In fact, basketball schedules have now become so perverse that few student-athletes are able to carry standard academic loads during the season and are forced to make up academic deficiencies during the summer.

This impact of the sport on academics becomes even more serious as the season-end conference tournaments and NCAA tournament approach. This schedule almost seems designed to place maximum pressure on student-athletes at the most critical period in their studies, between midterms and final examinations. Too many student-athletes have seen their studies flounder on the rocks of the NCAA tournament. But this makes all the better entertainment for the media, since perhaps these players will be forced to go into the pro draft early, with their chances for academic success eroded by the intensity of postseason play.

The season culminates in a fevered pitch at the circus the media call "The Road to the Final Four," the NCAA tournament. Actually, it looks more like a carnival than a circus, since there is usually a huckster character to most of the promotional activities. During my years as president, Michigan made it to the Final Four in three different venues: the Kingdome in Seattle in 1989, the Metrodome in Minneapolis in 1992, and the Superdome in New Orleans in 1993. All three events were remarkably similar, clearly designed to appeal more to the television audience and corporate sponsors than to the participating institutions or higher education more generally. A few lingering images will illustrate.

First, the NCAA's priorities with respect to audience are glaringly apparent if you count the number of rows of press desks surrounding the court, which push spectators far back from the action. Ironically, much of the time members of the sports press are milling around outside enjoying the various hospitality areas where they get free eats and free drinks. When they do actually return to their tables, they are frequently standing, chatting among themselves and generally annoying spectators. Of course, this probably does not make much difference anyway, since most spectators are so far from the court in these football stadiums the NCAA uses for its tournaments that they cannot see the competition itself and will have to read about the game later in the newspapers. The NCAA always reserves the only decent seats either for the college basketball coaches association, the NCAA Foundation members, or corporate sponsors.

Second, the tournament is surrounded by a carnival atmosphere, complete with amusement rides, barkers (sports commentators pretending to lead pep rallies), and hucksters promoting various products (particularly the "Just Do It!" crowd). Some of these events almost overshadow the games themselves: the practice "shoot-arounds" when the various teams exhibit their showboat skills, the contests of "power dunking" and three-point shooting, and the numerous and mandatory press conferences.

Finally, the players themselves are usually kept quarantined at distant hotels and can only be seen off the court as they walk through the lobby of hotels and boarding buses, most wearing the customary Discman earphones and dark sunglasses. The players have important roles to play beyond simply those of competitors: they are promoted as celebrities and obligated to satisfy the insatiable appetite of the sports media with press conference after press conference, all mandatory at the command of the NCAA.

The NCAA transformed what was once a two-week tournament to determine the national champion in basketball into the march to madness that we call the Final Four, a Super Bowl of entertainment. In the process, they retained iron-clad control over any and all associated activities capable of generating revenue: licensing, marketing, broadcasting, et cetera. The NCAA rode this lucrative new product to new heights of riches, commercialism, and bureaucracy, as well as to new depths of disregard for players, students, and higher education.

In many ways, the NCAA tournament represents all that is wrong with college sports: the showbiz atmosphere created by the sports media and sustained by the NCAA, the victimization of the student-athlete overwhelmed by both the scheduling and media demands of this event, the celebrity status given the power coaches at the expense of their players and their institutions, and the inconsistency of the values and images swirling about this spectacle and those of the academic enterprise that sponsors these sports programs. And, perhaps most ironic of all, this Frankenstein media monster, so much at odds with the most fundamental values of the academic enterprise, has been created, sanctioned, and nourished by the NCAA, the very organization responsible for the integrity of college sports. But then, perhaps this is not so surprising, since the NCAA tournament generates over $550 million a year that flows directly into coffers of the NCAA.

Case Study 2: Swimming and Diving

Imagine being a coach of a college sports program in which you were able to recruit the very best athletes in the world, win conference championships year after year, compete for the national championship every year, and periodically prepare your student-athletes to compete in the Olympic Games. Imagine you had access to state-of-the-art athletic facilities. And imagine, beyond this, your Olympic-caliber athletes were also outstanding students, able to achieve strong academic success in the most difficult academic programs in the university.

It sounds like nirvana, doesn't it? Look at the smiles on the faces of Michigan men's and women's swimming and diving coaches: Jon Urbancek, Jim Richardson, and Dick Kimball. Year in, year out, these coaches are able to recruit some of the world's greatest swimmers and divers, who are attracted to Michigan over schools in warmer climates as much for the quality of its academic programs as for that of its athletics programs. These are coaches who not only lead programs that compete with the nation's very best every year, but who also have occasional opportunities to coach in the Olympic Games.

Yet there are downsides. At a football school like Michigan, these sports programs usually go relatively unnoticed. In an Olympic year the sports press suddenly discovers Olympians such as Mike Barrowman, Gustavo Borges, or Tom Dolan. But in other years, the swimming and diving teams typically draw only several hundred hard-core fans to their events—even when competing

The men's swimming team. (UM Photo Services.)

against national powers such as Stanford or Texas. Even a national championship draws only brief notice. And, while the coaches do have some opportunities to benefit financially from camps and coaching clinics, they make only a fraction of the income of their football and basketball colleagues.

The same is true for many other sports programs such as gymnastics, cross-country and track, soccer, and crew. All of these sports attract world-class athletes who also perform academically at the highest level. All are low profile. And yet, these programs probably represent much of the best in college sports, achieving a true combination of athletic and academic excellence, even if in obscurity.

Case 3: Men's Ice Hockey

There is yet a third model of a sport that commands high visibility and loyalty on the campus, yet also seems to blend athletic competition with academic values: ice hockey. On the athletics side, it is a fast, rough, and entertaining sport with both professional and Olympic opportunities. It engenders strong and loyal fan interest, with frequent sellout games. It benefits from a strong international character, with student-athletes not only from Canada but also from other nations with avid hockey interests such as Russia and Sweden. Because of the relatively small number of college hockey programs and the lack of a conference or NCAA divisional structure based on institutional size, one finds an unusual institutional diversity. Gigantic universities such as Michigan, Minnesota, and Wisconsin play competitively against small colleges such as Lake Superior State and Colorado College or Ivy League schools such as Harvard and Cornell. Indeed, in what other sport could you ever expect to see Michigan (with an enrollment of thirty-seven thousand students) play Colorado College (twelve hundred students) for the national championship?

Beyond these athletic characteristics, ice hockey also seems to attract student-athletes genuinely interested in the opportunity for a college education. To some degree this can be traced to the strong commitment of many hockey coaches to the academic success of their players. But it could also be due to the fact that so many

Honoring Michigan's 1996 NCAA Champion Ice Hockey Team at the White House. (White House Photo.)

hockey players, particularly those from small Canadian towns, view hockey as a unique opportunity to get a college education. Whatever the reason, the fact remains that an unusually high percentage of hockey players complete their education, even if they later go on to professional careers.

Perhaps hockey provides the most balanced model for intercollegiate athletics, a highly competitive sport drawing world-class athletes, generating high fan interest, and achieving a balance between athletic and academic priorities. What makes hockey different from sports such as football and basketball that have been overwhelmed by commercialism? First, the presence of minor professional leagues provides talented athletes with little interest in college a route to the NHL. Second, there is no national television market for college hockey. While there are local broadcasts of college hockey games, only the national championship game draws a national audience, and even this is small. This low profile has prevented college hockey from evolving into the commercial product, the cash cow, that football and basketball have become, although most programs do cover their expenses. But it has also protected hockey from the gross commercialization that threatens the integrity of the most visible programs.

Conclusion

Throughout the history of higher education in America, sports have always been closely identified with campus life and with academic institutions. Yet throughout this same history, there have always been charges against college sports' inherent professionalism, their stress on providing entertainment rather than educational opportunities for students, their commercialization, and their conflict with academic values.

In a very real sense, the problems in college sports that are of so much concern today are not significantly different than a century ago. The concerns about both the recruiting and academic welfare of student-athletes remain. Celebrity coaches continue to exploit their institutions for personal gain, and their power to pressure their universities continues unchecked. The relationship between college and professional sports continues to create many problems. And the integrity of higher education continues to be threatened by the enormous commercial appeal of college football and basketball.

Yet today there are some differences in the problems, both in character and intensity, from these earlier times. College sports have become a major source of public entertainment in America. Coaches and players have become media celebrities. Dollars from television have distorted institutional priorities and driven unnecessary growth in intercollegiate athletics programs. The media have created a feeding frenzy in which sports columnists rival gossip columnists in their efforts to pander to public curiosity. All these factors have distorted intercollegiate athletics from its original status as an extracurricular activity into just another form of show business, a commercial product of great value. The traditional organizations like the NCAA or the conferences should be resisting this trend, but are too unwieldy to be effective. They, too, have been co-opted by the lure of additional television dollars.

My hypothesis is simple. As long as higher education continues to allow the networks, the media, the sporting apparel companies, and the American public—not to mention celebrity coaches and ambitious athletic directors—to promote and pressure college sports to become an entertainment industry, there will be little progress toward true reform within the athletics programs. Until our universities insist on the primacy of academic objectives and values over those of athletic competitiveness, visibility, and the financial bottom line, true reform is impossible. My fear is that few universities, athletic conferences, and athletic associations will be able to withstand the tremendous pressure and rewards of "big-time athletics," a.k.a. big-time showbiz, not to mention their alumni, public, and governing boards. Few institutions—and few academic leaders—will have the resolve to insist on the dominance of academic principles over financial and entertainment objectives.

Chapter 5   **University 101**

Although I have argued that intercollegiate athletics today is excessively influenced and distorted by external pressures such as the sports media and the commercial marketplace, our athletics programs did not evolve independently from, but rather within, the university. They have been shaped, in part, by the policies and practices, the financing and governance, of the university itself. Therefore to understand the character of college sports in America and the challenge they pose to higher education, we have to understand the nature of the university itself.

For example, most NCAA Division I-A universities tend to regard their athletic departments as "auxiliary activities," responsible for generating most of the revenue to cover their costs through ticket sales, licensing, and broadcasting contracts. In part, this can be traced to the early history of college sports, in which students organized, conducted, and financed their games independent from their colleges. When universities began to take over the administrative and financial responsibilities for intercollegiate athletics, they continued this tradition of independence. Today, athletic departments are operated at arm's length, similar to university hospitals or residence halls, rather than like core academic activities such as teaching departments, research centers, or most student extracurricular activities. This more independent financial status has led in many instances not only to different rules and policies governing athletics, but to management values and cultures that depart quite significantly from those of the academic core of the university.

This independent financial status is compounded by the highly decentralized organization of the contemporary university. Both academic and administrative units are delegated considerable authority in the management of their activities. While there is line-reporting authority, such as faculty to deans, deans to the provost, and the provost to the president, there are not the intricate webs of interlocking controls such as internal audits or financial regulations one would find in a corporation.

The values, goals, and nature of intercollegiate athletics are so totally different from those of academic units that athletic departments generally lie at the periphery of the university. The focus of sports on immediate rather than longer-term results, the dictatorial power of athletic directors and coaches, and the enforcement of discipline through punishment—all are quite alien to the academy, where values such as freedom of thought and freedom of expression reign supreme.

Finally, it is important to realize that while the university has existed as a social institution for many centuries, it also has changed in profound ways in response to changing social needs. Today we have entered yet another period of rapid and profound change in higher education, driven in part by a shrinking resource base, changing societal needs, new technologies such as the computer, and new competitors. While the university will almost certainly continue to play a central role in our future, it is likely to do so on different terms and in different forms than we find today. For-profit colleges, cyberspace universities, global alliances, all are likely to be key elements in the higher-education enterprise of the twenty-first century. Any consideration of a particular activity of the university such as intercollegiate athletics must occur within this context of change and evolution.

What Is a University?

What is a university? There are perhaps as many different definitions as there are individuals who have attended, served, or been served by these marvelous and enduring institutions.[1] To some, the university is "a place of light, of liberty, and of learning" or "a place of instruction where universal knowledge is professed." To others, perhaps more skeptical of such lofty definitions, the university is a far more utilitarian entity, defined by the many roles it

plays in contemporary society: it provides an education for our citizens; produces the scholars, professionals, and leaders needed by
our society; performs the research necessary to generate new
knowledge critical to the progress of our nation; and provides a
number of services to society that draw on the unique expertise of
our institutions.

The most important role of the university in America has been
education. Unlike its European predecessors, America's system of
higher education extended far beyond the education of the elite
and attempted to provide an education to a significant fraction of
our population. A diverse array of institutions evolved to serve our
diverse population, from small colleges to big universities, from
religious to secular institutions, from single-sex to coeducational
colleges, from vocational schools to liberal arts colleges, from
land-grant to urban to national research universities.

To many students and families, this educational role has been
best symbolized by the university's power in granting degrees.
Today almost two-thirds of the public believe that the primary reason for attending college is to earn a degree so that one can get a
good job.[2] Most view the formal educational program as a ticket to
lifetime rewards and security rather than as a road to the lofty
goals of a liberal education.

Beyond formal education in the traditional academic disciplines and professional fields, the university has been expected to
play a far broader role in the maturation of students. It has provided a secure environment, a place where the young could spend
their first years away from their families, both learning and exploring without concern for the risks posed by "the real world." An
undergraduate education is designed to be a time of challenge and
curiosity, discovery, and intellectual development. Note that it is
this purpose that is most frequently used as a justification for
intercollegiate athletics in higher education. The argument is that
competitive athletics can be an important developmental experience, for both participants and spectators.

The second traditional role of our colleges and universities has
been scholarship: the production, criticism, reevaluation, dissemi-
nation, systematization, and preservation of knowledge in all

forms. While the academy would contend that knowledge is important in its own right and that no further justification is required for this role, it is also the case that such scholarship and research have been essential to the university's related missions of instruction and service. The public willingly supported this activity in anticipation of eventual application and benefit to key priorities such as national defense, health care, and social well-being.

The third traditional mission of the university has been to provide service to society. American higher education has long been concerned with furnishing special expertise to address the needs and problems of society. For example, a unique type of institution, the land-grant university, was created in part to respond to the needs of our agricultural and industrial base. The commitment of our universities to the development of professional schools in fields such as medicine, nursing, dentistry, law, and engineering is adequate testimony to the importance of this role. In fact, in one sense, intercollegiate athletics has evolved from a student extracurricular activity to a service activity, with a function of providing public entertainment.

Finally, higher education in America has been expected to provide leadership for society more generally. Public opinion generally holds that the university should serve both as a laboratory and a model, where the major problems of our society can be addressed. In this way, the students and faculty of the university have been challenged to become an intellectual community in which the human mind can be brought to bear on the largest and most enduring questions that confront us.

The nature of the contemporary university and the forces that drive its evolution are complex and frequently misunderstood. The public still thinks of us in very traditional ways, with images of students sitting in large classrooms listening to faculty lecture on subjects such as literature or history. Faculty members think of themselves as Oxbridge dons, and their students as serious scholars. The federal government sees the university as just another R&D contractor or health provider, a supplicant for the public purse. And armchair America sees the university on Saturday afternoon as yet another quasi-professional athletic franchise. Needless to say, the reality is far more complex.

With an annual budget of $3 billion and an additional $3 billion of investment assets under active management, the *U of M, Inc.* would rank roughly 490th on the Fortune 500 list. We educate roughly fifty thousand students on our several campuses, an educational business amounting to about $1 billion per year. The university is also a major federal R&D laboratory, conducting over $500 million a year of sponsored research, supported primarily by federal contracts and grants.

We also run a massive health-care company. Our university-owned hospitals and clinics currently treat almost a million patients a year, with a total medical center income of $1.2 billion. We have a managed-care corporation with over one hundred thousand "managed lives." In 1994, we formed a nonprofit corporation, the Michigan Health Corporation, that will allow us to make equity investments in joint ventures to build a statewide integrated health

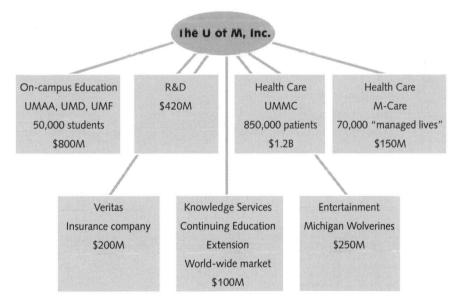

The various business lines of the U of M, Inc.

care system of roughly 1.5 million subscribers, the patient population necessary to keep our university hospitals afloat.

We are already too big and complex to buy insurance, so we have our own captive insurance company, Veritas, incorporated in New Hampshire. We have become actively involved in providing a wide array of knowledge services, from degree programs offered in Hong Kong, Seoul, and Paris, to cyberspace-based products such as the Michigan Virtual University. And, of course, we're involved in public entertainment: the Michigan Wolverines. The $250 million associated with the Michigan Wolverines is not our athletic budget—our operations amount to "only" $45 million per year. But, when we include licensing and marketing, including even the "block M," which the athletic department copyrighted many years ago, our sports activities become a far larger enterprise. It is big-time show business!

This corporate organization chart would compare in both scale and complexity with many major global corporations. And it is not unique to the University of Michigan. Most of the major universities in America have very similar organizational structures, indicative of their multiple missions and diverse array of constituencies.

Financing the University

The operation of a university, just as other enterprises in our society, requires the acquisition of adequate resources to cover the costs of its activities. This is a somewhat more complex task for academic institutions, because of both the wide array of their activities and the great diversity of the constituencies they serve. The not-for-profit culture of the university, whether public or private, leads to a somewhat different approach to the development of a business plan than one would find in business or commerce.

Universities usually begin with the assumption that all of their current activities are both worthwhile and necessary. They first seek to identify the resources that can fund these activities. Beyond that, since there are always an array of worthwhile proposals for expanding ongoing activities or launching new activities, the university always seeks additional resources. It has only been in recent years that the possibility of reallocating resources away from ongoing activities to fund new endeavors has been seriously considered. Strategies from the business world aimed at cutting costs and increasing productivity are relatively new to our campuses.

For most universities, one can identify the following revenue sources:

Tuition and fees paid by students
State appropriations
Federal grants and contracts
Gifts and endowment income
Auxiliary activities (such as hospitals, residence halls, and athletics)

The availability and importance of each of these resources vary greatly, depending upon the nature of the institution and the environment it faces. Most public institutions are heavily dependent upon state appropriation. Small private institutions with modest endowments depend heavily upon tuition and fees, and issues such as enrollments and tuition pricing play a key role in financial strategies. Highly focused research universities such as MIT and Caltech are heavily dependent upon federal research support.

More broadly, however, it is important to recognize the very real financial pressures on most colleges and universities, since these provide a context for understanding college sports. Since the late 1970s, higher education in America has been caught in a financial vise.[3] On the one hand, the magnitude of the services demanded of our colleges and universities has increased considerably. Enrollments have grown steadily. University research, graduate education, and professional service have all grown in response to societal demand.

Yet the costs of providing education, research, and service per unit of activity continue to grow at a rate somewhat faster than inflation. Furthermore, higher education has had difficulty in taking the bold steps to constrain cost increases that have been required in other sectors of our society such as business and industry. This is in part because of the way our colleges and universities are organized, managed, and governed. However, even if our universities should acquire both the capacity and the determination to restructure costs more radically, it is debatable whether those industrial sector actions designed to contain cost and enhance productivity could have the same impact in education. The current paradigm of higher education is simply too people- and knowledge-intensive.

As the demand for educational services has grown and the operating costs to provide these services have risen, public support for higher education has flattened and then declined over the past two decades.[4] The growth in state support of public higher education peaked in the 1980s and now has fallen in many states in the face of limited tax resources and the competition of other priorities such as entitlement programs and prisons. While the federal government has sustained its support of research, growth has been modest in recent years and is likely to decline as discretionary domestic spending comes under increasing pressure from the impact of unconstrained entitlement programs such as Medicare and Social Security. Federal financial aid programs have shifted increasingly from grants to loans and tax incentives as the predominant form of aid.

To meet growing societal demand for higher education at a time when costs are increasing and public support is declining, most institutions have been forced to sharply increase student tuition and fees. This has provided short-term relief, but it has also triggered a strong public concern about the costs of, and access to, a college education, and it has accelerated forces to constrain or reduce tuition levels at both public and private universities.

A Restructuring of the Higher-Education Enterprise

Universities operate in a competitive marketplace. Society seeks services such as education and research. Academic institutions must compete for students, faculty, and resources. To be sure, the market is a strange one, heavily subsidized and shaped by public investment so that prices are always far less than true costs. Furthermore, if "prices" like tuition are largely fictitious, even more so is much of the value of educational services based on myths and vague perceptions. The idea of a college degree as a surefire ticket to success and the prestige associated with certain institutions are perfect examples of this mythology. Ironically, the public expects not only the range of choice that a market provides but also the subsidies that make the price of a public higher education much less than the cost of its provision.

In the past, most colleges and universities served local or regional populations. While there was competition among institutions for students, faculty, and resources, the institutions' power to award degrees, that is, credentialing, led to a tightly controlled competitive market. Universities enjoyed a monopoly over advanced education because of geographical location and their monopoly on credentialing through the awarding of degrees. However, today all of these market constraints are being challenged. The growth in the size and complexity of the postsecondary enterprise is creating an expanding array of students and educational providers. Information technology eliminates the barriers of space and time, and new competitive forces are entering the marketplace to challenge credentialing. We have already seen this technology-driven restructuring in industries such as telecommunications, entertainment, broadcasting, and retailing. Today we see the first waves of restructuring lapping on the shores of higher education.

As a result, higher education is rapidly evolving from a loosely federated system of colleges and universities serving traditional students who live nearby to, in effect, a global knowledge and learning industry. With the emergence of new competitive forces and the weakening influence of traditional regulations, the higher-education enterprise is evolving like other deregulated industries, like health care or communications or energy. Yet, in contrast to these other industries that have been restructured as government regulation has disappeared, the global knowledge industry is being unleashed by emerging information technology—computers, networks, software—that releases education from the constraints of space and time, even as the academic credentialing monopoly begins to break apart.

As our society becomes ever more dependent upon new knowledge and educated people, upon knowledge workers, this global knowledge business must be viewed clearly as one of the most active growth industries of our times. But the learners of our future society will demand that their educational experiences prepare them for a lifetime of learning opportunities, fused both with work and with life. They will seek just-in-time and just-for-you learning through networked organizations. They will seek the integration of timeless and timely knowledge.

The system of higher education that emerges in the decade ahead will almost certainly be far different from today's. Higher education will either transform itself or be transformed, as financial imperatives, changing societal demands, emerging technologies, and new competitors reshape the knowledge enterprise, changing in the process how colleges and universities organize and deliver learning opportunities as well as how they structure and manage their institutions. Universities will have to learn to cope with the competitive pressures of this marketplace while preserving their character and the most important of their traditional values.

Governance

Another topic of interest and relevance to intercollegiate athletics is the governance of the university. American higher education has been relatively free from the centralized federal governing bodies, such as ministries of education, that characterize most other nations, although it is certainly subjected to federal laws, regulation, and bureaucracy. Public colleges and universities are frequently caught in a web of state governance, exercised through legislative controls, state governing or coordinating boards, and statewide systems of higher education. Although such external forces can have considerable impact on the academic mission, available resources, and quality of a university, they rarely intrude into the operation of specific activities such as intercollegiate athletics.

The lay board has been the distinctive American device for "public" authority in connection with universities.[5] The use of lay boards of trustees or regents, comprising citizens appointed or elected to this role, to govern universities evolved in large measure to protect the university from political interference.[6] The function of governing lay boards in American higher education is simple, at least in theory. The board members have final authority for key policy decisions. They accept both financial and legal responsibility for the welfare of the institution. And they select and appoint the university president.

However, in practice, most American colleges and universities have a tradition of "shared governance."[7] Because of the lay board members' very limited expertise, they are expected to delegate the responsibility for policy development, academic programs, and administration to professionals with the necessary training and experience. For example, essentially all governing boards delegate their authority over academic matters to the faculty, generally ceding to the academy the control of academic programs. Furthermore, the day-to-day management of the university is delegated to the president and the administration of the university, since it comprises professionals with the necessary experience in academic, financial, and legal matters.

The heart of the governance of the academic mission of the university is actually not at the level of the governing board or at the presidential level but rather rests in the academic unit, typically at the department or school level. Universities have long accepted the premise that faculty members should govern themselves in academic matters, making all decisions about what should be taught, whom should be hired, and other key academic issues such as the admission and retention of students. Beyond this, faculty have long cherished and defended the tradition of being consulted in other institutional matters, of sharing governance with the governing board and university officers.

A second level of faculty governance occurs at the university level and usually involves an elected body of faculty representatives, such as an academic senate, which serves to debate institution-wide issues and advise the university administration. In sharp contrast to faculty governance at the unit level, which has considerable power and influence, the university-wide faculty governance bodies are generally advisory on most issues, without true power. Although they may be consulted on important university matters, they rarely have any executive authority. The university administration or governing board makes most key decisions.

There are several reasons for this. While the faculty has been quite influential and effective within the narrow domain of their academic programs, the very complexity of their institutions has made substantive involvement in the broader governance of the university difficult. The current disciplinary-driven governance structure of the academy, broken into departments such as English and history, law and medicine, makes it very difficult to deal with broader, strategic issues.[8] Since universities are highly fragmented and decentralized, one frequently finds a chimney organization structure, with little coordination or even concern about university-wide needs or priorities. The broader concerns of the university are always someone else's problem, for example, the president's or the governing board's. And, as we shall see, intercollegiate athletics has become one such area with little direct faculty oversight or participation.

Beyond the fact that it is frequently difficult to get faculty committed to—or even interested in—broad institutional goals that are not necessarily congruent with personal goals, there is an even more important characteristic that prevents true faculty governance at the institution level. Responsibility and accountability always accompany authority. Deans and presidents can be fired. Trustees can be sued or forced off governing boards (at least in private universities). Yet the faculty, through the important academic traditions of academic freedom and tenure, are largely insulated from the consequences of their debates and recommendations. It would be difficult if not impossible, either legally or operationally, to ascribe to faculty bodies the necessary level of accountability that would have to accompany executive authority.

The Role of the President

There is a well-worn definition of the modern university president as someone who lives in a large house and begs for a living. And, to be sure, many presidents do live in large, stately houses on their campuses, while all presidents are expected to be actively involved in fund-raising. But there are other roles. In a sense, the president and spouse are the first family of the university community, in many ways serving as the mayor of a small city of thousands of students, faculty, and staff. This public leadership role is particularly important when the university is very large. As the university's most visible leader, the president must continually grapple with the diverse array of political and social issues and interests of concern to the many stakeholders of higher education: students and parents, state and federal government, business and labor, the press and the public at large, and, of course, the faculty.

The president of a large university also has a significant role as its chief executive officer, responsible for the management of a diverse collection of activities, ranging from education to health care to intercollegiate athletics. However, unlike the corporate CEO, who is responsible primarily for shareholder value, the university president as CEO is held responsible for everything that happens in the university—at least, everything bad. The old expression "the buck stops here" is chiseled in the cornerstone of the university administration building. Anything that happens, whether it involves the president—or, indeed, whether it is even *known* by the president—from student misbehavior to financial misdeeds to town-gown relations to the location of football seats for trustees—eventually ends up on the president's desk.

Further, unlike most corporate CEOs, the president is expected to play an active role generating the resources needed by the university, whether by lobbying state and federal governments, by seeking gifts and bequests from alumni and friends, or by clever entrepreneurial efforts. There is an implicit expectation on most campuses that the president's job is to raise money for the provost and deans to spend, while the chief financial officer and administrative staff watch over their shoulders to make certain they all do it wisely.

The presidential family also plays a pastoral role. Students look to them for parental care, even as they emphasize their rejection of *in loco parentis*. Faculty and staff also seek nurturing and understanding during difficult times for the university. To both those inside and outside, the presidential team is expected always to cheer for the university, be upbeat and optimistic, even though they frequently share the concerns and are subject to the same stresses as the rest of the campus community.

The president is expected to be the defender of the faith, both of the institution itself and the academic values so important to a university. One might think of this latter role as roughly akin to that of a tired old sheriff in a frontier western town. Every day a president has to drag his or her bruised, wounded carcass out of bed, strap on guns, and go out into the main street to face whatever gunslingers have ridden in to shoot up the town that day. Sometimes these are politicians; other times the media; still other times various special interest groups on campus; occasionally even other university leaders such as deans or regents, coaches or athletic directors. And, each time presidents go into battle to defend their university, they know that one day they will run into someone faster on the draw than they are.

The president of a major university, particularly a large public university, is in an unusual leadership position in other respects. Although the responsibility for everything involving the university usually floats up to the president's desk—the buck stops there—the direct authority for university activities almost invariably rests elsewhere. There is a mismatch between responsibility and authority that is unparalleled in other social institutions.

The academic organization of a university is best described as a creative anarchy. Consider it for a moment. A faculty member has two perks that are extraordinary in contemporary society: academic freedom, which means that faculty members can say, teach, or study essentially anything they wish; and tenure, which implies lifetime employment and security. Faculty members do what they want to do. And there is precious little one can do to steer them in directions where they do not wish to go. There is an old expression that leading the faculty is a bit like herding cats.

The corporate side of the university, the professional staff responsible for its financial operations, plant maintenance, public relations, and intercollegiate athletics, might be expected to behave according to the command-communication-control hierarchy of a business. After all, major universities are in reality very complex multi-billion-dollar enterprises, with all of the accountability and demands of a modern business. Yet here too one finds an erosion of the normal lines of authority, almost as if the "I'll do it only if I choose to" culture of the faculty has also infected professional staff. Indeed, this blurring of academic and corporate cultures has been one of the great challenges in putting into place the programs to enhance productivity so successful in the business world.

Little wonder then that recent studies have concluded that the contemporary university president operates from one of "the most anemic power bases of any of the major institutions in American society."[9] They often lack the clear lines of authority they need to act effectively, and are compelled to discuss, negotiate, and seek consensus. And all too often, when controversy develops, presidents find that their major partners, their governing board and the faculty, do not back them up. With trustees and faculty immersed in a broad range of everyday decision-making processes, presidents are bogged down by demands for excessive consultation, a burdensome requirement for consensus, and a fear of change. In practice, either of the two groups—governing boards or faculty—can effectively veto proposals for action, either through endless consultation or public opposition.

Hence governance in higher education is far more complex than in business or government, particularly in a world in which various constituencies, including faculty bodies and governing boards, may occasionally drift away from the best interests of the university. This poses a particular challenge in the control of a highly visible activity such as intercollegiate athletics. As the Knight Commission put it, "The current practice of shared governance leads to gridlock. Whether the problem is with presidents who lack the courage to lead an agenda for change, trustees who ignore institutional goals in favor of the football team, or faculty members who are loath to surrender the status quo, the fact is that each is an obstacle to progress."[10]

The Athletic Department

So where does the athletic department fit into the complex organization of the university? As I have already noted, the principle of institutional control of intercollegiate athletics adopted by the NCAA requires that the president assume ultimate responsibility for the integrity of the athletics program. Hence, the reporting lines of the athletic department must at some point arrive at the office of the president.

But there are many different paths. Some universities put the reporting line of the athletic director and the athletic department with a vice president, such as the vice president for academic affairs (provost) or vice president for finance. Actually, if sports were mainstreamed rather than treated as a special activity, the athletic department would logically report to the vice president for student affairs, since in a sense it is simply another student extracurricular activity. But most presidents believe that intercollegiate athletics is far too visible, far too politically sensitive, and far too hazardous both to them and to their institution to have it managed as simply another student activity.

Although universities are highly decentralized, there is nevertheless an intricate set of controls, of checks and balances, that provides guidance to most academic and administrative units. For example, the chief financial officer has the authority to supervise financial and business matters, including contracting, outsourcing, and expenditures. The personnel office has the authority to make certain that university policies are observed in both hiring and management. The public relations office is expected to coordinate interactions with the media, and the development office coordinates fund-raising activities. The admissions and financial aid officers handle all these key student services functions. And the faculty has its own intricate set of rules, procedures, checks and balances, to govern academic matters.

Yet, in many universities, the athletic department is allowed to operate relatively autonomously from these controls. University practices such as affirmative action and equal opportunity are sometimes bypassed in recruiting and hiring coaches. Contracts with sports apparel companies or broadcasters are negotiated and signed without university approval. Coaches largely ignore the conflict-of-interest rules that restrict other university faculty and staff and benefit financially from commercial endorsements or contracts that exploit the name or reputation of the university. As many universities have learned from bitter experience, and as we will discuss in later chapters, athletic departments that are allowed to operate in such an independent and cavalier fashion can walk the universities far out on a limb that threatens the integrity of their academic mission.

At Michigan, there has been a long-standing practice of having the athletic director and the athletic department report directly to the president. In theory at least, the athletic director was supposed to work closely in day-to-day matters with a faculty body, the Board in Control of Intercollegiate Athletics, which usually contained a vice president as representative of the administration. The athletic director would then consult with the president on major policy issues such as the stance of the university on pending NCAA legislation. In practice, however, the interaction between the athletic director and the president depended very much upon personalities. Sometimes there was a close relationship between the two, which served the university well in both the leadership of the university's athletics programs and its relationship with bodies such as the Big Ten Conference and the NCAA. However, occasionally the university would encounter an athletic director with a more independent streak, who preferred to run the department much like an independent, feudal kingdom. Needless to say, such excessive independence usually spelled trouble.

Chapter 6   # The Governance
                   of Intercollegiate
                   Athletics

During my term as chairman of the Big Ten Conference Council of Presidents (i.e., its board of directors), the conference celebrated its one hundredth anniversary in 1995 with a black-tie gala in the Palmer House Hotel in Chicago. Exactly a century earlier, in the same hotel, the presidents of several major midwestern universities had come together, under the leadership of an earlier Michigan president, James Angell, to form the Western Conference. Their goal was to put into place policies and rules to address the corruption that was then plaguing college football. (It was rumored at the time that most of the players on the Michigan football team were not even students.)

The early years of the Western Conference, which eventually became known as the Big Ten, were difficult. The famous Michigan football coach Fielding Yost, concerned about the conference rules that forbid him to accept outside income, went over Angell's head to lobby the Michigan regents successfully to withdraw from the conference.[1] Eventually, sanity returned and Michigan rejoined, albeit with occasional lapses, such as when Michigan lobbied to prevent Michigan State from joining in the 1950s.

At about the same time that the Big Ten Conference was taking shape, there was action at the national level, initiated by President Theodore Roosevelt, to form an alliance to control injuries and brutality in college football. The result was the National Collegiate Athletics Association, the organization that today has the major responsibility for protecting the integrity and the revenue stream of college sports.

Both the conference structure and the broader NCAA federation are important elements in the current organization and culture of intercollegiate athletics. But so too are the internal mechanisms universities use to govern and control intercollegiate athletics. Intercollegiate athletics today is a highly political enterprise, with an ever-changing balance of forces involving coaches and athletic directors, faculty, presidents and governing boards, conferences and the NCAA, the sports media and the entertainment industry, government and public opinion. This chapter will focus on the governance of intercollegiate athletics, its politics and its politicians.

The Command, Control, and Communications Hierarchy

At the competitive level, the responsibility for program control and integrity rests firmly with the coach. Competitive sports, by nature, demand a clear sense of discipline and direction from the head coach, and in many sports, this discipline has become almost an obsession. Many coaches seek to gain total authority over their programs and their athletes—at least until they run into trouble, when they seek help from all quarters.

In the next level of institutional control, the athletic director is responsible for the administration of the athletic department, for example, hiring and firing coaches, managing budgets and athletic facilities, and interfacing with organizations such as the athletic conference and the NCAA. In the past, many athletic directors have attempted to rule the athletic department as a feudal empire, separate from the university, subject to its own laws and practices, with little need or desire to consult with others. The dictatorial, command-control-communications structure of most athletic departments stands in sharp contrast to the highly consultative, collegial, and occasionally anarchical culture of the academic units of the university.

Many members of the faculty believe that the true control of intercollegiate athletics should be their responsibility, either through specific bodies such as faculty athletics boards or through more general faculty governance. After all, the principal participants are students—or at least one would hope—and these are of concern to the faculty. Faculty members reason further that intercollegiate athletics are presumed to have an educational benefit. Yet, in reality, institutional control does not rest at this level. While many faculty members are concerned about athletics, few have the time to understand the intricacies of contemporary intercollegiate athletics. And rare are those among the faculty who are willing to accept the responsibility and accountability that must accompany the authority for true control.

University governing boards sometimes devote unusual attention to the control, and even occasionally the management, of intercollegiate athletics. Since this is the most visible element of most universities, the more political board members are naturally as attracted to athletics as moths to a flame. Yet, here again, the level of understanding, experience, and accountability of most board members is rather limited and not well aligned with the needs of college sports.

Many external forces challenge and sometimes even subvert institutional control of college athletics. At the least organized level are alumni and sports fans who seek not only to link themselves with successful programs, but also actually to influence these programs through inappropriate involvement in recruitment or other player activities. The media clearly seek to influence college sports, if not control it, since this is usually the part of the paper or news broadcast that most influences circulation or the size of the viewing audience. Universities must contend with the entertainment industry more broadly, which views the broadcasting of college sports as a highly lucrative business, and college sporting events as commercial products. Similarly the sports apparel industry bases much of its advertising and marketing on the endorsements of successful coaches, players, and programs. Even government occasionally gets into the act when legislatures and Congress flex regulatory muscles to demonstrate their concern about intercollegiate athletics by requiring further paperwork and reporting, for instance of student-athlete graduation rates.

Next in the hierarchy of governance are the official bodies actually charged with developing the rules and regulations for college sports: the conference offices and the NCAA. Although these organizations represent themselves as critical regulatory bodies, designed to maintain the integrity of intercollegiate athletics, in fact they tend to focus primarily on promoting and marketing college sports and maintaining competitive balance.

And finally there is the role of the university president. Perhaps to the consternation of the other internal and external constituencies seeking to influence college sports, both the conferences and the NCAA, as well as the organizational structure of the university, place the final responsibility for intercollegiate athletics clearly, firmly, and inescapably with the president of the university.

Coaches

While the public sees the coaches of successful big-time athletics programs as high-paid celebrities, in reality much of the job can be grueling, full of monotonous routines and high stress. So too, the public stereotype of the behavior of college coaches is quite at odds with reality. The camera focuses on the celebrity coach stalking the sideline, deciding on strategies, and entertaining the media in postgame press conferences. But the media also show, perhaps fairly, the dark side of coaching, and we see coaches berating officials, chastising players, or throwing tantrums (and sometimes headsets, linemarkers, and even chairs). While many coaches complain about the pressure to win, in reality, most of this pressure is self-generated. Coaching, by its very nature, attracts type A personalities, driven to win by almost perverse levels of expectations both for themselves and their players.

For the most part, coaches are honest and dedicated professionals, doing what they think is right, motivated to win and intensely loyal to their players. Their actions are, nonetheless, all too frequently at odds with the values and objectives of the university. As part of the highly artificial world of competitive athletics, their decisions are governed by totally different objectives and standards than the academy's. For them, obedience is more important than creativity, the team is more important than the individual, and winning, provided it is according to the rules, is more important than anything else. Integrity is defined in terms of "the rules," which are better designed to regulate competition than to safeguard the welfare of student-athletes and their educational institution. They are all too often stretched, bent, or even broken when the excuse that "everybody else is doing it" becomes a fully functional belief.

Furthermore, today's head coaches are all too frequently publicists or managers of the commercial entertainment businesses their programs have become. They handle the administration of the program, the hiring and firing of assistant coaches, the press conferences, the television and radio appearances, the speaking engagements, and other marketing activities designed as much to promote their personal careers as to benefit their programs. The more routine details such as the conduct of practices, the details of recruiting, the personal relationships with players, and even the development and execution of game strategies are all too frequently assigned to assistant coaches.

For many coaches, these management and public relations responsibilities are an annoyance, drawing them away from those aspects of their profession they most enjoy: working with young people, athletic competition. But for a few of the most visible coaches, the celebrity status seems to reshape not only their behavior but their values. It is not just that these coaches become hypocritical when they lecture their players or the public on the value of loyalty, sacrifice, and dedication, and then demonstrate just the opposite when they exploit their celebrity status for personal gain or break an agreement—whether by honor or by contract—with their university or their players and leave to accept a better job. The bigger problem is that many celebrity coaches have become so isolated from their universities that they no longer can tell the difference between right and wrong. They actually believe they have the right to behave with such blatant self-interest. Few even know of university regulations governing conflict of interest and external compensation that constrain the activities of other university employees. Many are blind to the academic purpose of the university.

Many years ago, most coaches were also members of the teaching staff of universities. In today's high-pressure world of big-time college sports, coaching has not only become highly professionalized, but it operates in a marketplace that accepts the assumption that big-name coaches will move from university to university, or perhaps even to the professional leagues, if such mobility enhances their personal prosperity or status. Although celebrity coaches preach the importance of loyalty to dear old State to their players and staff, most are all too willing to break a personal commitment or contract to achieve personal gain. Sometimes the offers and counteroffers can become not only amusing but even ludicrous. During the peak of his success as Michigan's head football coach, Bo Schembechler agreed to consider an offer from Texas A&M. Not only was Michigan forced to come up with an attractive counteroffer, but pizza king Tom Monaghan offered Schembechler a Domino's Pizza franchise if he would stay. In Columbus, Ohio, no less!

Some would argue that the competitive marketplace for coaches is no different than for star faculty or even academic administrators, and that a truly outstanding coach benefits a university through the visibility and riches attracted by winning programs. Yet we should keep in mind that universities never attempt to compete with the private marketplace, with business or industry, to retain top faculty, so the comparison is uneven at heart. And from a financial perspective, while there are always a few great coaches, their impact on either the reputation of a university or its finances is marginal at best. After all, the real reputation of a university is determined by academics, not athletics. Finally, we also know that essentially all the revenue generated by athletics simply flows back to pay the expenses of the athletic department. We have seen too many instances of talented assistant coaches stepping successfully into the void left by a departing celebrity coach to support the marketplace contention that coaching draws from a sufficiently small talent pool to merit such star treatment.

The cult of the celebrity coach is a serious problem. In reality, many coaches have little connection with their university. At the same time, they are also frequently popular community figures, better known than anyone else in the university. Hence, they are surrounded by powerful legions of loyal boosters and supporters, ready to defend the celebrity coach against any who would challenge his or her authority. Little wonder that many presidents are reluctant to act against this booster coalition since it might compromise their own political support. When celebrity coaches attempt to pressure the university through the influence of powerful financial contributors, politicians, or even members of governing boards, both the president and the university can be at great risk.

The Athletic Director

Although the university president has the ultimate responsibility for the athletic department, on a day-by-day basis this authority is delegated to the athletic director, much as authority is distributed in other key areas of the university. As I said earlier, most athletic directors carry considerable authority. They hire and fire coaches. They manage the business operations of the athletic department. They are responsible for the welfare of student-athletes. And they are responsible for the integrity of the university's athletic programs, including its compliance with institutional, conference, and NCAA policies and regulations.

Most athletic departments operate much as athletic teams do, with a military style of command and control hierarchies, where coaches report to and take direction from the athletic director. To some degree the nature of college sports itself demands this, since coaches are authority figures to both players and assistants and naturally respond to athletic directors in the same way. But the power of the contemporary athletic director is also a consequence of the historical independence of athletics programs from the university, since the athletic director's decisions and actions are seldom questioned by those in the university administration. Many athletic directors do exercise this power behind the scenes, avoiding the press, and leaving a more visible role to their coaches and players. However some athletic directors prefer to assume a more visible role, sometimes even overshadowing coaches and programs as a symbol of the athletic department.

In theory, the athletic director has line responsibility for coaches and staff in the athletic department. In practice, this can sometimes be a challenge when one of the programs has a celebrity coach, with popularity and influence that extends far beyond the campus. The authority of the athletic director must therefore be clearly specified and understood by all so that coaches do not use their power and influence to advance their own interests at the expense of the department or the university.

These responsibilities create a serious conflict of interest in situations where an athletic director also wears the hat of a head coach. Beyond the simple fact that both jobs are extremely demanding and complex, some of the director's responsibilities and decisions are incompatible with the responsibilities of a coach for a particular team. Such dual appointments clearly undermine the concept of institutional control. Yet they continue to occur from time to time when a coach becomes so powerful that the search for an athletic director becomes impossible.

The athletic director is responsible for both the integrity and the financial health of the athletic department. In years past, athletic directors were selected from the ranks of coaches. While these individuals brought experience and understanding of competitive athletics, they also tended to bring with them many aspects of the coaching culture: a dictatorial management style, a desire for absolute control that all too often isolated athletic departments from the rest of the university, and a total lack of understanding of financial management. A standing caution passed on from president to president these days is never to hire an athletic director who has worn a whistle around her or his neck. Instead, presidents are increasingly looking for people with far broader experience in leading and managing the type of complex organization that modern athletics programs have become. The management of a modern intercollegiate athletics program involves a broad range of skills and experience: leadership, fiscal management, personnel relations, public relations, and, perhaps most important, a deep understanding and acceptance of academic values as preeminent in a university. Few university presidents lament the disappearance of the "AD" (athletic dinosaur) athletic director, a term used by some of my Big Ten colleagues.

Many universities have turned to the business world in their search for the leaders of their athletic departments. And to be sure, certain aspects of intercollegiate athletics are similar to a business enterprise: the need to generate adequate revenue to cover expenses, cost containment, facilities management, marketing and advertising. In fact, some contemporary athletic directors would portray their roles as essentially chief executive officers of self-supporting entertainment businesses, loosely affiliated with their universities. They view their role primarily as running a commercial entertainment business, in which the customer is the spectator and the objective is competitive and financial success. In such cases, the needs of the student-athlete and the broader roles and responsibilities of the university are sometimes ignored or swept aside.

While this is certainly important to the financial integrity of the athletic department, too great a focus on the business nature of intercollegiate athletics can be very dangerous to a university. One must never lose sight of the fact that athletic departments, for all of their business characteristics, are nevertheless part of academic institutions. Their primary participants are students, whose participation in sports should (ideally) be an extracurricular experience that is beneficial to their education. Student-athletes are not commercial entertainment products.

As I will suggest later in this book, I believe that the qualifications of an athletic director need to be reordered. Beyond an understanding of competitive athletics and business acumen, an athletic director should have both experience in and appreciation for the fundamental activity of a university, education.

The Faculty

At the most fundamental level the operational responsibility for the intellectual and academic integrity of a university must rest with the faculty. To the degree that intercollegiate athletics is supposed to be related to the educational mission of the university, the faculty should certainly have a role in the development and monitoring of broad athletics policies governing intercollegiate athletics. Faculty control is generally achieved through two mechanisms: faculty bodies formed to govern intercollegiate athletics, and faculty representatives to athletic organizations such as the conferences and the NCAA.

The primary means for faculty involvement in intercollegiate athletics has been through the former: governing or advisory bodies associated with athletic departments. For example, since its earliest days, the Big Ten Conference insisted on faculty control of sports. (In fact, the earliest name of the conference was the Intercollegiate Athletic Conference of Faculty Representatives.)[2] To this end, the conference required that each university form a faculty governance council, responsible for the integrity of the athletics programs. At Michigan, this body is known as the Board in Control of Intercollegiate Athletics (BICIA). In theory, it plays an important role not only in governing intercollegiate athletics at the university, but also in assuring the integrity of its programs and the welfare of its student-athletes through subcommittees such as its Academic Standing Committee.

But there is a problem here. A strong athletic director can influence the membership of such faculty bodies, both by shaping their general composition and by influencing the selection of its particular members. For example, over the years, faculty influence on the Michigan board was diluted by adding alumni members, selected by several of the more athletics-dominated alumni clubs (e.g., Detroit, Grand Rapids). There were instances of alumni with particularly strong interests in athletics lobbying both the athletic director and the regents to be selected for the faculty board. Furthermore, the athletic director would sometimes attempt to stack the board with faculty members who shared an unusual interest in or sympathy for college sports. Even faculty on the BICIA have felt strong incentives to be sensitive to the concerns of the athletic director, since they were showered with perks: preferred seating and other special consideration at major athletic events and the long-standing practice that the members of the BICIA and their spouses were included as part of the official party to bowl games.

At Michigan, faculty influence was diluted even further by the fact that the athletic director chaired the BICIA, determining its meeting schedule and its agenda. There were times that the athletic director actually used the BICIA to further isolate the athletic department from the university. Although the board was rarely engaged in key issues facing the athletic department (e.g., budget, gender equity, Big Ten Conference negotiations), it did serve as a convenient excuse for not touching bases with the university administration on key issues. Important decisions such as broadcasting- and licensing-contract negotiations and personnel policies did not flow through the usual business or personnel channels of the university. This occasionally caused great havoc in the university more broadly, such as when the athletic department negotiated a new radio broadcasting contract that cut out the campus radio station or when a bowl game was scheduled during finals week without the president's knowledge.

There is one further wrinkle in the faculty governance of intercollegiate athletics at the university. Each Big Ten institution has, by conference rules, a faculty athletics representative, appointed by the president, who plays a very key role not only in the governance of athletics programs on campus, but also in serving on a faculty body to oversee intercollegiate athletics at the conference and the NCAA level. The faculty athletic representative serves as the principal interface between the university and the conference in critical matters such as rules violations and athletic eligibility. This faculty member also plays an important role in representing the university at the NCAA level. Several of Michigan's most distinguished faculty members have served in this role, usually for periods of several years to gain the necessary experience.

Since the faculty athletics representative reports directly to the president, it is inevitable that there are occasionally issues that put the faculty athletic representative at odds with the athletic director. In fact, without the cooperation of the athletic director, the faculty athletic representative would have great difficulty in performing her or his role. At Michigan, this situation was made somewhat more complex by the presence of two faculty athletics representatives, one for men's sports and one for women's sports. Both faculty representatives, along with the athletic director and president, were involved in governance issues at both the Big Ten Conference level and NCAA level, so careful coordination was required to make certain that the university spoke with a single voice on key issues. Today the men's and women's faculty athletic representatives have been merged, but this difference in perspective from men's and women's sports remains.

The Athletic Conference

Athletic conferences such as the Big Ten are supposed to operate under faculty control, with faculty members from conference universities controlling both the conference and the athletic departments on their respective campuses. Yet from the earliest days of the conferences, the real power has resided with the coaches and the athletic directors.

Most athletic conferences were originally organized by the university presidents of their member institutions. In the past the responsibility for managing conference activities was delegated to the conference commissioner working with the athletic directors and faculty representatives of each institution. Presidents would meet on conference matters each year, but the detailed governance of the conferences was delegated to others.

Today things are very different. Beyond the fact that the risks associated with intercollegiate athletics demand the direct participation and oversight of university presidents, the financial operations of major athletic conferences have required them to become legal corporations, with the presidents of its member institutions designated as their boards of directors. The size of the broadcasting contracts negotiated by major athletic conferences and their increasing financial responsibility—and liability—requires such a formal legal structure. Through the new articles of incorporation, the presidents have both authority over and responsibility for the matters of the conference similar to those held by other boards of directors.

For example, the Big Ten Conference became incorporated in 1985. Although it was evident that this would require the presidents to play a more direct role in the governance of the conference through their duties as its board of directors, there were other important implications not immediately apparent to most. With incorporation, all other conference constituencies that had traditionally controlled conference activities, such as athletic directors, coaches, faculty representatives, and even the governing boards of the member institutions, became advisory in nature. Only the presidents, sitting as the conference board of directors, had legal authority in conference structure, financing, policy, and so forth. And with both legal and financial responsibilities, the presidents were obliged to be active participants in the governance of the conference.

The amount of time university presidents devote to the governance of intercollegiate athletics at the institution, conference, and NCAA level may seem excessive to some. Beyond the regularly scheduled two-day meetings held by the Big Ten presidents each winter and summer, there are also frequent half-day meetings at other presidents' gatherings, retreats, teleconferences, and committee meetings held to deal with conference matters. NCAA matters generally required a multiday commitment for the national convention in January, along with various committee meetings on specific issues throughout the year. And, of course, within the institution, presidents are actively involved throughout the year, whether in governance, personnel matters, or just flying the flag through their attendance at numerous athletic events. But intercollegiate athletics is so visible, and the consequences of missteps so serious, that such presidential attention is almost mandatory.

The issues that presidents deal with at the conference level range from the cosmic to the mundane. During my years as president, among the more significant were the decisions on conference expansion (e.g., adding Penn State), renegotiating revenue-sharing policies, efforts to control the escalating costs of sports, the structuring of the major broadcasting contracts, the negotiation of the Rose Bowl's merging with the football Bowl Championship Series alliance, and the decision to commit to a timetable for the achievement of gender equity. However, as in all such activities, there is also a tendency to delve into microdetails, particularly when it came to reaching conference positions on the myriad proposed changes in the NCAA rules.

Beyond their concern about the future of intercollegiate athletics, the Big Ten presidents were also drawn together by some other challenges. For example, many presidents had inherited athletics programs dominated by powerful athletic directors or power coaches who were strongly resistant to an active role of the presidents. The presidents were unanimous in their conviction that true reform in intercollegiate athletics required that their universities regain control of athletics, and they were determined to achieve this. One by one the old guard of independent athletic directors were replaced by a new generation of young leaders, generally coming from outside the traditional world of college sports, and more capable of dealing with the complex management, financial, personnel, legal, and educational issues swirling around today's intercollegiate athletics programs.

The nature of the commissioners selected by the major conferences has undergone a similar transformation. In years past, the principal role of the commissioner was to work with the athletic directors. However, today, the responsibilities and activities of the commissioner of a major athletic conference such as the Big Ten are quite similar to those of the commissioner of a major professional league. Commissioners need the people skills to work with the varied interests of the presidents of the conference's universities, who, after all, form the board of directors, as well as with athletic directors, coaches, faculty representatives, and student-athletes. They need the business acumen to negotiate broadcasting contracts, bowl relationships, and licensing agreements worth hundreds of millions of dollars. They need to have an understanding of the myriad legal issues surrounding intercollegiate athletics. And, of course, they need to have strong skills in public relations and dealing with the media.

Because most modern conferences are incorporated, the conference commissioner has become ever more involved in working directly with university presidents in their role as board of directors of the conference corporation. The relationship between the modern conference commissioner and the university presidents is not unlike that of the commissioner of a major professional league and team owners. It requires great skill, agility, and a sense of humor. Furthermore, since today's modern university presidency is not a particularly stable situation, with the average tenure of public university presidencies now less than five years, the conference commissioner has to be able to tolerate rapid change.

Today's major athletic-conference office functions more like a business enterprise than an association of academic institutions with primary responsibility for the integrity of college sports. To be sure, these offices do assist institutions in understanding and complying with the ever more complex rules of the NCAA. They provide compliance programs, rules seminars, and help in evaluating complex issues. However, the investigation and handling of serious violations is generally bumped up to the NCAA level, which is far better equipped to handle these matters. Today, a primary activity of the conferences has become the negotiation of television contracts, the management of conference championship events, and the provision of a coordinated interface with the NCAA.

The National Collegiate Athletics Association

As I noted in the introduction to this chapter, the National Collegiate Athletics Association was formed in 1906 to counter the brutality and professionalization then characterizing college football. Although this association of colleges and universities was charged with protecting the integrity and amateurism of intercollegiate athletics, in reality the NCAA played a rather minor role in college sports until the late 1940s. As growing scandals in football and basketball began to stimulate calls from educators and the media to de-emphasize college sports, the commissioners of several of the major conferences decided in 1946 to use a strengthened NCAA to promote "an enforced policy of amateurism" as a mechanism for damage control.[3] Although the NCAA portrayed itself as the defender of the integrity of college sports, in reality this was primarily a public relations effort, aimed at deflecting criticism rather than exploring more fundamental reforms.

These contradictory roles both characterize and define the NCAA today. On the one hand, it is charged with establishing and enforcing rules that maintain both the competitive balance and integrity of college sports. Yet it is also responsible not only for promoting, selling, and occasionally defending college sports, but also for serving as a university cartel to negotiate broadcasting rights for major events such as the NCAA basketball tournament. In this latter role the primary objective of the NCAA is to maximize profits for colleges and universities in the negotiation of broadcasting rights and the management of national championship events. Put another way, the NCAA has been charged with the formidable—and perhaps impossible—task of simultaneously guarding the integrity of intercollegiate athletics while generating hundreds of millions of dollars in income for its member institutions.

Throughout its long history, the NCAA has tried to accommodate these dual and conflicting roles. It has attempted to lead (or to at least appear to lead) major efforts to reform and regulate intercollegiate athletics. At the same time, the NCAA has been a major force in driving the evolution of college football and basketball into an entertainment industry, particularly with its control and promotion of the televising of football and the NCAA basketball tournament.

Over the past two decades, the NCAA has increased its revenues by over 8,000 percent, with major broadcasting contracts such as the $6 billion contract with CBS for broadcast of the NCAA men's basketball tournament in 1999.[4] Although the NCAA was created as a nonprofit educational organization, each year it generates over $550 million in revenue. Operating far more like a professional league than an educational association, it now pays high salaries to its administrators, conducts its meetings at expensive resorts (where a nearby world-class golf course is a requirement), strokes its various oversight committees with first-class air travel to events, and wines and dines corporate sponsors and business prospects. In fact, about the only characteristic that distinguishes the NCAA from the NFL or the NBA is that it does not pay income taxes on its millions of dollars of television revenue, licensing, and sponsorship.

The NCAA also faces another practical challenge: coping with the great diversity in perspectives and goals of the various representatives of the 983 member institutions that comprise the association. These range from gigantic public university campuses to elite private universities, from commuter campuses to small liberal arts colleges. Each of these institutions is also represented by a diversity of views, from coaches, athletic directors, faculty representatives, and presidents. It is understandable that in the effort to accommodate the diverse views of these institutions and their representatives, the NCAA should become more and more unwieldy.

Before 1996 this was thrown into sharpest relief at the NCAA's annual meetings and conventions, events more like a political party convention in a presidential election year than a meeting of educators. This is not surprising, since the stated purpose of the NCAA is to secure in college athletics "a consensus legislative plan on the ground rules to guide amateurism and its values in an ethical sense."[5] Here, wildly disparate views of almost a thousand diverse institutions came together and were processed into the rules and regulations governing intercollegiate athletics. Rules were proposed, passed, revised, and appealed on every aspect of college sports, from recruiting constraints to eligibility standards to team travel arrangements. And, as they say about the making of laws in legislatures or Congress, the process was like making sausage: you only wanted to see the final result.

The spectacle of the convention itself was something to behold. Not only was each institution represented by athletic directors, faculty representatives, and, frequently, presidents, but beyond this, hundreds of coaches descended to the lobby with their particular agendas. Hundreds more staff members from the conferences and the NCAA joined the crowd. In fact, few convention centers—even cities—were capable of holding this annual event. In days past, voting on particular issues always occurred using paddles, one per institution. However, in more modern electronic times, electronic voting was used, with each institution using a radio-transmitter to send its vote to a central computer, which, almost instantaneously, computed vote totals. Despite this technology, the NCAA convention was a very human and intensely political phenomenon. People believed deeply about the hundreds of issues that swirled about each convention, and they fought hard to have their viewpoint accepted. There were complex motions, amendments, and intricate parliamentary maneuvers. In fact, frequently the real outcome and consequences of a convention were not known until long afterward. Most conferences and even the presidents themselves had meetings throughout the convention to better understand the issues and to develop agendas and strategies.

Like political conventions, the events surrounding the conference seemed like a bit of a circus. Members of the press were everywhere, trying to find a sensational story or stir up some gossip. Coaches and athletic directors were wheeling and dealing, not infrequently to find new jobs. The faculty representatives wandered about trying to find where their next meeting was scheduled—or the nearest hospitality suite. And the presidents in attendance did their best to prevent the old athletic establishment from controlling the NCAA agenda and intercollegiate athletics.

Throughout most of its history, the NCAA has been strongly influenced by power coaches and athletic directors. Influential faculty representatives have managed on occasion to deflect if not control the evolution of college sports from time to time. But until the early 1980s, it is fair to say that on most issues, the coaches and athletic directors usually had their way. However, forces were also building within other higher-education organizations such as the American Council on Education to shift power away from the athletic directors and coaches to the presidents. After years of frustration in attempting to push reform through the established athletics bureaucracy, the presidents came together, first by forming in 1986 a Presidents' Commission to develop a reform agenda for the NCAA, then by taking a more active role in the NCAA convention. The strong attendance by university presidents at the NCAA convention in recent years has been both to demonstrate visibly their support for the reform agenda of the Presidents' Commission and to make certain that the delegation from their university votes in the appropriate fashion. In earlier years, when presidents were not so visible, delegations could sometimes be hijacked by forceful athletic directors or coaches and persuaded to vote on a particular issue in a manner at odds with broader institutional interests. After all, the NCAA convention was a *political* convention, and politics reigned supreme.

In 1996 the NCAA was completely restructured, transforming it from an association controlled by athletics interests to a federation of universities clearly controlled by their presidents. The growing role of the presidents in governing the NCAA has been more visible—and more strongly resisted—than their takeover of athletic conferences. But both were equally significant and similarly inevitable.

Today, the aspects of the NCAA convention that resemble a political convention have been replaced by a series of committees within each division that consider various rule changes. Although most decisions are made at the division level, those that would affect NCAA members as a whole are referred to a Management Council, comprised of athletics officials and faculty representations, and finally to a Board of Directors comprised of university presidents. Although there is an opportunity for broad consultation with the membership, decisions are made by these governance panels and not by NCAA-wide votes at annual conventions as in the past. To be sure, the process remains complicated, but at least it avoids much of the politics and tyranny of the majority that paralyzed the NCAA in the past.

Throughout almost a century of existence, the NCAA has existed essentially as a trade association, with the primary objective of defending the status quo of college sports as a commercial entertainment industry, largely for the benefit of those who profit, such as coaches and athletic directors, and those who exploit, such as the television networks, the commercial sponsors, and the sports press. Although some looked to the NCAA for reform, in reality this could not have happened as long as it was controlled by coaches and athletic directors. The chickens would never be safe as long as the foxes were in the henhouse.

Today the restructuring of the NCAA into a federation has given the university presidents, particularly of Division I, firm control of the new NCAA federation, albeit challenged at times both by internal constituencies such as coaches and athletic directors, and external forces such as the sports media. For the first time in decades, there is a real opportunity to control and perhaps even to reform intercollegiate athletics. That is, there is the opportunity for reform if there is the will among university leaders.

The Role of the President

Though the final responsibility and authority for intercollegiate athletics should and usually does end up on the president's desk, the president's function is neither well understood nor frequently accepted by members of the university community and its supporters. The fundamental principle of integrity in intercollegiate athletics is based upon presidential control and accountability. This has been reaffirmed time and time again by formal governing bodies ranging from the NCAA to the conferences to university governing boards.

Of course, this should not be surprising since the president has broad responsibility for the welfare of the university including its academic quality and integrity, its financial strength, and its public accountability. One would think that in view of the immense size and complexity of the contemporary university and the issues that swirl about it, sports would be only a peripheral concern. Yet if we were to corner any major university president in a candid moment, he or she would likely admit that many of the problems arising with the various internal and external constituencies of the university could be traced to intercollegiate athletics. Whether it is a concern about program integrity, or a booster-driven pressure for team success, or media pressure for access to coaches and players, or overinvolvement by trustees, presidents are frequently placed in harm's way by athletics. Whether they like it or not, most presidents learn quickly that they must become both knowledgeable and actively involved in their athletics programs. As Peter Flawn, former president of the University of Texas, put it in his wonderful "how-to" book on university leadership "If you are a sports enthusiast and enjoy intercollegiate athletics, so much the better; if you are not . . . fake it."[6]

The principle of presidential authority and responsibility for intercollegiate athletics as the key to institutional control has caused a sea change in the governance of college sports in recent years. Although most universities have long had a formal system in place wherein the athletic department reports to the president, it was not uncommon in years past for powerful athletic directors to keep the president and the institution at arm's length. However, by the 1980s, it became clear that the days of the czar athletic director and independent athletic department were coming to an end. College sports were becoming simply too visible and their impact on the university too great for their control and management to be left entirely to the direction of the athletics establishment, its values, and its culture.

This shift in control was reinforced by changes in the governance of athletic conferences. As the major conferences became more directly involved in negotiating large broadcasting contracts, it was necessary for them to incorporate to provide the necessary financial and legal structure. Today in most major conferences, university presidents serve as the board of directors in a legal sense, with both ultimate authority and fiduciary responsibility. As we noted earlier, when the Big Ten Conference incorporated, the university presidents assumed the role of its board of directors responsible for both policy and financial oversight. This effort demands a great deal of time; since the operations of the conference are quite extensive and more like a professional league such as the NFL or NBA than an academic association. Big Ten Conference presidents spend many days each year over at the conference offices in Chicago or elsewhere about the country, working—or sometimes jousting—with other presidents on intercollegiate athletics matters.

However, while the responsibility for intercollegiate athletics is consistent with the president's other duties, it is also clear that no president can or should play a hands-on role in directing college sports. As with most other activities, control depends on the delegation of authority to key leaders such as the provost, chief financial officer, or athletic director and the establishment of a careful system for monitoring compliance with institutional, conference, and NCAA policies.

Such a leadership philosophy is well accepted and effective in most other areas of the university, such as its academic programs. But the relative newness of this approach to athletics, the long tradition of athletic departments' relative independence from the rest of the institution, and the maelstrom of external forces upon college sports raise serious questions as to whether this leadership approach is now adequate. When the president focuses attention on the athletics enterprise, with the support of the governing board, there is usually sufficient authority available for adequate control. However, as the president's other duties call for attention, there is the serious possibility that the old culture of independence of intercollegiate athletics may once again reappear, to the detriment of both sports programs and the university that hosts them.

Chapter 7   Financing College Athletics

The sports media fuel the belief that money is the root of all evil in college athletics. And, indeed, the size of the broadcasting contracts for college football and basketball events, the compensation of celebrity coaches, and the professional contracts dangled in front of star athletes make it clear that money does govern many aspects of intercollegiate athletics.

For example, Michigan, along with many other universities with big-time athletics, claims that football is a major money-maker. In fact, Michigan boasted that it made a profit of $14 million from its football program in 1997, the year it won the national championship. Furthermore, Division I-A football programs reportedly averaged profits of $5 million in this year. Yet at the same time, most athletic departments plead poverty when confronted with demands that they increase varsity opportunities for women or financial aid for student-athletes. In fact, many athletic departments in Division I-A will actually admit that when all the revenues and expenses are totaled up, they actually lose money.

What is going on here? Could it be that those reporting about the economics of college sports have difficulty understanding the Byzantine financial statements of athletic departments? Are accounting tricks used to hide the true costs of intercollegiate athletics? Or perhaps those who lead and manage college sports have limited understanding of how financial management and business accounting works in the first place?

It is probably all of the above, combined with the many other myths about the financing of college sports, which confuse not only outsiders such as the press and the public, but even those insiders such as the university administration, athletic directors, and coaches. Before we dive into a discussion of how college athletics are financed these days, I want to straighten out several of the more common misperceptions.

Stripping Away the Myths

First, most members of the public, the sports press, and even many faculty members believe that colleges make lots of money from sports. In reality, essentially all of the revenue generated by sports is used by athletic departments to finance their own operations. Indeed, very few intercollegiate athletics programs manage to balance their operating budgets.[1] The revenue from gate receipts, broadcasting rights, postseason play, licensing, and other commercial ventures is rarely sufficient to cover the full costs of the programs. Most universities rely on additional subsidies from student fees, booster donations, or even state appropriations. Beyond that, college sports benefit from a tax-exempt status on operations and donations that represents a very considerable public subsidy.

The University of Michigan provides an interesting case study of the financing of intercollegiate athletics, since it is one of only a handful of institutions that usually manages to generate sufficient revenue to support the cost of operations (although not the full capital costs) for its intercollegiate athletics programs. Even for Michigan, financing intercollegiate athletics remains an ongoing challenge. For example, during the 1988–89 fiscal year, my first year as president, the University of Michigan won the Big Ten football championship, the Rose Bowl, and the NCAA basketball championship. The university also appeared in seven national football telecasts and dozens of basketball telecasts, played in a football stadium averaging 105,000 spectators a game, and sold out most of its basketball and hockey events. Yet it barely managed to break even that year, with a net profit on operations of about $1 million on $35 million of revenue. We should have been thankful for even this small operating "profit" since in more recent times, Michigan has begun to experience significant operating deficits.

Michigan's 1997–98 operating budget for intercollegiate athletics amounted to roughly $45 million based on revenues from gate receipts of $16 million; sponsorship, signage, and licensing revenue of $8 million; and private gifts of $7 million. This sounds like a large budget, but it is less than 2 percent of a total university budget of roughly $3 billion. When I was provost, football coach Bo Schembechler once complained to me about the enormous pressures to keep Michigan Stadium filled. He pointed to the losses that we would face if stadium attendance dropped 10 percent. I responded that, while this loss would be significant, it paled in comparison to the loss we would experience with a 10 percent drop in bed occupancy in the University of Michigan hospitals, which have an income more than twenty times larger than that of Michigan football ($1.2 billion in 1997). Even football revenue has to be placed in perspective.

The University of Michigan, as one of the nation's most successful athletics programs, generates one of the highest levels of gross revenue in intercollegiate athletics. Despite this fact, in some years, the expenditures of our athletic department actually exceed revenues. For example, in the 1998–99 fiscal year following the football team's national championship season, the athletic department actually ran an operating deficit of $2.8 million. This paradox is due, in part, to the unique "business culture" of intercollegiate athletics. The competitive nature of intercollegiate athletics leads most athletic departments to focus far more attention on generating revenue than on managing costs. There is a widespread belief in college sports that the team that spends the most wins the most, and that no expenses are unreasonable if they might enhance the success of a program. A fancy press box in the stadium? First-class travel and accommodations for the team? A million-dollar contract for the coach? Sure, if it will help us win! Furthermore, the financing of intercollegiate athletics is also complicated by the fact that while costs such as staff salaries, student-athlete financial aid, and facilities maintenance are usually fixed, revenues are highly variable. In fact, in a given year, only television revenue for regular events is predictable. All other revenue streams, such as gate receipts, bowl or NCAA tournament income, licensing revenue, and private gifts, are highly variable.

While some revenues such as gate receipts can be accurately pre-
dicted, particularly when season tickets sales are significant, others
such as licensing and private giving are quite volatile. Yet many
athletic departments (including Michigan, of late) build these speculative revenues into annual budgets that sometimes crash and
burn in serious deficits when these revenues fail to materialize.

Needless to say, this business philosophy would rapidly lead to
bankruptcy in the corporate world. It has become increasingly
clear that until athletic departments begin to operate with as much
of an eye on expenditures as revenues, universities will continue to
lose increasing amounts of money in their athletic activities, no
matter how lucrative the television or licensing contracts they may
negotiate.

Well, even if athletic departments essentially spend every dollar they generate, don't winning programs motivate alumni to
make contributions to the university? To be sure, some alumni are
certainly motivated to give money to the university while (and,
perhaps, only when) basking in the glow of winning athletic programs. But, many of these loyal alumni and friends give *only* to
athletic programs and not to the university more generally. And
the amounts they give are relatively modest. For example, the total
gifts to Michigan's athletics program amount to only about $5 mil-
lion per year. By way of comparison, the annual gifts to the university more generally are currently about $180 million a year. In
1997 we finished a $1.4 billion fund-raising campaign, with less
than $10 million of this amount given to intercollegiate athletics.

University fund-raising staff have known for many years that
the most valuable support of a university generally comes from
alumni and friends who identify with the *academic* programs of
the university, not its athletic prowess. In fact, many of the university's most generous donors care little about its athletic success
and are sometimes alienated by the attention given to winning
athletics programs.

The staggering sums involved in television contracts, such as
the $6 billion contract with CBS for televising the NCAA tourna-
ment, suggest that television revenue is the goose that lays the
golden eggs for intercollegiate athletics. But for most institutions,

ticket sales are still the primary source of revenue. Indeed, there is some evidence that television can have a negative impact on the overall revenues of many athletic programs by overexposing athletic events and eroding gate receipts. Lower game attendance brought on by television has been particularly harmful to those institutions and conferences whose sports programs are not broadcast as primetime or national events, since many of their fans stay home from university events in order to watch televised events involving major athletic powers.

The additional costs required to mount "TV quality" events tend to track increasing revenue in such a way that the more one is televised, the more one must spend. More and more institutions are beginning to realize that there is little financial incentive for excessive television coverage. While exposure can convey the good news of successful athletic programs and promote the university's visibility, it can also convey "bad news," particularly if there is a major scandal or a mishap with an event.

If the financial and publicity impact of television is not necessarily positive, why is there then such a mad rush on the part of athletics programs for more and more television exposure? Speaking from the perspective of one of the most heavily televised universities in the country, my suspicion is that the pressure for such excessive television coverage is not coming from the most successful and most heavily televised institutions—the Michigans, Ohio States, and UCLAs. It is, instead, coming from the "have-not" institutions, those who have chosen not to mount competitive programs but who have become heavily dependent on sharing the television revenue generated by the big box office events through conference or NCAA agreements.

Stated more bluntly, the television revenue-sharing policies of many conferences or broader associations, such as the NCAA, while implemented with the aim of achieving equity, are failing. They are, in reality, having the perverse effect of providing strong incentives for those institutions that are not attractive television draws to drive the system toward excessive commercialization or exposure of popular events. While the have-not universities share in the revenues, these institutions do not bear the financial burden or disruption of providing television-quality events. In a sense, the revenue-sharing system does not allow for negative feedback that might lead to more moderate approaches to television broadcasting.

What about the suggestion that student-athletes deserve some share of the spoils? The argument usually runs as follows: College sports is golden—witness, for example, the $550 million paid each year by CBS for the NCAA tournament or the $12 million payout per team for the football Bowl Championship Series games. And yet the athletes do not even get pocket money. Look at how much Chris Webber and Juwan Howard make in the pros. And what about college coaches, some of whom make over a million dollars a year? Shouldn't we pay the athletes who generate all this money? Late in his long tenure as executive director of the NCAA, Walter Byers argued that since colleges were exploiting the talents of their student-athletes, they deserved the same access to the free market as coaches. He suggested letting them endorse products, with the resulting income going into a trust fund that would become available only after they graduated or completed their eligibility.[2]

These myths are firmly entrenched not only in the public's mind but in the culture of the university. We need now to separate out the reality from the myth, to better understand the real nature of the financial issues facing college sports.

Reality I: What Do Universities Really Make from Athletics?

As we noted earlier, in 1997, the University of Michigan generated $45 million from its athletics activities, of which only about $3 million came from television. Although the university actually generated far more than this from the broadcasting of events such as football and basketball games, the Rose Bowl, and the Big Ten and NCAA basketball tournaments, most of this revenue was shared with the other Big Ten and NCAA schools. How much of this revenue can we attribute to the efforts of students? This is hard to estimate. On the one hand, we might simply divide the entire revenue base by the number of varsity athletes (seven hundred) to arrive at about $45,000 per athlete. But, of course, coaches and staff also are responsible for generating revenue, by building winning sports programs or marketing or licensing sports apparel. Certain unusual assets, like Michigan Stadium, attract sizable crowds and generate significant revenue regardless of how successful the team is. Finally, we have not said anything yet about expenses. Operating expenditures at Michigan, as at every other university in the nation, are sometimes larger than revenues. As a result, the net revenues, the profit, is zero! While it is admittedly very difficult to estimate just how much income student-athletes bring to the university, it is clear that it is far less than most sportswriters believe.

Reality 2: What Do the Players Receive from the University?

At Michigan the typical instructional cost (not "price" or tuition) of our undergraduate programs is about $20,000 per student per year. When we add to this support for room and board and incidentals, it amounts to an investment of about $30,000 per year per fully tendered student-athlete, or between $120,000 to $150,000 per athlete over four or five years of studies. The actual value of this education is far higher, since it provides the student-athlete with an earning capacity far beyond that of a high school education (and even far beyond that of most professional sports careers, with the exception of only the greatest superstars). Of course, only a few student-athletes will ever achieve high-paying careers in professional sports. Most do not make the pros, and most of those who do are only modestly compensated for a few short years.

The real reward for student-athletes is, of course, a college education. Despite having somewhat poorer high school records, test scores, and preparation for college, athletes tended to graduate at rates quite comparable to those of other students.[3] The reasons for their academic success involved both their strong financial support through scholarships and their academic support and encouragement through programs not available to students at large. Yet it is also the case that recruiting college athletes based entirely on physical skills rather than academic promise undermines this premise. As William Dowling, professor at Rutgers, has noted, "Problems will remain as long as players in the so-called revenue sports represent a bogus category of students, recruited on the basis of physical skills rather than for academic or intellectual ability."[4]

Those who call for professionalizing college athletics by paying student-athletes—and they are generally members of the sports media—are approaching college sports as show business, not as part of an academic enterprise. Only in show business do the stars make such grossly distorted amounts. In academics, the Nobel Prize winner does not make much more than any other faculty member. In the corporate world, the inventor of a device that earns a corporation millions of dollars will receive only a small incentive payment for her or his discovery. The moral of the story is that one simply cannot apply the perverse reward system of the entertainment industry to college sports—unless, of course, you believe college sports is, in reality, simply another form of show business.

A Primer on College Sports Financing

Most business executives would find the financial culture of intercollegiate athletics bizarre indeed. To be sure, there are considerable opportunities for revenue from college sports. In 1997–98 NCAA Division I schools generated almost $2 billion, almost entirely from football and men's basketball. In terms of their revenue-generating capacity, three college football teams, Michigan, Notre Dame, and Florida, are more valuable than most professional football franchises.[5] Such statistics have lured college after college into big-time athletics, motivating them to make the investment in stadiums, coaching staffs, scholarships, to join the big boys in NCAA's Division I-A.

Yet most intercollegiate athletics programs at most colleges and universities require some subsidy from general university resources such as tuition or state appropriation. Put another way, most college athletics programs actually lose money, to the tune of $245 million for Division I schools in 1995–96.[6] And, while football coaches might like to suggest that the costs of "nonrevenue" sports are the problem, particularly those women's sports programs mandated by Title IX, before blaming others, they should first look in a mirror. While football generates most of the revenue for intercollegiate athletics, it also is responsible for most of the growth in costs. More precisely, when college sports is transformed into an entertainment industry, and when its already intensely competitive ethos begins to equate expenditure with winning, one inevitably winds up with a culture that attempts to spend every dollar that it is generated, and then some.

Stated another way, the costs of intercollegiate athletics within a given institution are driven by decisions concerning the level of competition (e.g., NCAA Division, regional, or nationally competitive), the desire for competitive success, and the breadth of programs. Although football generates most of the revenue for big-time athletic programs through gate receipts and broadcasting, it is also an extremely expensive sport. Not only does it involve an unusually large number of participants and attendant coaching and support staff, but the capital facilities costs of football stadiums, practice facilities, and training facilities are very high. Furthermore, many of the remaining costs of the athletic department, such as marketing staff, media relations, and business are driven, in reality, primarily by the needs of the football program rather than the other varsity sports. In this sense, football coaches to the contrary, big-time football programs are, in reality, cost drivers rather than revenue centers.

It is instructive to take a more detailed look at the various revenue streams and costs associated with intercollegiate athletics in order to get a sense of scale. The following are the principal sources of revenues and expenditures:

Revenues
  Ticket sales
  Guarantees
  Payouts from bowl games and tournaments
  Television
  Corporate sponsorships, advertising, licensing
  Unearned revenues
    Booster club donations
    Student fees and assessments
    State or other government support
    Hidden university subsidies

Expenditures
  Salaries
  Athletic scholarships
  Travel and recruiting
  Equipment, supplies, medicine
  Insurance
  Legal, public relations, administrative
  Capital expenditures (debt service and maintenance)

Furthermore, intercollegiate athletics is highly capital intensive, particularly at a big-time program such as Michigan. Few
athletics programs amortize these capital costs in a realistic fashion. Including these imbedded capital costs on the balance sheet
would quickly push even the most successful programs far into the
red.

To illustrate, let us walk through the budget of the University
of Michigan Department of Intercollegiate Athletics. First let me
note that it is the practice of the university that intercollegiate athletics be a self-supporting enterprise, not consuming university
resources. It receives neither state appropriation nor student
tuition. Furthermore, this financial firewall works in both directions: any revenue balance earned by the athletic department cannot, under normal circumstances, be transferred to the academic
side of the university. They must pay for what they cost the university, and they keep what they make. The department revenues
and expenditures in 1997–98 are shown in table 1.

Not included in these figures were onetime expenditures of
roughly $18 million to expand Michigan Stadium, to decorate it
with a gaudy maize-and-blue halo designed by the noted architect
Robert Venturi, complete with the ten-foot-high words to the
Michigan fight song, "Hail to the Conquering Heroes"; to install $8
million worth of "Jumbo-tron" television scoreboards; and to build
a sophisticated control room for Internet broadcasts. These onetime
expenses were charged against (and largely decimated) the flexible
reserve funds of the department. Lest you think these latter
expenses were unusually extravagant, Ohio State is in the midst of
several construction projects that will leave their athletic depart-

TABLE 1. Revenues and Expenditures, University of Michigan Department of Intercollegiate Athletics, 1997–98 (millions of dollars)

Revenues		Expenditures	
Ticket sales	18.1	Salaries, wages, benefits	13.1
Facilities revenues	1.9	Student financial aid	7.6
Television and radio	4.7	Other team and game expenses	6.4
Royalties	5.7	Postseason play	2.1
Concessions, parking, etc.	1.3	Plant operation and maintenance	4.1
Postseason play	4.7	Other operating	4.2
Investment income	1.0	Administrative	1.4
Endowment income	1.0	Debt service	5.3
Gifts	3.2		
Corporate sponsorship	2.3		
Miscellaneous	1.0		
Total revenues	44.2	Total expenditures	44.2

Source: Year-End Financial Statements for Department of Intercollegiate Athletics, University of Michigan (1998).

ment saddled with a $277 million debt, to be paid over the next thirty years.[7] (And you wonder why people believe that the financial culture of intercollegiate athletics is wacko?)

As I noted earlier, the financial strategy in intercollegiate athletics is strongly driven by competitive pressures. The belief that those who spend the most win the most drives institutions to generate and spend more and more dollars. The prosperous programs at institutions such as Michigan, Penn State, and Notre Dame set the pace for the entire intercollegiate athletics enterprise, no matter what the size of the school.

As expenditures on athletics programs continue to spiral out of control, there have been increasing calls for action at both the national and conference level. Yet part of the problem is that many athletic departments hide the true nature of the financial operations not only from the prying eyes of the press and the public, but even from their own universities. Several years ago, the Big Ten Conference launched an effort to contain costs by restricting the growth of institutional expenditures on athletics to the rate of inflation. At that time, many universities were suffering as their athletics drained resources from the rest of the institution because athletics revenues were insufficient to cover costs. There were also concerns about competitiveness, since the wealthier schools tended to dominate most Big Ten sports, particularly football.

More specifically, Michigan and Ohio State, because of their very large stadiums, had considerably more gate receipt revenue than the other Big Ten members. Onetime football powers such as Wisconsin and Minnesota had fallen on hard times, with mediocre teams and low stadium attendance. Minnesota was in a particularly difficult bind since it had shifted its football games to the downtown Minneapolis Metrodome and torn down its on-campus stadium. Earlier attempts to address this discrepancy among institutions through revenue-sharing formulas had finally become burdensome enough to the larger stadium schools, particularly with the entry of Penn State, that the conference agreed to accept a more equitable formula.

Therefore, attempts to control expenditures rather than to redistribute revenues became the focus. But there was a big problem here. Nobody really knew how much the athletic departments in each university were spending. On top of that, no one seemed to know how much or where the revenue came from. And because most athletics programs were independent of the usual financial management and controls of their institutions, it was clear that this comparative information would be difficult if not impossible to obtain through the departments themselves.

Member institutions decided to form a special subcommittee to the Big Ten Council of Presidents comprised of the universities' chief financial officers. This CFO committee was charged with developing a system to obtain and compare annual athletics revenues and expenditures within the Big Ten. Needless to say, this decision to go outside of the athletic enterprise for supervision did not go down well in some schools where the athletic department had unusual autonomy. And while opening their books for examination was not particularly troublesome to most Big Ten universities, since as public institutions they frequently had to endure audits from state government, this was a very sensitive matter to the one private university in the Big Ten, Northwestern.

The first set of comparisons across all universities was eye-opening.[8] Among the factors of particular note was the distribution of revenues.

Ticket sales	38 percent
Television and radio	13
Gift income	13
Subsidies	11
Licensing, concessions, etc.	9
Game settlements, guarantees	8
Bowls and NCAA revenue	4
Miscellaneous	4

Although broadcasting and bowl revenues were important—and are becoming more so—the largest single revenue source (38 percent) remained gate receipts. This explains why the three universities with very large stadiums (Michigan at 105,000, Ohio State at 98,000, and Penn State at 96,000) stand out in revenues. Among the public universities, there was great disparity in the capacity to generate private support for athletics (with Michigan ranking, surprisingly enough, toward the bottom of the range) and in their subsidies from state support.

The financial studies revealed that 72 percent of total athletic department revenue is attributable to football. Another 23 percent comes from men's basketball. In other words, 95 percent is generated by football and basketball combined. (Ice hockey contributes 4 percent and women's basketball 1 percent.) A further breakdown of revenue sources shows the difference between men's and women's sports.

Men's sports	71.1 percent
Women's sports	4.3
Administrative operations	24.6

In terms of expenditures, 57 percent was spent on football and men's basketball, while 24 percent was spent on women's sports, and 14 percent on all other men's sports. Despite the Big Ten Conference's efforts to achieve gender equity, women's programs amounted to only one-quarter of expenditures in the 1990s. Financial aid was distributed 67 percent to men, 33 percent to women, roughly in proportion to their representation among varsity athletes.

Two universities stood out in terms of the breadth and comprehensiveness of their programs: Ohio State, with thirty-five programs, and Penn State with thirty. Michigan's twenty-three programs were only in the middle of the pack, despite the fact that Michigan ranked number one in revenues ($45 million).

There was a factor-of-two difference in athletic department revenues and expenditures, ranging from Michigan and Ohio State at $45 million to Northwestern and Purdue at $25 million. The analysis also quickly made apparent why Northwestern had been so reluctant to share its financial data. In sharp contrast to the public universities, Northwestern was subsidizing its athletics programs from general academic resources to the tune of about $8 million per year (almost half their revenues). Although today, after two Big Ten football championships, faculty and students might believe it was worth the roughly eight hundred dollars per student of tuition (or other academic income) it cost to remain in the Big Ten, at the time of the first CFO surveys, this was highly sensitive information. While Northwestern's hidden subsidy was the largest among Big Ten universities, it was certainly not unique. Some institutions provided hidden subsidies by waiving tuition or granting instate tuition rates for student athletes. Others received direct subsidies for their athletics programs through state appropriations (e.g., Wisconsin received $634,000 per year).

There were a number of other significant differences among the expenditure patterns of the various universities. For example, several of the public universities charged only in-state tuition to athletes, even if they were out-of-state residents, thereby reducing very significantly their costs for athletic scholarships. In contrast, Michigan charged full out-of-state tuition levels, which were comparable to those of private institutions, thereby driving up the costs of athletic grants-in-aid programs considerably. Labor costs also varied widely among institutions, ranging from urban and unionized wage scales to rural and nonunionized wage scales.

It was finally concluded, after several years of effort, that the great diversity among institutions in terms of the manner in which revenue was generated, expenditures were managed, and accounting was performed made it almost impossible to attempt conference-wide cost containment. Hence, the Big Ten presidents adopted a policy encouraging rather than requiring cost containment. However, they also decided to continue the annual CFO comparative analysis of revenues and expenditures, if only to provide visibility for unusual practices.

Show Me the Money!

Revenue flows into athletics departments from a number of sources and out again through a complex array of expenditures. University of Indiana historian Murray Sperber provides a fascinating analysis of the economics of college sports in his book *College Sports, Inc.*[9] In this brief discussion, I will focus only on a few items of particular interest.

One of the most expensive elements of sports is the current grants-in-aid system for the financial support of student-athletes. In contrast to the need-based financial aid programs for regular students, colleges are allowed to provide student-athletes with sufficient support to meet "all commonly accepted educational expenses"—a full ride, regardless of financial need or academic ability. This policy, first implemented in football in the 1950s, has spread rapidly to all varsity sports. As the costs of a college education have rapidly increased over the past two decades, the costs of grants-in-aid have risen dramatically. For example, the University of Michigan currently spends about $8 million a year on grants-in-aid. But there is considerable variation among institutions, as the Big Ten financial data indicate.

Michigan	$7.6 million
Northwestern	5.7
Ohio State	4.6
Penn State	4.5
Michigan State	4.3

Indiana	4.1
Illinois	3.4
Minnesota	3.4
Purdue	3.4
Iowa	3.3
Wisconsin	1.8

In some cases, this discrepancy is due to institutions that choose to subsidize financial aid by granting all athletes in-state tuition levels, in effect hiding the subsidy of the difference between in-state and out-state levels. Although some universities restrict the number or types of grants-in-aid they provide in various sports, the University of Michigan has long had a policy of fully funding all allowable grants-in-aid in all sports in which it competes. Since most student-athletes are subject to out-of-state tuition levels, the resulting cost of athletically related student aid is unusually high at $8 million.[10]

A second factor in the inflating costs was the rapid growth in size of football programs as coaches pushed through the unlimited-substitution rules in the 1960s. This system allowed college football to develop specialists for essentially every position and every situation in the game—offense and defense, blocking and tackling, kicking and passing. Although it was promoted as a way to make the game more exciting, it was not just a coincidence that it also made football far easier to play and to coach. More significantly, it transformed college football into a corporate and bureaucratic enterprise, with teams of over one hundred players, dozens of coaches, trainers, and equipment managers, and even technology experts in areas such as video production and computer analysis. Furthermore, unlimited substitution not only transformed college football into the professional football paradigm, but it also demanded that high school football follow the colleges and the pros down the same expensive path.

The third factor driving the rapid expansion of the program's cost and complexity has been the insatiable desire of football coaches for any additional gimmicks that might provide a competitive edge, either in play or competition. Special residences for football players became common, some resembling country'clubs more than campus dormitories. Many football programs have built not only special training facilities but also even museums to display their winning traditions to prospective recruits. A visit to the sports museum in Schembechler Hall at the University of Michigan provides an excellent example of these shrines. Teams usually travel in high style, with charter jet service, four-star hotels, and even special travel clothing such as team blazers. And, of course, each time a coach at one university dreams up a new wrinkle, all of the other coaches at competing universities have to have it, no matter how extravagant or expensive.

This competitive pressure from coaches—and fans and even the media—has made it very difficult for athletic departments to control costs. Each time actions are proposed to slow the escalation of costs in the two main revenue sports, football and basketball, they are countered with the argument that the more one spends, the more one will win and hence the more one will make. The relative financial inexperience of those who manage athletic departments

A symbol of the arms race in football expenditures: Schembechler Hall

makes it even more difficult to resist these competitive forces. They tend to develop a one-dimensional financial culture, in which all attention is focused on revenue generation, and cost controls are essentially ignored.

A conversation with any athletic director soon reveals just how much of their attention is devoted to generating revenue to cover ever-increasing costs. This preoccupation with revenue generation propagates up through the hierarchy, to university presidents and governing boards, athletic conferences, and even the NCAA. Far more time is spent on negotiating broadcasting contracts or licensing agreements than on cost containment, much less concern about the welfare of student-athletes or the proper role of college sports in a university.

Though most of the revenue for college sports has traditionally come from revenue associated with football and basketball events, several of the most popular programs have generated very extensive licensing income from the use of institutional logos and insignia. A number of major athletics programs, Michigan among them, have signed lucrative contracts with sports apparel companies. Many athletic departments have also launched extensive fund-raising efforts involving alumni and fans, both for ongoing support and endowment. In fact, both athletic scholarship pro grams and key athletic department staff such as athletic directors and football coaches are supported by endowments in some universities.

Athletic departments go to great lengths and considerable creativity to find new sources of revenues. For example, when Michigan decided to replace its artificial turf in Michigan Stadium with natural turf in 1992, the athletic department got the bright idea that people might want to purchase a piece of the old carpet for nostalgic reasons. They chopped up the old artificial turf into an array of souvenirs, ranging from coasters to doormats to large rugs containing some of the lettering on the field. To their delight, these sold like hotcakes, and the department made over two hundred thousand dollars. In fact, some of the more enterprising staff wanted to purchase old carpets from other stadiums and sell this under the Michigan emblem. Fortunately, wiser heads prevailed.

Another example is the construction of an elegant new plaza and fence surrounding Michigan Stadium in 1995. The athletic department decided to sell paving bricks at a premium (one hundred to one thousand dollars apiece) and allow people to inscribe their names and perhaps even a brief message. Again, demand soared for the opportunity to become "a part of Michigan Stadium," and the department rapidly raised the several hundred thousand dollars required for the project.

Licensing provides a more standard means for generating revenue for the athletic department. Michigan moved early into a more direct merchandising effort, placing retail shops (the M–Go Blue Shops) in various athletics venues, so that it could participate directly in the profits from athletic or signature apparel. It was always a fascinating experience to browse through these shops to see what the fertile creativity of the marketing side of the athletic department had devised or approved for licensing: maize-and-blue toilet seats that play "The Victors" when raised, the Michigan football helmet chip-and-dip bowl, and hundreds upon hundreds of different sweatshirt designs. The catalog mail-order business became particularly lucrative.

Sometimes there is a more altruistic purpose to these financial ventures. For example, our athletic directors, Jack Weidenbach and Joe Roberson, established the tradition of an annual "garage sale" held in Crisler Arena to sell old athletic equipment as memorabilia, with the proceeds going to the University Library.

We have noted earlier the extreme volatility of most revenue sources for intercollegiate athletics. While a New Year's Day bowl appearance or success in the NCAA Basketball Tournament can provide a windfall, a poor season can trigger rapid declines in gate receipts, licensing income, and private gifts. Catastrophe awaits the naive athletic director who builds an expenditure budget based on such speculative income, since disaster awaits when the books are finally closed at year end. During my tenure as president, we not only required the athletic department to budget very conservatively, but it also was encouraged to build a reserve fund with sufficient investment income to compensate for any uncertainty in the operating budget. In fact, our athletic director generally measured financial performance in terms of the growth of the reserve fund from year to year.

Financial Accountability

The athletic department at most NCAA Division I-A universities is treated as an auxiliary activity, separated by a financial firewall from the budgets of academic programs. This strategy allows athletic directors to offer up the excuse that the sometimes flamboyant expenditures of the department are not being made at the expense of the university. But it also creates major problems. It tends to focus most of the athletic department's energy (not to mention the conference's and NCAA's) on revenue generation rather than cost management. It subjects coaches and staff to extreme pressures to generate additional revenue in the mistaken belief that it will enhance the competitiveness of their programs. And, perhaps most significantly, it further widens the gap between the athletic department and the rest of the university.

Despite the boasts of athletic directors and football coaches to the contrary, intercollegiate athletics at most institutions—perhaps all institutions, if rigorous accounting principles were applied—is a net financial loser. All revenues go simply to support and in some cases expand the athletic empire, while many expenditures that amount to university subsidy are hidden by sloppy management or intricate accounting. Put more pointedly, college sports, including the celebrity compensation of coaches, the extravagant facilities, first-class travel and accommodations, VIP entertainment of the sports media, shoddy and wasteful management practices, all require subsidy by the university through devices such as student fees, hidden administrative overhead support, and student tuition waivers.

Yet our athletic departments not only tout their self-supporting status, but they vigorously seek and defend their administrative and financial independence. And well they should, since their primary activity is, increasingly, operating a commercial entertainment business. As college football and basketball become ever more commercial and professional, their claim on any subsidy from the university is diminished.

Of course, few of our sports problems are self-supporting. If we illuminate hidden costs and subsidies, we find that all intercollegiate athletics burden the university with considerable costs, some financial, some in terms of the attention required of university leadership, some in terms of the impact to the reputation and integrity of the university, and some measured only in the impact on students and staff. Experience has also shown that expenses always increase somewhat more rapidly than the revenues generated by college sports.

In conclusion, the mad race for fame and profits through intercollegiate athletics is clearly a fool's quest. Recognition on the athletic field or court has little relevance to academic reputation. Nebraska can win all the national championships it wishes, and it will never catch fair Harvard's eye. Indeed, fame in athletics is often paradoxical, since it can attract public scrutiny, which can then uncover violations and scandal. As the intensity and visibility of big-time athletics build, the university finds itself buffeted by the passion and energy of the media and the public, who identify with their athletics programs rather than their educational mission.

Yet every year, several more universities proudly proclaim they have decided to invest the resources to build sports programs that will earn them membership in NCAA's Division I-A. Sometimes lessons are never learned.

PART III
Cracks in
the Facade

Chapter 8

The Commercialization of College Sports

Several years ago at a Big Ten Conference meeting, I decided to shake up things by offering a radical (if tongue-in-cheek) proposal. I proposed that all of the Big Ten universities agree to a five-year moratorium on television broadcasting of our sports events. I argued that this moratorium would provide our universities with the opportunity to determine the purpose and priority of athletics on our campuses, without the glare of media attention or the pressure of the entertainment industry. Our universities could then restructure or realign their intercollegiate athletics programs in a manner consistent with their priorities.

During the moratorium, the sports media and the public would be chased out of the locker rooms and the lives of our student-athletes and coaches. With the loss of television revenue, universities would have to learn how to live on a revenue diet by controlling the costs of intercollegiate athletics and scaling back their programs (and their aspirations) to more realistic levels. We would have to learn to live without athletic dormitories, shoe contracts, and big-time promotion. And we would have to learn how to treat coaches as normal staff and athletes as students. At the same time, the media would have to find other fodder to satisfy America's appetite for armchair sports entertainment, perhaps even joining the rest of the world in promoting popular professional sports such as soccer or cycling.

After the five-year moratorium, television, the sports press, and the public would be invited back as spectators (rather than producers) of college sports, but only on terms set by the universities, in a manner consistent with their academic priorities. There would no longer be late-night basketball every night of the week, or football games starting in the gathering gloom of the late afternoon, or television commentators shrieking in a fevered pitch to hype the action. Nor would national championship tournaments or bowl games interfere with critical periods of the academic calendar such as examinations.

In short, my proposal was to take "showbiz" out of intercollegiate athletics and to allow academic priorities to determine the nature of sports. Of course, my proposal, although put forward partly in jest, was also designed to trigger some more serious discussion. Needless to say, my colleagues did not greet my proposal with overwhelming enthusiasm. They immediately returned to their discussions of television contracts, bowl alliances, and conference expansion.

In a sense, the content of this proposal and my colleagues' reaction to it illustrate the degree to which we have lost sight of the fundamental purposes of intercollegiate athletics. It was then my belief that the commercialization of college sports, while bringing new revenue to the enterprise, had seriously undermined the integrity and the credibility of intercollegiate athletics, driving them far away from the values and purpose of the university.

Show Business

We generally identify intercollegiate athletics as an integral part of college life. The football games in the fall, the NCAA basketball tournament in the spring, the participation of college athletes in the Olympic Games, all seem as naturally a part of the university as student examinations, fraternities and sororities, and campus protests. Yet, while sports at many colleges and universities may indeed be just another extracurricular activity for students, whether as participants or spectators, for the 192 institutions comprising the NCAA Division I, it is something far more. For these institutions, intercollegiate athletics is both big-time entertainment and big business.

Long ago the marquee sports of football and men's basketball

were transformed from mere opportunities for students to participate at the varsity level in competitive athletics into commercial
products produced primarily for public entertainment. To a very
significant degree this transformation was driven by the broadcast
media, particularly television, although there were other pressures
on the university from external forces such as alumni interest, the
sports press, and community merchants. Although the athletic
departments of colleges and universities happily seized opportunities to commercialize intercollegiate athletics with the strong support of university administrations, trustees, and students—although
not necessarily the faculty—the primary driving forces were external.

Today we find that big-time college sports most closely resembles the entertainment industry. To be sure, intercollegiate athletics still does involve students, albeit with many preparing for pro-
fessions in athletics rather than the typical career objectives of
other students on the campus. Coaches have long since ceased to
be governed by the rules and values of the rest of the university,
and now are regarded by those both on and off campus as media
celebrities. While universities "own" their athletic franchises, they
are far from actually controlling these activities in the face of
intense media, market, and political pressure.

We see many signs of this commercialization. College football
and basketball games at major universities have become almost
indistinguishable from professional events. Stadiums and arenas
are saturated with advertising and marketing. The events themselves are largely staged as television productions, with broadcasting directors controlling the flow of the game in order to accommodate the necessary commercials and updates on other ongoing
games of major interest. Athletes and coaches are required to open
their locker rooms and make themselves available to the sports
media. The games themselves are scheduled at all hours of the day
and night to accommodate broadcasting schedules. Even the
choice of competing teams has been greatly influenced by public
interest, media pressure, and market-share implications. As a
result, conferences have been reorganized, end-of-season playoffs
and tournaments are juggled, and the intense media drive to rank

teams and build hype and public interest in national championship events reaches higher and higher pitches.

Those who control, or at least are responsible for, intercollegiate athletics are increasingly more focused on broadcasting contracts, product value, and market share than on the integrity of college sports, much less the welfare of athletes. Whether it is at the level of the NCAA, the governing boards of the athletic conferences, or the university administration, so-called revenue sports are now commonly managed much as if they were professional franchises.

And what could be more logical, at least to those who benefit most from the commercialization of college sports. After all, in 1998 the television networks signed up to purchase the rights to broadcast the National Football League for the next eight years for the sum of $17.6 billion.[1] They will pay $2.4 billion for the National Basketball League over the next four years, and $600 million for the National Hockey League for the next five years. Rupert Murdoch offered $1 billion for England's Manchester United soccer club. And while the $36 million that Michael Jordan made during his last season in the NBA is impressive, perhaps even more so are the average salaries of professional athletes: $2.6 million in basketball, $1.4 million in baseball, and $1.2 million in hockey. The staggering sums bid for professional sports and paid professional athletes make it very clear: live, unscripted programming has become a valuable commodity for the broadcasting networks, as they compete in an increasingly global marketplace. And this will propagate very rapidly to college sports. In the face of the staggering sums paid for professional sports, the current contracts for college football and basketball appear to provide only chump change. They will, however, grow very rapidly.

Celebrity Coaches

It is certainly no surprise that as college football and basketball have become commercial products for the entertainment industry, the key participants in these activities have acquired celebrity status. Actually, we have long had college players and coaches whose prowess and personalities achieved national prominence: Red Grange, Tom Harmon, Knute Rockne, Bear Bryant, and Woody Hayes to name a few. But the celebrity culture of college sports today is unprecedented. It poses one of the most serious challenges to the integrity of higher education because of the distorted images and values it conveys about the academic enterprise and the inappropriate pressure it can exert on institutions.

Ironically enough, today's celebrities in college sports are not the players but the "power coaches," those whose success, endurance, or mere personality has elevated their visibility above the teams they coach and, sometimes, even the institutions they represent. Joe Paterno, Bobby Bowden, and Steve Spurrier in football, or Mike Krzyzewski and Bobby Knight in basketball transcend their teams, their institutions, and even the sport itself. As the new heroes of the sports media, these celebrity coaches have their own television programs, their own sports camps, even their own lines of clothing fashions. And they are the ones who get paid—big time!

For example, star football coaches such as Steve Spurrier of Florida and Bobby Bowden of Florida State now make well over one million a year, and they are not alone.[2] With the recent trend of college basketball coaches being recruited by the NBA, their salaries will probably go even higher. The contracts for celebrity coaches now are as complex and, in some cases, as lucrative as those for movie stars, and they increasingly are attracting a swarm of agents and lawyers to assist in the negotiations. Celebrity coaches now expect bonuses for winning, deferred (tax-shielded) compensation, home loans, automobiles, and country club memberships. Beyond this, big-name coaches are allowed to generate staggering dollars from external sources, such as consulting or contracting with sports apparel manufacturers, running sports camps for precollege students, or making paid speaking engagements.

Of course, athletic directors would defend the coaches' astronomical compensation by claiming that these successful coaches generate millions in revenue. Yet in the previous chapter we noted that, at least from the perspective of full-cost accounting, almost none of these programs truly makes a profit. Furthermore, even the most successful coach generates only $20 million in revenues (not profits). This should be compared not only to the billions of dollars of revenue or shareholder value generated by a modern corporate executive, but to the tens of millions of dollars brought to the university by the faculty member directing a major research laboratory, the clinical faculty member treating patients, or the fundraising officer soliciting gifts from donors.

Does the market drive these compensation packages? To be sure, the college coaching profession looks like a game of musical chairs, as big-name coaches jump from one institution to another as each more lucrative offer is put on the table. But, again, this market is based as much on illusion as substance. Recall the success of many assistant coaches who have stepped into the void left by a departing celebrity coach. During my first year as president, when basketball coach Bill Frieder jumped ship to accept a more lucrative offer from Arizona State, assistant coach Steve Fisher stepped in and won the national championship!

In show business, the more people who know who you are, the more you get paid. It really does not matter much whether you are any good or not; but name recognition is key. Apparently this rule seems to apply as well for prominent coaches. Usually the highest-paid people on their campuses, coaches, make several times more than top professors or university presidents. Tom Everhart, former chancellor of the University of Illinois, put it well in a farewell address to his faculty as he was leaving to become president of Caltech. He observed that he was looking forward to going to an institution where the president got paid more than the football coach. Certainly very few Division I-A presidents can make the same claim.

Although the base salaries of head football and basketball coaches—that is, the numbers acknowledged by most institutions—are comparable to those of top professors in professional schools such as business or medicine (typically $150,000 to $200,000 per year), these coaches benefit from significant income from other sources such as sports camps, television programs, speaking engagements, and the notorious "shoe contracts." This extra income, in many cases paid through the university, can bring their annual compensation to $1 million or more. Most universities allow coaches to use campus facilities and the university name to run lucrative summer camps for grade school and high school students. While some head coaches use this income to supplement the rather low pay of assistant coaches, many others benefit personally.

Most football and basketball coaches at major universities also have lucrative radio and television programs. In return, the sponsors of these programs frequently receive special benefits like preferred seating at events and direct access to players and coaches. Actually, this special relationship to sponsors is necessary for another reason, since most of these coaching programs are dreadful in content and rarely generate much of an audience. Rather the sponsors are in reality simply acting as loyal boosters, helping to fund the coach's income through the television program.[3] Beyond this, many coaches are also offered special perks by the local business community, such as complimentary cars, country club memberships, corporate board memberships, real estate, or even business opportunities. Some coaches' celebrity status also provides them with lucrative speaking opportunities and commercial endorsements, in a sense allowing them to market their university's reputation for their personal gain.

Perhaps the most controversial form of compensation for college coaches is the shoe contract, a practice in which various sports apparel companies such as Nike, Reebok, or Adidas hire a coach as a "consultant" at payment levels of hundreds of thousands of dollars a year. In return, the coach agrees not only to appear in promotional events for the company, but also requires the team to wear its products, usually in a highly visible fashion. For some of the most prominent celebrity coaches, these shoe contracts have become astronomically lucrative. And, unfortunately, for some student-athletes, the requirement to wear a particular product has sometimes caused damage to their health or their athletic career from improperly fitted equipment.

The shoe contracts raise one of the most serious issues in the management of intercollegiate athletics. To what degree should coaches be allowed to profit personally by exploiting the reputation and resources of their institution and perhaps the well-being of their athletes? After all, while Nike executives certainly want the names of celebrity coaches such as Bobby Knight, Lloyd Carr, and Mike Krzyzewski associated with their products, they want even more to be associated with universities such as Indiana, Michigan, and Duke. While some kids are attracted to Bobby Knight's basketball camp or Lloyd Carr's football camp, they are even more drawn to Indiana and Michigan. While the coach's personality contributes to the popularity of a television program, shows such as *Michigan Replay* will continue, year in, year out, regardless of who is Michigan's head football coach.

Some would argue that these additional sources of income are appropriate since they reward many activities that extend far beyond simply coaching. In a sense, this income is analogous to the consulting fees that some faculty members earn. Yet for all but the most prominent celebrity coaches, essentially all of this additional income is derived from marketing not their own expertise but rather the reputation and prominence of their institution. And unlike faculty consulting, which is limited both in duration (typically two to four days a month) and amount (typically 20 percent of one's base salary), there are no limits on coaches' additional compensation from outside activities such as endorsements or speaking engagements nor the time they put into hustling this extra income.

In a world in which a Michael Jordan earned a salary of $36 million per year (eight thousand dollars a point) or a Barry Sanders made $7 million (four thousand dollars per yard gained), the compensation of celebrity college coaches may seem modest. Even the faculty has become numb and rarely challenges this practice. When an occasional concern floats up from faculty governance, all too frequently the athletic director or the sports press responds that, relative to the world of professional sports, such compensation seems reasonable. College sports and professional sports are both part of the same market for top coaches.

While the compensation of celebrity coaches may seem reasonable from the perspective of the sports media, it is certainly not consistent with the practice and values of the academy. Few faculty members expect their compensation to be comparable to that of colleagues in professional practice. For example, business and engineering faculty earn only a small fraction of what they could earn in industry. Coaches in varsity sports other than football and basketball are compensated at only nominal levels, comparable to or less than the faculty. Assistant coaches in the revenue sports also are at the low end, most receiving less than one-tenth of the compensation of the celebrity head coach. Furthermore, student-athletes on athletic scholarships receive only the minimal level of financial aid necessary for their education, typically money to cover tuition and room-and-board, along with a very small spending allowance. While these sums are not insignificant, they are a far cry from the extravagant income of the head coaches.

It is ironic, indeed, that among all of the members of the university community, athletics coaches are the only ones allowed to profit personally from the reputation and activities of the university. Faculty and staff face stiff conflict-of-interest regulations that prevent them from benefiting personally through the marketing of the institution. Student-athletes, of course, are limited by NCAA and conference regulations. Yet coaches use the university's name and reputation for personal benefit in a variety of ways: radio and television broadcasting contracts; highly visible sports camps promoted by the university's reputation; and, perhaps most insidiously of all, through apparel contracts that not only link the university's name with particular products, but actually require student-athletes and staff to wear this apparel, while only the coach benefits financially. Clearly any of these activities would be a serious violation of the conflict-of-interest policies for anyone else in the institution. Yet universities have traditionally tolerated this practice among coaches.[4] As the Knight Commission put it, "Coaches are selling something they don't own, the universities' name and image. If a school's purchasing agent did the same thing he would be led off in handcuffs."[5]

Certain signs point to the fact that the celebrity coach culture may be headed for the edge of a cliff. As professional sports begin to include coaches in their perverse superstar compensation culture, there will inevitably be new pressures on college sports. We are already beginning to see mega-offers to lure college coaches to the pros, such as that which persuaded Rick Patino to leave Kentucky for the Boston Celtics or P. J. Carlesimo to the Golden State Warriors. Despite the temptation to respond with similar contracts in an effort to retain their celebrity coaches, few universities will have the resources to compete with professional offers. Furthermore, since faculty and staff salaries have eroded as a result of declining public support, it is not difficult to imagine how the faculty would react if they were to suspect that the astronomical compensation of their coaches was actually coming out of their own pockets. How would the courts react if it was brought to their attention that many head football coaches make more than the total combined salaries of *all* women coaches at their institution? This is a rather clear case of gender discrimination.

Fortunately, other forces may slow down the celebrity coach culture before it crashes and burns. Several years ago, the NCAA began requiring universities not only to be knowledgeable of but also to authorize the total compensation of their coaches, including all outside income. Some universities took the next step and began to require that all such income, from sports camps, broadcasting, and even sports apparel contracts, flow through the institution rather than directly to coaches. Coaches were then put on fixed compensation contracts, although some of these are still astronomical, approaching $1 million a year.

The institutions and universities designed to oversee intercollegiate athletics have demonstrated remarkably little courage in taking this sacred cow to market. A recent NCAA committee report revealed this reluctance when it acknowledged that on the one hand "Philosophical questions arise when coaches receive total compensation far in excess of that received by any member of the faculty or staff, including the president." But it finally concluded, "We do not believe it is possible or appropriate to develop specific guidelines or legislation to address compensation."[6] The NCAA's equivocal reaction should not be particularly surprising. After all, the NCAA itself compensates its senior administrators at levels comparable to executives of professional sports, complete with perks such as country club memberships, automobiles, and golden parachutes. Members of its numerous committees are stroked with first-class travel to meeting locations in resorts like Hawaii, Lake

Tahoe, and Jackson Hole, usually with nearby world-class golf courses, in sharp contrast to the modest, utilitarian sites chosen by other higher-education organizations. Most telling is the NCAA's rationale for such behavior, as expressed by its former executive director Dick Schultz, "We're schmoozing with heavy-hitter business donors and corporate sponsors and all of that, so we have to be like them."[7]

Celebrity Players

The stereotypical image of the "big man on campus," usually an athlete, often the captain of the football or basketball team, is going the way of the dinosaur. Aside from the fact that an increasing fraction of varsity athletes today are women, there are many other things wrong with this image today.

Most athletes at NCAA Division I institutions live lives of relative obscurity, at least compared to their high-profile celebrity coaches. To be sure, every once in a while a superstar athlete emerges, a Heisman trophy winner or a basketball All-American with celebrity potential. But while the press may try to make media celebrities of these individuals, their lives on campus are far more mundane. In the first place, most college campuses are very large and complex communities, and the likelihood of having a high-profile athlete in one's class or residence hall is remote. Second, the web of rules and regulations woven about college sports seriously constrains differential treatment of student-athletes, at least within the academic arenas of the university.

Some college athletes do, however, live in a fishbowl. Universities allow members of the press postgame access to locker rooms. Many require their athletes to participate in press conferences. Sometimes athletes are also asked to participate in promotional events on behalf of the university or the NCAA, for instance, to tape TV public service announcements on topics such as substance abuse or college entrance requirements. As a result, many college athletes become quite adept at dealing with the media and speaking before large audiences. It has always struck me as somewhat ironic that at the annual football and basketball banquets at the end of each season, I could always distinguish between the outstanding athletes and the outstanding students on the squads by how they handled their speaking duties in front of the large crowds attending these banquets. The outstanding students would generally read carefully scripted remarks, clearly nervous and occasionally stumbling. The outstanding athletes would simply approach the podium and wing it with the polished confidence of one who had faced dozens of press conferences and interviews.

Licensing and Advertising

The next time you tune into a college football or basketball game, look carefully at the amount of advertising—not during the commercial breaks but rather during the competition itself. Count the number of times you see the Nike "swoosh" prominently displayed on uniforms, coaches' hats, and scoreboards. Look for other signs of advertising—on scoreboards or other places in the stadium or perhaps announced over the public address system droning on in the background.

Universities have been involved in advertising for years, but they used to confine it to promoting themselves, albeit with the added benefit of earning a bit of cash on the side. Sweatshirts, T-shirts, hats, pennants, and flags all carried the university logo or mascot. Some trace the more aggressive licensing effort back to the early 1970s when Michigan's athletic director Don Canham introduced many of the marketing tricks we now take for granted: souvenir stands at games, mail-order catalogs, et cetera. In fact, the Michigan athletic department even copyrighted the Michigan "block M." (Only an athletic department would have the audacity to copyright a letter of the alphabet.)

For years, Michigan and Notre Dame have run neck and neck in licensing activity. Whenever Michigan would have a year of athletics successes, a Rose Bowl or Final Four, licensing income would rise. In my international travels, I would frequently see Michigan paraphernalia in the countries I visited. I used to run little surveys of university popularity by doing simple counts of the number of times I spotted a college logo. One time I tried this survey while walking across the Harvard Yard. The score was Michigan—7, Duke—3, and Harvard—1. Go Blue!

As Michigan teams became more successful in the 1990s, licensing revenue rose rapidly into the millions of dollars and became an ever larger component of the financial support base of the athletic department. Once the *Wall Street Journal* pegged the gross level of our licensing activity at roughly $250 million,[8] although in reality we only netted about $5 to $6 million per year. However, much of this activity was uncoordinated and rather unsophisticated. In 1995, we entered into a comprehensive licensing agreement with Nike, in which Nike would pay us a certain fee while providing all of our athletics equipment and uniforms in return for the right to license the Michigan athletics logo. Within a few months, not only did the Nike swoosh appear on all of our uniforms, but the Nike motto ("Just do it!") began to appear on signs and billboards sprinkled about our athletics complex.

Signs of the Michigan's Faustian bargain with Nike

Needless to say, this contract was a highly controversial step. While other universities had signed broad licensing agreements associated with various commercial products (e.g., Penn State's agreement with Pepsi-Cola) and although about a dozen other universities signed with Nike shortly after Michigan, many people believed we had sold out. To be sure, many of the Nike ads were of questionable taste. Others expressed concern about the rumors that Nike ran sweatshop factories in poor countries, a concern that has erupted more broadly among sporting apparel companies in recent years.

Yet the pressures for more strategic licensing were inevitable. Furthermore, the athletic director believed that by entering a broader agreement, the department could better control the commercial agreements, the "shoe contracts," with individual coaches. Since these were provided by Nike, by signing a broader licensing agreement, we hoped we could gradually eliminate these additional sources of personal income.

However, in retrospect, I believe we were very naive. Today our football and men's basketball coaches are compensated even more excessively than they were with the old shoe contracts. The Nike contract did not significantly expand the resources available to nonrevenue sports. What is more, the association with an aggressive marketing company such as Nike, with its emblem plastered over players, coaches, and facilities, has harmed rather than protected the reputation of the university. In hindsight, I am now convinced that the contract was a mistake, a Faustian bargain, rather than shrewd marketing decision.

Equally controversial was the issue of advertising. While many universities had long allowed advertising of commercial products, particularly on scoreboards, Michigan had remained aloof. However, our athletic directors, Bo Schembechler and Jack Weidenbach, were convinced that we needed to tap this source of income, and a large scoreboard with advertising went up in our basketball arena. Shortly after that beachhead was established, advertisements began to appear on the boards surrounding our hockey rink. While I managed to keep advertising out of Michigan Stadium, it became commonplace outside the stadium in concession areas, which soon looked like a shopping mall. Once I suggested that if the athletic department was going to accept advertising from automobile companies or banks, perhaps they should also provide pro bono advertising for university purposes—perhaps signs that would invite students to "Consider Majoring in Philosophy" or "Explore Art History!"

Even with these changes, Michigan remained an amateur compared to the commercial activities of many other universities. I remember a football game in a newly expanded stadium in the East where advertising was plastered on every available space, and every minute or so the public address announcer would proclaim another sponsor, almost as if to say, "This play has been brought to you by Budweiser!" Major events such as the football bowl games have not only been swamped by advertising, but they have even sold their names. Now we compete for an invitation to the Nokia Sugar Bowl or the Frito-Lay Fiesta Bowl.[9] Michigan and Notre Dame were once approached by General Motors, which wanted to purchase the name to our annual game. Can you imagine the Cadillac Bowl?

Incidentally, I believe that the value of college sports "properties" as advertising platforms has been one of the strongest forces driving the NCAA toward a national championship playoff for Division I-A football. Several years ago the Disney Company tried to drum up support for a Disney-sponsored national championship game. They distributed a promotional tape, in which Disney CEO Michael Eisner promised that Disney would use the occasion to celebrate the importance of higher education, by inviting outstanding students and faculty from colleges and universities across the country for a weeklong festival of academic achievement—just coincidentally capped, of course, by a football game between the number one and number two ranked teams in the nation. In an interview about this with the *Chicago Tribune,* I noted that if one watched Eisner's sales pitch carefully, you could make out a small statuette of Pinocchio on the credenza behind his desk. Perhaps it was just my imagination, but I could have sworn that Pinocchio's nose got longer as Eisner explained the Disney proposal.

The Sports Media

Spring is a traumatic month for many university presidents. Across the nation a strange disease begins to appear: March Madness. The sports media intensify their promotion of college basketball, whipping fan interest into a frenzy, aided by the insane schedule of conference tournaments. And the NCAA does its part by building anxiety to high levels of intensity prior to the weekend when the seedings are announced for the Big Dance, the NCAA tournament.

While I was president of the University of Michigan, we always dreaded this moment. As certain as a snowstorm in late March was the inevitable attack on the Michigan basketball program launched each year at this time by the local newspapers. After all, what could stimulate circulation and sell advertising more than a juicy story about suspected scandals at Michigan, long a symbol of integrity in college sports, appearing just before the NCAA tournament. The allegations were wide-ranging and always sketchy: A Michigan basketball player rumored to hang out with drug dealers; an unidentified booster rumored to have been slipping cash to players; someone—always unidentified—arranging for players to drive fancy cars. Never mind that the accusations were usually unsubstantiated rumors obtained from anonymous sources, or that they involved presumed incidents that had occurred months earlier, or that weeks later, in small print on a back page, they would be acknowledged as false by the papers. The mission had been accomplished. The newspapers had been first with a scandalous story. The sports reporters had increased their personal visibility. The Michigan basketball team had been distracted. And the long-standing principle of the sports media had been upheld: Never let the truth stand in the way of a good story!

Yet our times represent a sharp departure from the past traditions of the sports press. From the early days of reporters such as Grantland Rice, writers have served more to promote and glorify college sports than to criticize them. Sports writing became almost a classical genre of fictional prose that frequently found its way to Hollywood. In fact, the Carnegie study of the 1920s made it a point to condemn the many newspapers that treated sports as if they were the main purpose of the university.[10] Although newspapers launched occasional efforts to expose the sordid underside of college sports, such as during the basketball gambling scandals of the early 1950s, these investigative efforts rarely appeared on the sports pages since they might undermine the cozy relationship between sportswriters and coaches.

News about college sports clearly sells newspapers and television advertising. The sports sections of most newspapers are generally the best staffed, the most up-to-date, and the most lavish in their use of headlines, color photographs, and other eye-catching devices. The news media have clearly identified America's obsession with sports as the key to circulation and profits. For example, a survey conducted during 1997 found that over 40 percent of the front pages of the two major Detroit newspapers carried headline sports stories and over 70 percent of the daily website home pages of these two papers began with a sports story or photograph.[11] Although newspaper circulation is generally determined by subscriptions, in an intensely competitive market a given paper's reputation is determined more by who is first with a story than who is most on target with accuracy. This is particularly true in a community like Ann Arbor, where the university is covered not only by the local newspaper, but as well by Detroit's two major newspapers, several television stations, and national papers such as the *Chicago Tribune*, the *New York Times*, and *USA Today*.

While armchair America's fascination with college sports is, to some extent, understandable, the attack mentality that has recently been emerging among many members of the sports media is harder to fathom. To be sure, many college athletes and coaches are celebrities, and along with celebrity status goes a certain risk of becoming a media target. Yet college athletes are also young college students, in many cases still in their teen years, who are still learning from all of the experiences of college life, both good and bad. Unfortunately, they must all too frequently endure these learning experiences under the harsh scrutiny of the sports press.

The difficulty of this situation is compounded by the fact that many student-athletes come from less fortunate backgrounds—limited family incomes, educational opportunities, and experiences—

that make college even more of a challenge for them. While their athletic abilities may be extraordinary, their academic and social skills sometimes need considerable maturation. Yet the sports media can create an artificial world, treating the better-known student-athletes much as if they were high-paid professional celebrities.

It is increasingly apparent, therefore, that we should add to our list of concerns about college sports the behavior of the sports media themselves. We have already noted the role of the broadcast media, particularly television, in commercializing college football and basketball, transforming them into just another form of show business. This is understandable, if unfortunate, since the aim of the broadcast media is to sell advertising, and entertainment clearly sells better than education.

But there is another problem, and that is the culture of the sports media themselves—the sportswriters and broadcasters who create the public images of college sports. This culture has always seemed more characterized and driven by the values of the entertainment industry than journalism. Indeed, for much of the history of college sports, the sports media have done more promotion than news investigation and reporting. But this character is also due, in part, to the nature of those attracted to this profession. Few sportswriters have ever had the experience of competing in varsity athletics, at least at the level of college or professional sports. More typically, they have developed an interest in sports as spectators, hanging around sports programs for years as managers or school newspaper reporters. Furthermore, like most of the rest of the news media, sportswriters are overwhelming white and from middle-class or affluent backgrounds, with experiences far removed from the talented black student-athletes dominating college football and basketball.

My first hypothesis is that most sportswriters and broadcasters are attracted to this activity because of their longing to become a part of something they can never really understand through direct participation, since most have always sat on the sidelines as observers.[12] Woven through much of their writing and reporting is a clear sense of envy of the public adoration of athletes, of their privileged status, beginning in secondary schools, then college, and finally culminating in the celebrity status of professional athletes. This jealously creates a love-hate relationship between sportswriters and athletics, athletes, and coaches.

My second hypothesis can be summarized as the "Pulitzer Prize" syndrome. Most sportswriters—indeed, most journalists—strive for the one big story, the big hit, that will bring them fame and fortune. The fact of life of modern journalism is that these award-winning efforts are almost uniformly investigative efforts that expose corruption or failure, rather than positive stories about heroics and success. Furthermore, in competitive markets such as Detroit, the pressures to be first with the story all too often trample the truth.

Editors and publishers also deserve to share the blame for this culture. These media executives realize that college sports generate much of their market, as evidenced by the prominence of sports news in most major newspapers. While editors can become shrill in their complaints about the ills of intercollegiate athletics, they rarely acknowledge that their own reporting has contributed significantly to the problem.

The media simply do not apply the same journalistic standards to sports reporting as they do to other fields such as politics. Even *Sports Illustrated* has acknowledged that the media have failed college sports and, because of this failure, are as much to blame for the moral and ethical wasteland intercollegiate athletics have become as the people who break the rules.[13] To be sure, there are occasional instances in which editorial boards elevate sports reporting to the standards applied to areas of journalism, such as the recent series on the NCAA conducted by the *Kansas City Star* in 1997.[14] But, for the most part, sports reporting tends to be lumped more with entertainment reviews than with substantive issues such as economic policy or international diplomacy. The quality and accuracy of sports reporting reflects this.

The media tend to widen the gap between athletics and academics. Few reports on college sports ever acknowledge the broader educational mission of the institutions that sponsor them, unless it is to make a point during a moment of scandal. Beyond this, both reporters and editors generally lump together college and professional sports, thereby implying that both share the same values. Perhaps even more hypocritical is the degree to which newspapers continue to publish betting lines on college sports, clearly appealing to gambling interests.

Perhaps there is no more conspicuous example of the conflict between the media's role as the watchdogs of college sports and their role as the promoters of college sports than in the voluminous reporting about the recruiting of high school football and basketball players. No element of intercollegiate athletics is more subject to abuse than recruiting. Yet the media focus on this in such a way as to place even more pressure on coaches and institutions and to create a climate in which violations occur.

Case Study 1: Showtime

Let me illustrate the growing commercialization of college sports with some personal experiences and observations. The Rose Bowl and the Final Four have long been the glamour events of college sports. Each year millions of fans look forward to watching these events on television, long viewed as the pinnacle of success for college football and basketball. Both events also have the highest commercial value in college sports.

Most fans can only watch these sporting events on television. For those students and alumni fortunate enough to be associated with a participating university, they may have a once in a lifetime opportunity to attend one of these events in person. Yet the president of a major university such as Michigan frequently has the opportunity to attend such events as a participant, thereby gaining an unusual personal perspective on just how college sports really functions as big-time show business.

The Rose Bowl

Although we think of the proliferation of bowls today as unusual, there were over sixty such events in the 1940s, including such monumental spectacles as the Glass Bowl in Toledo, the Vulcan Bowl in Birmingham, the Yam Bowl in Dallas, and the Papoose

Bowl in Oklahoma City. There were numerous unsuccessful attempts by the university presidents to control or even eliminate such events, both because they were highly commercial and because they conflicted with academic calendars.

The Big Ten Conference shunned the bowls from 1920 until after World War II for these same reasons. However, in 1946, they agreed to begin sending the Big Ten champion to the Rose Bowl, with the understanding that the bowl receipts would be distributed evenly among all Big Ten universities (including an extra share to the participating team to cover travel expenses, which it never did).[15] This practice of sending only the champion to a bowl ended in the early 1970s, when the intense competition between Michigan and Ohio State—rather, between Bo Schembechler and Woody Hayes—finally generated pressure to send more than one Big Ten team to a bowl each year. In fact, in recent years, the Big Ten has sent as many as six teams to bowl games.

The Rose Bowl, the granddaddy of the bowls, has always been a class event. Born and sustained by civic pride in Pasadena as part of the city's Tournament of Roses, it has long matched the champions of the nation's two most powerful athletic conferences, the Big Ten and the Pac-10, on New Year's Day. On five different occasions during my presidency, we had the opportunity to lead the Michigan expedition to the Rose Bowl for New Year's Day. For my wife Anne and me, it was always a homecoming of a sort, since we had spent several years in Pasadena while I completed my doctorate at Caltech. Yet during our years living in California, we never made it closer to the Tournament of Roses than looking over the heads of the crowds lined up along Colorado Boulevard for the Rose Parade. And like hundreds of millions of others around the world, we watched the Rose Bowl on television, since most tickets were reserved for either the participating institutions or corporate sponsors.

Our trips to the Rose Bowl with the Michigan football team had all the logistical complexities of a military invasion. Typically several thousand students, staff, alumni, and other fans would fly out on dozens of charter flights a few days before New Year's Day. The team was usually housed as far away from Pasadena as possible—

The Michigan Marching Band takes the field at the Rose Bowl.

Newport Beach, Pomona, Manhattan Beach—so that coaches and players could get away from the noise and activity of the Tournament of Roses and enjoy some decent practice time (albeit, accompanied by the sports press, of course). The alumni tours were assigned to a complex of hotels in Century City, with the Century Plaza being the headquarters hotel. And the Michigan Marching Band was usually looking for cheap eats and cheap sleep alongside something that resembled a football practice field. On several occasions I had to step in and insist that the band and cheerleaders be put in a quality hotel, one time even getting them into a new Loews hotel on the beach in Santa Monica.

The Tournament of Roses and its Rose Bowl are, in reality, a weeklong circus of events: promotional press conferences, black-tie dinner dances, luncheons, and other activities. Beyond this, the team itself has a number of events: special luncheons and banquets, public relations trips to places like Disneyland, the "beef bowl" at Lawry's Prime Rib in Hollywood, pep rallies, and press conferences. Finally, because of the large turnout of alumni and

Presidential labor at the Rose Bowl

friends, we viewed the Rose Bowl as a major development opportunity, and we always scheduled a number of special events for donors. As a result, my wife and I would spend much of our time on Rose Bowl trips driving about the Los Angeles freeway system from one event to another. We usually set up a command center at the Century Plaza to coordinate this broad array of activities. Needless to say, it was always a very hectic period for us, and by sundown on New Year's Day, we were usually as tired as the players and coaches.

Although the Rose Bowl was and remains the class of the bowl events, in some ways it always played second fiddle to the Tournament of Roses Parade, which drew millions to Pasadena. Its high commercial value allowed it to negotiate sufficiently lucrative broadcasting contracts that it was never forced to share its name with a corporate sponsor, as in the Nokia Sugar Bowl or the Fed-

A Rose Bowl pep rally at Century City

eral Express Orange Bowl, at least until 1999 when it allowed "AT&T to bring you the Rose Bowl." Yet here too there were many signs of commercialism, including a large circus of hospitality tents adjacent to the Rose Bowl stadium for pre- and postgame parties of corporate sponsors and extensive advertising through the stadium.

The Final Four

It used to be that March in the Midwest signaled the arrival of the thaw in the weather. Today there is another sign of March: the media frenzy that begins to build about the approaching NCAA basketball tournament. While the sports media generally exaggerate most issues, they do have an apt description for the phenomenon: "March Madness."

Finally the game begins.

And, indeed, madness it is. Although CBS has owned the rights to the NCAA men's basketball tournament for some time, it has now been joined by ESPN and the other networks in promoting the tournament. The conferences join in this circus by scheduling special tournaments at the end of the conference season to select the conference representative to the NCAA tournament, thereby obliterating the significance of the conference championship earned by competition throughout the season. Even the Big Ten Conference now has joined in this end-of-season charade, launching a conference tournament in 1998. Here I hasten to add that during the years of my presidency, the Big Ten presidents were unanimous and steadfast in their refusal to allow such a conference tournament. Of course, we were lobbied hard by many of the athletic directors seeking the additional revenue and the basketball coaches seeking yet another route into the NCAA tournament. Unfortunately, the year after I stepped down as president of the university and chair of the Big Ten Conference Council of Presidents, the presidents caved in and agreed to a conference tournament, first held in 1997. And won by Michigan, incidentally.

During the latter weeks of the regular season, sportscasters begin to analyze each game from the perspective of how it will affect the selection or seeding of teams in the NCAA tournament. Personalities—not the players' personalities but rather the celebrity coaches'—begin to dominate the discussion, overshadowing the teams themselves and their host institutions. It is always "How will Bobby Knight or Mike Krzyzewski do this year?" never "How will Indiana or Duke fare?" Sports commentators like Dick Vitale, Billy Packer, and Digger Phelps endlessly speculate about which coaches will dominate the tournament. They are invariably wrong, of course, but somehow entertaining, at least to basketball-addicted viewers. While every aspect of college basketball is shamelessly promoted by advertisers, the ironic and tragic fact that success in the NCAA tournament will likely bring to a premature end the college education of many players goes unmentioned. The list of grievances goes on and on; some of the actors change; but the stories remain the same.

Perhaps there is no more symbolic example of the crass commercialization of college sports than the NCAA basketball tournament. The tournament now poses the greatest danger to the integrity of intercollegiate athletics. A recent series of articles on the NCAA by the *Kansas City Star* put it well:

> Can you tell the difference between the college basketball finals and the NBA championship? One group stages its games before medium sized crowds at modest ticket prices. The other group plays in arenas so huge that spectators need binoculars, and tickets cost as much as a hotel room. Referees lengthen timeouts so that television can sell more commercials. (Note that the manual for cities holding the Final Fours requires a series of gifts to be delivered every night to the hotel rooms of NCAA officials.)[16]

The climax of the NCAA men's basketball tournament, the Final Four, becomes a cosmic event and entails a command performance from the president. However, unlike a bowl trip, in which one has a month or more to prepare, the Final Four descends on one at the very last minute, since the final games sending teams to the Final Four occur the week before. Hence there is a certain spontaneity—and almost panic—surrounding the event.

Our first experience with the Final Four was totally unexpected. During our first year in the presidency, 1988–89, Michigan had had a rather mediocre season—lots of talent on the team, but certainly not dominant in the Big Ten. The team was selected among the sixty-four that would play in the NCAA tournament, but nobody expected them to get very far. Indeed, just before the tournament began, Coach Bill Frieder announced that he had accepted another coaching position at Arizona State, and so the team would be led by the unknown assistant coach, Steve Fisher.

There was mild surprise when Michigan won its first two games to go on to the regionals in Lexington. But everybody knew we would run into a strong North Carolina team, and, just as in previous years, it would be lights out. And it was, but rather for North Carolina. Michigan tore through the regional, upsetting both North Carolina and Virginia to win the trip to the Final Four in Seattle. It was a shocking turn of events, but, again, most suspected the team would go no further. After all, both Duke and Illinois (a team that had already destroyed Michigan twice) were also in the Final Four.

The Final Four itself is almost anticlimactic for the participants. It is really designed for television and the corporate sponsors. At Seattle, as at our other Final Four experiences in Minneapolis and New Orleans, the games were played in an indoor football stadium, in which most people were seated miles from the court. This was made even worse by the NCAA decision to seat row upon row of press around the court, so that the true spectator seating began even farther back. The teams and their schools are treated almost as an afterthought, usually placed in hotels on the outskirts of the city, given a small number of poor tickets, and otherwise essentially ignored, except for the frequent and mandatory press conferences.

Since the 1989 Final Four in Seattle was our first, we did not really know what to expect. We arrived right before the semifinal game against Illinois, and after speaking at a pep rally, we went to the game in the Kingdome. The game itself was exciting, with Michigan upsetting Illinois on a last-second shot to move on to the championship game against Seton Hall.

We then learned the next quirk of Final Fours. You can only purchase tickets—if you can find them—and hotel reservations in blocks for the entire Final Four series, both the semifinals and final. Since the semifinal is played on Saturday, and the championship final is not played until Monday night, that leaves you with Sunday and the better part of Monday without much to do. This is bearable for winning teams looking forward to the championship game. But it is a dismal experience for those teams and fans that lose on Saturday, since they are required to stay through Monday or forfeit the investment in tickets and accommodations.

Of course, many of the losing fans just want to get out of town. Immediately following the semifinal games there are always large numbers of scalpers waiting by the exits where the losing fans are seated, offering to buy their unused tickets to the championship game. Incidentally, this is the reason why tickets to the semifinals are scalped at hundreds of times face value, while those to the championship round sometimes go begging.

The 1989 NCAA championship game in Seattle was another cosmic event. After a seesaw battle, the game went into overtime. Trailing by one point with only three seconds to play, Michigan's guard, Rumeal Robinson, was fouled. He calmly stepped to the line and made both free throws to give Michigan an 80 to 79 victory and the national championship. After a rather sleepless evening of celebration—although nothing like the riots they had in Ann Arbor—we flew back with the team on the charter flight. The Michigan State Police provided an escort for the team buses from the airport to a gigantic pep rally in Crisler Arena, with fans honking and cheering at every intersection along the way.

Quite an experience. Indeed, perhaps a once-in-a-lifetime experience, anyplace else but Michigan. As fate would have it, three years later we found ourselves back at the Final Four, this

Rumeal Robinson sinking the shot that won the 1989 NCAA Championship for Michigan

time with the Fab Five,[17] probably the most talented class of freshman basketball players in history. Although it took awhile for the team to jell—and for Steve Fisher to get enough nerve to play all the freshmen at once—by the end of the season, they had developed into a national powerhouse. In their last game they took apart a strong Indiana team and earned a berth in the NCAA tournament.

Nobody expected very much of Michigan in the tournament since the team was so young, but, again, Michigan was full of surprises. The Fab Five proceeded to knock off each opponent, including Big Ten champion Ohio State in the regionals, to earn the trip to the Final Four in 1992. Ironically, Michigan followed much the same route through the regionals to the Final Four as it had three years before, including playing its early games in Atlanta. Since most coaches are superstitious, Steve Fisher took no chances, and

The NCAA Champions visit the White House. (White House Photo.)

the team stayed in the same hotel and went on the same tours that the 1989 team had on its previous march through Atlanta.

This time we were prepared, and we knew what to expect, although none of the sports press did. Michigan beat a strong Cincinnati team to win the right to play Duke in the finals for the national championship. In the finals, Michigan came very close to beating Duke, leading at the half, but Duke finally wore them down to win the championship. The trip back on the team plane wasn't as enjoyable as the flight back from Seattle. But the team was young, and the chant was "We'll be back!"

And indeed they were. The next year, they once again beat a series of very good teams in the tournament to make it to the Final Four in New Orleans in 1993. This particular Final Four was even more showbiz that the first two, being played in the gigantic Superdome. The other teams were all traditional powers: Kentucky, Kansas, and North Carolina. Again, nobody gave Michigan much

The Duderstadts with the Fab Five plus. (UM Photo Services.)

of a chance, particularly playing number one ranked Kentucky in the semifinals. But in one of greatest games a Michigan team has ever played, they beat Kentucky in overtime. The championship game against North Carolina was evenly matched, with the lead seesawing back and forth throughout the game. Although Michigan held a five-point lead with two minutes left, North Carolina took the lead again on two long three-pointers. The ending was one of those unforgettable moments: Michigan struggling back to within two points in the last seconds, only to have its star player, Chris Webber, call an illegal timeout that iced the game for North Carolina. Although it was a disappointing ending, it again demonstrated, as did our earlier experiences, that the Final Four—who makes it and who wins it—is largely a matter of chance.

This was to be the last Final Four for this team and for our presidency. One by one, the precocious young players of the original Fab Five were lured into the pros, and the team withered away. The demise of the Fab Five was probably not a bad thing for the university. One of the unusual features of this team was its flamboyance and bravado—and its popularity. It was this Michigan team that introduced a new fashion to college basketball: baggy pants down to their calves, black socks and shoes. This was the team that suggested in their first year they were so good they could win four NCAA championships. The press was drawn to them like flies to honey.

But this fame came with a real price. While members of sports press reveled in the athletic talents of the Fab Five, they were always on the lookout for signs of misbehavior that they could splash over their newspapers. Because these were young students, there were inevitably such incidents. Some even believe that the Fab Five caused long-term damage to Michigan athletics. In a sense, these precocious athletic talents challenged every tradition of the old guard, among the fans and the sports media. Their street-culture style, their arrogance, and, perhaps most of all, their success triggered a bitterness among the college sports establishment that continues to haunt Michigan to this day.

While television turned the Final Four into the showy spectacle of March Madness, those of us who experienced it as participants developed a more cynical attitude. It represented the extreme of what can happen when one allows the media to transform college athletics into show business. And while several of our players eventually became big-time winners in this bonanza (Chris Webber's and Juwan Howard's professional basketball contracts for $78 million and $101 million, respectively) in the end I believe that most of the players, coaches, and the university itself were losers.

Case Study 2: Conference Expansion

The expansion of the Big Ten Conference by adding Penn State University provides yet another example of how commercialism can distort college sports. As the saying goes, you win some, and you lose some. The expansion of the Big Ten Conference was one of the battles Michigan lost, since we fought against it. We were not opposed to Penn State as an institution, but saw absolutely no reason beyond television market share that conference expansion made sense.

On the plus side, Penn State was an outstanding academic institution, on a par with other Big Ten schools. It was the flagship public university in its state; it was a member of the American Association of Universities; and it had strong athletic programs (including a celebrity coach, Joe Paterno). More to the point, it could also provide the Big Ten with an important entry into the eastern television market. But adding an eleventh university would cause almost as many problems. It would create an awkward schedule. The thousand-mile distance between Penn State and Iowa symbolized the travel difficulties. There was great uncertainty as to whether the addition of Penn State would add any revenue to the Big Ten Conference, or whether it would just add one additional mouth feeding at the same trough.

Although the early phase of the discussions concerning Penn State were held in strictest confidence, word soon leaked out. It was decided to announce that the Big Ten and Penn State would examine together this possibility, but that there were many issues that needed to be resolved before a decision would be made. Needless to say, the news caused great turmoil on many Big Ten campuses. The initial press reports portrayed the Penn State expansion as a fait accompli, even though the faculty and administrators on the campuses, including Penn State, had yet to discuss it. The financial, logistical, and academic studies of expansion were inconclusive.

The politics swirling around the Big Ten meeting at Iowa in 1993, where the decision would be made, were understandably complex. In the first round of discussions, following a dinner at the president's house, four institutions opposed expansion—Michigan, Michigan State, Indiana, and Northwestern—largely because they believed that the case had not been made that any expansion was necessary. Since seven votes were required for expansion (a two-thirds majority), it looked like the addition of Penn State was not to be.

The next morning, however, the president of Northwestern

suddenly announced that he had changed his vote, thereby creating the necessary majority for admission. What happened overnight to change his vote remains uncertain. But the outcome was that Penn State agreed to join the conference, subject to a number of conditions that only became apparent later (such as that their football team would receive a bye the week before playing Michigan and Ohio State for the first several years).

Once the decision was made to admit Penn State, Michigan joined in the welcome. We were particularly hospitable by losing three of our first four football games to Penn State. Today, Penn State is not only regarded as a full-fledged member, but moreover it has become one of our most important rivals, joining Ohio State and Notre Dame. And, in an interesting stroke of logic, the Big Ten Conference decided to keep its name, with a very creative logo, despite the fact that it had eleven members. As the then-president of the University of Minnesota, Nils Hasselmo, a scholar in Scandinavian languages, observed, the number eleven in Swedish is created by adding the adjective "big" to the word for "ten"!

The issue of conference expansion, however, was not over. The conference realized the awkwardness of scheduling an odd number of teams, and there was extensive analysis given to further expansion, to twelve or perhaps more teams. This occurred in the midst of other conference shake-ups, such as the demise of the Southwestern Conference, the addition of Florida State to the Atlantic Coast Conference, and the formation of the Big East. A special committee put together a number of possible options. As word leaked out that the Big Ten was considering such possibilities, we began to be courted by a number of universities including Pitts-

The Big Ten Conference logo

burgh and West Virginia from the east and Missouri and Nebraska from the Big Eight.

After a thorough analysis, it became clear that if we were to expand, only two institutions would be real assets to the conference. Texas was the only public university in the central United States comparable in scale and character to the Big Ten universities. Unfortunately, Texas was tied politically to Texas A&M and Texas Tech, and we certainly did not want to expand to sixteen members. The most attractive possibility was Notre Dame. While Notre Dame had an extremely lucrative contract with NBC as a football independent, its other sports were atrophying. Notre Dame also depended on competition with the Big Ten for many of its football games (notably Purdue, Michigan, and Michigan State). Although the Notre Dame trustees expressed considerable interest, the administration opposed joining out of respect for what is known as "the little Leprechaun theory." They believed that the independent nature of Notre Dame football gave the institution a visibility and loyalty from the subway alumni that would be lost as a member of a conference. From the Big Ten perspective, although Notre Dame had a strong reputation for the quality of its undergraduate programs, its graduate and professional programs were not sufficiently distinguished to earn membership in the American Association of Universities, a key characteristic of all of the Big Ten universities. Hence, after a few preliminary discussions, both parties backed away, and the Big Ten Conference decided to remain the "Swedish Big Ten" (namely, eleven).

Case Study 3: The Mad Rush toward a Division I-A Football Championship Playoff

The litmus test of the depth of a given university presidents' commitment to true reform in intercollegiate athletics may be how he or she reacts to the proposal for a national championship playoff for Division I-A football. For most of the history of college football, the holiday bowl games were the ultimate measure both of team success and market strength. The major conferences had long-standing tie-ins with the major New Year's Day bowls: the

Big Ten and Pac-10 with the Rose Bowl, the Southeastern Conference with the Sugar Bowl, the Big Eight with the Orange Bowl, and
so on. In the 1970s, the floodgates were opened when conferences
began to allow strong teams other than the conference champions
to play in postseason bowls.

The number of bowls expanded rapidly, spanning the period
from mid-December until New Year's Day. Since bowl income was
determined primarily by television revenue, bowl organizers
tended to seek those teams with large market draw rather than
strong seasons. The NCAA eventually had to impose a requirement
that a team had to have at least six wins during the season against
Division I-A teams to qualify for a bowl. And, in fact, in recent
years it has been common for powerful conferences such as the Big
Ten to send teams with six-and-five records to bowl games—quite
a contrast with the old days in the 1970s when undefeated Michigan and Ohio State teams would play each year in late November
for the Rose Bowl berth, with the loser destined to spend a cold
New Year's Day home in the Midwest winter.

But, even this proliferation of the bowls was not enough for
the sports press, who clamored for a national championship playoff, similar to the National Football League. The conference tie-ins
with specific bowls prevented the top-ranked teams from facing
one another in competition, and the mythical national champion
was selected by a coaches' or sportswriters' poll at the end of the
bowl season. In editorial after editorial, sportswriters and broadcasters pressed for a playoff of the top eight or sixteen teams,
which would begin before the Christmas holidays and extend
beyond New Year's Day. To be sure, the financial success of NCAA
basketball tournament suggested that such a playoff would be very
lucrative, particularly to the television networks and sports press
selling advertising, the cities hosting the events, and perhaps even
to some of the participating institutions. One recent plan envisions
a sixteen-team playoff over a month following the regular season,
with a broadcasting value of $3 to $4 billion over several years.

Yet there were serious problems. Most college presidents realized that such a playoff would have detrimental academic implications, since competition would run right through the final exami-

nation period for the fall academic term. It would subject not simply players but entire institutions to intense media hype and commercial engagement right at the time when they should be focusing on academic matters. Furthermore, while the few bowl sites chosen for the playoffs would benefit from enormous television and spectator revenue, the traditional bowl system would be decimated. The traditions, the holiday season opportunities offered to countless fans and alumni, not to mention the revenue generated by the dozens of bowls, would be lost. Indeed, many of the bowls were already in trouble in more ways than one. The proliferation of bowl games and the quality of the opposing teams had already eroded market share and broadcasting values.

As the media pressure intensified, and the dollars promised by the entertainment industry increased, university leaders began to cave in. First, several of the bowls and conferences joined together into the Bowl Championship Series alliance aimed at arranging bowl pairings so that the teams ranked number one and number two would meet in one of the bowls, scheduled on January 2. However, the Rose Bowl, the Big Ten, and the Pac-10 refused to join the alliance, thereby creating a situation in which the top two teams might play in separate bowls if one was in the Rose Bowl. Although the networks and sports press did their best to manipulate the national rankings so that this would not happen, it did in fact occur in 1994 when Penn State was ranked number two, again in 1997 when Ohio State was ranked number two, and in 1998 when Michigan tied Nebraska for the national championship.

The lure of riches also weakened the resistance of many college presidents, who saw in a championship playoff a distribution of revenues to all NCAA colleges and universities even larger than that for basketball. As with the NCAA basketball tournament, colleges that would never get close to being in the playoff (thereby preserving their academic integrity) began to lobby to share in the potential riches. These colleges were supported by the NCAA bureaucracy who saw in a Division I-A football playoff yet another source of vast revenue and power.

Some athletic directors and university presidents offered up the usual rationalizations: that athletics was on the verge of bankruptcy or that the public demanded the playoff. In perhaps the most extreme example of a hypocritical rationalization, some even suggested that the revenue generated by the playoff might be used to help institutions move toward gender equity. But in reality, the weakening resistance of both the presidents and their institutions was driven once again by greed. Once again the commercial opportunities of intercollegiate athletics jeopardized the educational mission of their institutions.

To their great credit, the presidents of the Big Ten and Pac-10 Conferences continued to resist the pressure, although other conferences attempted to explain away this opposition by suggesting that the Big Ten and Pac-10 wanted to preserve their very lucrative, ongoing relationship with the Rose Bowl. As a participant in these discussions, however, I believe that the opposition of the Big Ten and Pac-10 presidents to a playoff was driven primarily by their concerns about academic integrity. Beyond the impact on the players and institutions participating in the proposed playoff, they saw looming before football the same media circus, the same March Madness, that basketball has to contend with.

In the end, the Big Ten, Pac-10, and Rose Bowl decided that they had to take some steps to accommodate the Bowl Championship Series if the bowl system was to be preserved. In 1996, they agreed to allow the Rose Bowl to enter the alliance, hosting the mythical national championship game every fourth year, with the participants being selected through polls rather than a playoff competition. In the off years, the Big Ten and Pac-10 champions would continue to meet in the Rose Bowl, unless one of these teams were selected for the national championship game.

It was our hope that by agreeing to participate in the bowl alliance, by providing a symbolic national championship game for the media and the public, we could forestall the march toward a football playoff. It was also our hope that the Big Ten–Pac-10 agreement with the Rose Bowl would encourage other conferences to reestablish their own long-standing relationships with other key bowls. This arrangement would allow a return to the traditional bowl system, albeit at the expense of subjecting two institutions and one bowl each year to the frenzy of the national championship game.

Although all of the Big Ten and Pac-10 presidents supported this compromise, Michigan's athletic director, Joe Roberson, strongly opposed it since he believed it was yet another step down the slippery slope toward a national championship playoff. Although I was chair of the Big Ten presidents at the time and supported their stance, I believed it was important that Roberson's concerns were considered, and I encouraged him to speak out about his opposition. This was one of those situations in which a fundamental academic value, the freedom of expression, was more important than portraying a united front. And besides, I had a hunch that Roberson might be right.

Conclusion

Despite the fact that in America, sports have always been closely identified with campus life and with academic institutions, there have always been charges of inherent professionalism of college sports. Universities have had to answer to charges that their athletics programs' emphasis on providing entertainment rather than educational opportunities for students and their susceptibility to commercialization conflict with academic values. The relationship between intercollegiate athletics and their academic hosts has long been an uneasy one.

In a very real sense, the problems in college sports that are of so much concern today are not significantly different than those a century ago. The concerns about both the recruiting and academic welfare of student-athletes remain. Celebrity coaches continue to exploit their institutions for personal gain, and their power to influence their universities continues unchecked. The relationship between college and professional sports still continues to create many problems. And the integrity of higher education continues to be threatened by the enormous popularity of college football and basketball.

Yet today there do seem to be some differences, in both the

nature and the intensity of the concerns characterizing intercollegiate athletics. College sports have become a major source of public entertainment in America, and coaches and players have
become media celebrities. Dollars from television have distorted
institutional priorities and driven unnecessary growth in intercollegiate athletics programs. The media have created a feeding frenzy
in which sports columnists rival gossip columnists in their efforts
to pander to public curiosity. All these factors have distorted intercollegiate athletics from its original status as an extracurricular
activity into another form of show business. Those institutions and
organizations traditionally responsible for the integrity of college
sports—the host universities, the athletic conferences, the NCAA—
have been co-opted by the lure of spectator, media, and licensing
revenue. One could well make the case that big-time college football and basketball today have become greedy, self-indulgent, and
exploitative entertainment businesses bringing little value and
very great danger to their host universities.

Today we have entered a period in which the American university itself is being challenged by our changing society to reex-
amine every aspect of its mission, from undergraduate education
to research to public service. Long-standing academic traditions
such as tenure, the value of a liberal education, and the balance
between teaching and research are being questioned. It is within
this context of self-examination and change that it has become
time once again to question whether there is any legitimate role for
the commercial entertainment enterprise we call big-time college
sports in the future of the American university.

Chapter 9 The Student-Athlete

Several years ago, the Michigan athletic department started an important tradition by hosting a banquet each spring to honor those athletes who had distinguished themselves in the classroom. It was my privilege as president to attend this banquet and offer congratulations to these students, all of whom had earned honors status in their various academic programs. It was gratifying to see many of our top athletes in attendance. In fact, some teams such as gymnastics and swimming sent a very high proportion of their athletes to the academic honors banquet. At each banquet, the university would also honor alumni who had been distinguished in both athletic and professional careers in order to make the point that the combination of outstanding athletic and academic performance would serve the student-athletes well later in life.

The academic honors event underscores the most important rationale for intercollegiate athletics: the belief that athletic competition can and should play an important role in the university's central mission of education. While the values learned in athletic competition are decidedly different from those learned in the classroom, they are no less important. Values of character, such as dedication, sacrifice, teamwork, integrity, and leadership can be learned on the field, both from coaches dedicated to their teaching roles and from the experience of athletic competition itself. It is clear that college sports have the capacity to provide students with important opportunities to develop these qualities so essential in later life.

Of course it takes great dedication and commitment to balance the demands of intercollegiate athletics with the demands of a college education. Excelling in academics is challenging enough without the additional pressures of participating in highly competitive athletics programs. Yet those student-athletes who manage to keep an appropriate balance between their athletic activities and their academic objectives have the opportunity for an extraordinary education, in the most complete sense of the word. It has sometimes been said that the purpose of a college education is to learn the art of life. If this is the objective, then our student-athletes may have a certain edge, since most of them benefit from a full range of experiences on our campus—from the intellectual, to the athletic, to the cultural. The value of athletics, when combined with commitment to receiving a quality college education, becomes all the more apparent when meeting former Michigan student-athletes who have gone on to great success—indeed leadership—in their careers as teachers, executives, doctors, lawyers, engineers, and even as president of the United States.

Yet there are two teams that are always underrepresented at our academic honors events: football and basketball. To be sure, a few outstanding student-athletes from these sports always attend, but they are clearly the exception. Football and basketball are not holding their own when it comes to student academic honors.

Retiring the Michigan football jersey number of President Gerald R. Ford. (UM Photo Services.)

Here again, the story of college sports breaks into two separate chapters. In the majority of sports programs, athletes are students first and athletes second. They achieve academic honors just as frequently as other undergraduates do. However, football and basketball are different. These sports have developed cultures with low expectations for academic performance. For many student-athletes in these sports, athletics are clearly regarded as a higher priority than their academic goals. Hence, to discuss athletics and academics, we are obliged once again to focus on where the problems really exist: in football and basketball.

In this chapter, we will focus on the concept of the student-athlete and the relationship between athletics and academics. At the outset we should acknowledge that, like much of the rest of college sports, this subject is shrouded in myths and misperceptions. Even the name used throughout this book to describe the participants in college sports, *student-athlete,* is contrived. In a creative public relations move designed to thwart efforts in the 1950s to make college athletes eligible for workman's compensation, the director of the NCAA, Walter Byers, decreed that all future NCAA publications would refer to college athletes as "student athletes."[1] This, along with the oxymoron *athletic scholarship,* was designed to prop up the myth that college football was an amateur activity designed for student benefit. The strategy worked; athletes were viewed as students and not as employees; and the term *student-athlete* has been used ever since.

We begin by discussing the recruitment and admission of athletes. We then turn to a consideration of their academic experiences. Finally we consider some issues of particular importance to today's student-athlete: sports injuries, gender equity, and race.

Recruiting and Admissions

Recruiting Pressures

The problems begin with the process of recruiting and admitting athletes. At many universities such as Michigan, the tradition of athletic success requires coaches to produce not only competitive but championship-winning teams. In some cases, even their employment contracts contain clauses specifying bonuses for winning conference championships or going to postseason bowl games or NCAA tournaments. Coaches are under enormous pressure to recruit the most outstanding high school athletes each year, since this has become the key determinant of competitive success in major college sports. The intensely competitive nature of the recruiting process is aggravated by the perception, real or imagined, that many coaches and institutions use negative or illegal recruiting tactics.

Sportswriters even rank the quality of the recruiting classes in football and basketball, and coaches strive to make the top ten on this list long before the season begins. However, this can also be a mixed blessing, since fans and the sports press can be merciless with a coach who has a great recruiting year and then a disappointing competitive season. What happened to all that talent? Must have been the coach's fault.

This pressure is particularly intense in college basketball, since one or two great players can make a program. Of course, such great players may only stay a couple of years before being lured away by the pros. But even this momentary brilliance is sometimes enough to raise a mediocre program into the stratosphere of a top-ten ranking.

The recruiting situation is a bit different in football. While the blue-chip athletes are important, football is far more of a team sport. To become a nationally ranked program, one must recruit a large number of outstanding players. This task is made more difficult by the great uncertainty about whether a player who has excelled at the high school level can make it in college. This uncertainty compels coaches to recruit more top athletes than they really need, much the same way that airlines overbook seats, with the end result usually being many frustrated students who would have been far happier at another university.

The coaches of most major college sports programs have become full-time recruiters, always on the lookout for new talent. Their networks of coaches, friends, and alumni reach back into the elementary and middle-school programs to begin tracking young athletes with potential. They monitor the development of these youngsters both through school programs and summer sports camps. By the time they approach the end of their high school careers, the best athletes are well known to and sought after by most of the major colleges. In fact, some athletes are effectively "signed" by coaches even before their senior year.

One of the most insidious recruiting mechanisms that has appeared on the scene in recent years is the use of a network of summer basketball camps for high school students, sponsored by the sporting apparel companies. It has become almost a requirement that aspiring young athletes attend these summer camps, both to develop their skills and to show off their talents, playing in scores of games throughout the summer. Coaches, also sponsored by companies, participate in these programs in an effort to identify and recruit the strongest players. Agents hang around the periphery, tempting players with free merchandise and benefits. Again, the commercial character of the sport has overwhelmed common sense.

Of course, recruiting athletes is only part of the process. After all, they are being recruited to participate as athletes in programs at a university where they are enrolled as students. Hence, the next phase is admissions.

Admissions Standards

Coaches and admissions officers have long known that the pool of students who excel at academics and athletics is simply too small for Division I institutions to fill their basketball and football rosters with players who meet the usual admissions criteria. All too frequently, the competitive pressure on coaches leads them to recruit athletes who are clearly unprepared for college work or who have little interest in a college education. While few of the universities engaged in big-time sports have truly competitive admissions processes, most do have certain minimum standards that must be met for admission. In all too many cases, recruited athletes fail to meet even these minimum standards.

The push to recruit blue-chip athletes has led to a practice at many institutions in which coaches actually negotiate for a certain number of "wild card" admissions. They argue that to land the very best athletes, they need far more flexibility than the university admissions process can typically provide. Hence, they seek a certain number of "no questions asked" admits, so that they can confidently go after the very top athletes. Of course, the vast majority of NCAA Division I-A universities do not have highly competitive admissions anyway, though they do usually insist on a certain level of academic attainment before admitting and enrolling a student. Turning over the admissions decision entirely to the coaches corrupts even these standards.

In 1986 the NCAA attempted to deal with the most serious cases of academic deficiency through Proposition 48, which required that all entering athletes score a minimum of 700 on their SAT and achieve a minimum high school grade point average in core academic courses of 2.0, or sit out their first year. This was a highly controversial rule, since many believed it discriminated against those racial minorities that do not traditionally perform well on standardized tests. Yet it is also the case that since Proposition 48 went into effect, the graduation rates of all athletes in football and basketball, minority and majority alike, have risen somewhat.[2]

The NCAA has been under pressure to weaken the requirements of Proposition 48 ever since its inception. In 1990, for example, a category of "partial qualifiers" was created that would allow the recruitment of athletes who fell below the SAT criterion but had a 2.0 high school grade point average in all courses. An interesting wrinkle here was that these students could receive financial support, provided it was not from athletic department funds, and also with the proviso that the grants-in-aid for partial qualifiers would not count against the NCAA limits on the number of varsity athletes. In 1992, the standards were modified slightly though Proposition 16, which kept the SAT minimum standard at 700 (although this was subsequently raised to 820 when the College Board changed the way the tests were scored), but raised the minimum grade-point average to 2.5 and the number of required high-school core courses to thirteen. The NCAA subsequently established a central clearinghouse to determine initial eligibility.[3]

The old practice, of recruiting athletes who are clearly unqualified for admission with the hope that their contributions on the field will be sufficient before their inadequacy in the classroom, has been slowed somewhat by the NCAA admissions requirements. But, ever-creative coaches have come up with an alternative: junior college transfers. The requirements for transfers from junior or community colleges are not nearly so rigorous. Furthermore, a coach can see more clearly how a junior college player has developed. Coaches disregard the fact that the transition from junior college to upper-division status in a major university is often so traumatic that many transfer students will drop out after their first year. What counts (at least to some institutions and some coaches) is that the transfer students be allowed to compete before their academic shortcomings are discovered. There is a strong correlation between the number of transfer student-athletes and the athletic success of many Division I-A universities in football and basketball. Little wonder that neither the conferences nor the NCAA has been able to close this loophole. Too many institutions benefit from it.

At many institutions the difference (in terms of grade point averages and test scores) between admitted "at risk" student-athletes and the general student body is negligible. Thus there are few problems associated with the admission of most student-athletes. At many, the university's admissions office is simply given a list of the students the coaches are recruiting with the understanding that they will be admitted. At one time, the only responsibilities of the admissions officer was to determine if the recruits were going to be eligible to play, though this is now done by the NCAA Clearinghouse. Even if the students were not eligible to compete, their admission would still be processed.

Even within a university, there is great diversity among the admissions standards of various programs. Those cynical about the academic standards of student-athletes always ask those institutions with selective admissions where they hide the athletes. Some simply admit at-risk athletes to "general studies" programs, hiding them among the total class. Others admit athletes to special programs characterized by less rigorous academic requirements or better academic support services. Common examples include programs such as physical education, sports management, sports communication, or recreational life.[4]

Yet all of these rules and dodges related to the admission of athletes were made moot in 1999 when a federal court struck down NCAA freshman eligibility standards as racially discriminatory, since it relied heavily on standardized tests such as the SAT and ACT that some contend discriminate against minority students. The ruling noted that the NCAA had not produced any evidence demonstrating that the cutoff score used in Proposition 16 serves, in any significant way, the goal of raising student-athletic graduation rates. At this point in time, the NCAA has not developed acceptable alternatives. Without such standards, however, the lack of coherence among the admissions standards of NCAA colleges and universities will create chaos.

Financial Aid

The professionalization of college sports is reflected in the evolution of the mechanisms for providing financial aid to student-athletes. Prior to World War II, it was common for well-to-do alumni or boosters to support outstanding athletes, Michigan's Tom Harmon being a good example. However, by the 1950s, the NCAA realized that this approach could lead to serious abuses, and it attempted to develop standards. The first approach was to follow the pattern of financial aid used in the rest of higher education, awarding scholarships to student-athletes based on need and academic performance.

However, football coaches resisted this policy. Using their influence within the NCAA, they pushed through the "grant-in-aid" system in which athletes were provided with grants sufficient to cover the cost of their college education, regardless of their financial need or their academic performance. Although this system was sometimes referred to as "athletic scholarships," in many ways it was a return to the old "pay for play" practice of the past. In return for athletic performance, students were provided with scholarships to cover tuition and fees, room and board, travel, and a small monthly allowance for incidental expenses.[5]

The athletic grant-in-aid system became even more of a tool for coaches to control their players when they managed to push through NCAA rules that allowed them to provide financial support on a year-to-year basis. Prior to 1973, grants were for four years and could not be revoked. But the coaches wanted more control over their athletes, including the ability to terminate their scholarship for poor athletic performances. They pressured the NCAA to allow them to terminate grants with the proviso that the institution would notify each student-athlete on or before July 1 period to the academic year whether the grant was to be renewed or not. Hence, if a student was unable to play, a coach could cut off the grant-in-aid and shift it to another athlete with only a two-month notice. The NCAA itself placed further pressure on the student-athlete by making it clear that any violation of their complex array of rules could lead to the loss of an athletes' eligibility and thus their grant-in-aid, that is, their capacity to continue to attend college. Little wonder that the priorities many student-athletes gave to athletic competition frequently dominated those given to academic performance. And little wonder as well that many people and institutions, although not the courts, began to view the grant-in-aid as in effect a contract, providing compensation to the student in the form of a college education.

From time to time the NCAA and various other athletic conferences have tried to modify the grants-in-aid system to align it better with educational values. As I mentioned earlier, the NCAA effort to eliminate athletic scholarships and shift to need-based scholarships was defeated, although the Ivy League did adopt this system as part of its effort to de-emphasize sports. The coaches also strongly resisted efforts to extend the term of financial support and make it less dependent on athletic performance—or the whim of coaches. Instead, they made financial support even more directly dependent upon athletic performance by eliminating students' opportunities for support from other sources such as federal student aid programs or work-study programs. Financial support for students during the period before or after their athletic eligibility was also prohibited. In each case the colleges' concern for student welfare was outweighed by the coaches' concern about competitive advantage.

Put another way, today's student-athletes are, in effect, employees of the athletic department, working at the job of athletic competition while being paid an amount just sufficient to cover their tuition, room, and board. Although college sports has been able to persuade the courts over the years that their participants are students, in fact in most other areas of the university such student "pay for performance" would be recognized as an employment agreement. At many universities, including Michigan, graduate student teaching assistants, who are compensated for assisting in classroom teaching, not only are recognized legally as employees but allowed to form unions for collective bargaining. It is ironic that those students compensated for academic activities are considered employees, while those students compensated for performing in highly profitable athletic "businesses" are not.

Academic Standing

Certainly one of the most serious issues facing college sports is the academic performance of student-athletes. If intercollegiate athletics are to have any place within the university, student participants must have the opportunity for a college education.

Yet all too often, student-athletes are really athlete-students. Many enter universities with very limited academic skills, passed on by their secondary skills because of their sports prowess. Instead of improving their academic deficiencies, they are swept into the intensive world of college sports, with exhaustive practices, disruptive competition schedules, and course selections designed primarily to maintain their academic eligiblity. The demands of their athletic programs deprive them of the broader opportunities of the undergraduate experience—and of the opportunity for a meaningful college education.

It is true that the academic success of most athletes is comparable to that of the student body more generally. In 1997, Division I athletes graduated at 58 percent, compared to 56 percent for the student body at large.[6] However in marquee sports of football and basketball, the situation is different. The average academic achievement of student-athletes in football and basketball programs ranks below that of the student body in general. In basketball, only 41 percent of all students graduate. The graduation rate of black basketball players has dropped to 33 percent, the lowest level in 15 years. This is not surprising, since the NCAA has found the same disparity at the national level. The average athlete on a top football or men's basketball team enters college in the bottom quarter of his class.[7] Even at the most elite competitive private universities, there is a considerable difference between the entering academic statistics of the football team and the student body in general.

Many athletics programs have made major investments in academic support services for student-athletes. For example, at Michigan the Student Athlete Support Program consists of a director, six full-time advisors, three assistant advisors, seventy tutors, ten specialized writing instructors, and fifteen proctors for supervised study sessions. The program provides assistance with the development of academic schedules, academic performance monitoring, tutorials, specialized writing instruction, supervised evening study sessions, and assists in relationships with academic instructors. Yet such academic support programs usually report to the athletic department rather than to an academic unit, and hence tend to place more emphasis on keeping varsity athletes eligible for athletic competition than on track for academic success.

Academic advisors face the challenge of keeping players eligible while trying to enable them to receive a college education. Since many are totally unprepared for and uninterested in college work, they are all too frequently steered to soft majors or soft faculty. Although most students major in a specific program such as English, chemistry, or business administration, all too often varsity athletes major in eligibility. Some coaches go so far as to demand that even good students be steered toward a less demanding course of study so that they will have more time for athletics. One continues to hear stories of academically able student-athletes being advised by coaches or academic counselors in the athletic department to steer clear of certain demanding courses or majors. It may therefore be impossible for student-athletes to have "typical" college experiences.

Most coaches profess a strong commitment to the academic success of their student-athletes. For many coaches, this goes beyond public rhetoric and reflects their sense of personal responsibility for the total college experience of their student-athletes, not only athletic but academic and even social as well. Several of our Michigan coaches spend hours every week meeting one-on-one with each of their players to make certain they took their studies seriously. Even when it is clear that accepting a professional contract prior to graduation was in the best financial interests of the player and his or her family, many coaches work hard to encourage players to complete their degrees.

Despite the fact that most coaches believe strongly in the academic success of their student-athletes, factors deeply imbedded in the cultures of college football and basketball hinder such success. And these exist not only in major athletic powers, but even in the most elite and prestigious academic institutions. A personal case in point: Many, many years ago, as a very young and very naive kid from a Missouri farm town, I attended Yale University to get an education—and to play football. The first year was a rough one. I believed football practice was more important than chemistry lab, until I received my first "D" grade. In my sophomore year, I learned that there are times when one must miss practice for academic reasons, although even at Yale, coaches found this hard to accept. When I told some of the other players that I intended to major in electrical engineering, one of Yale's most difficult academic programs, they strongly urged me to opt for something less demanding. Eventually I was forced to drop out of varsity sports because of its incompatibility with my academic objectives. The local newspapers suggested I must be crazy, and many of my teammates agreed. However in the long run, I still believe I made the right decision, although at the time none of my teammates or coaches understood it. Even at a top-flight academic school such as Yale, there was a clash between a sport like football and the academic goals of students.

Coaches eat, live, and breathe their sport, and they expect their student-athletes to do the same. Demanding academic schedules only get in the way. Left to their own designs, many coaches would require student-athletes to spend every hour of the waking day in some form of training or practice or competition. While the NCAA attempted to throttle back these demands by restricting student participation in varsity athletics to twenty hours per week, there are not only ongoing efforts by coaches to relax these limits, particularly for Olympic sports, but also attempts to subvert them with other activities such as personal training, studying playbooks, or meeting with the sports press.

Freshman Eligibility

There is no better example of the conflict between educational and competitive values than the issue of whether first-year students should be eligible to compete at the varsity level. The transition from high school to college is challenging for all students. The pressures of more demanding academic requirements, the social complexity of the modern university, and the difficulties of being away from home for the first time all combine to make the first year a critical time in students' college experience.

On the surface, the issue seems quite simple. Student-athletes, especially those in highly visible, high-pressure sports like football and basketball, have great difficulty balancing the intense demand of their athletics activities with the academic requirements of their first year. It is hard enough to adjust to the academic and social pace of a modern university without the additional pressure of athletic competition. And the social and intellectual development of students in their early college experience can be critical not only to their future education but to their later life as well.

Throughout much of the history of college sports, it was accepted that first-year students should be ineligible for varsity competition, particularly in the high-intensity sports such as football and basketball. But coaches, concerned about competitive advantage, eventually had their way and in the late 1970s managed to push through first-year eligibility in intercollegiate athletics. They argued that being part of an athletics program could serve as an important anchor and stabilize a student's early academic experience. But the real driving force was not student welfare, but rather the desire to accommodate and exploit the skills of unusually talented athletes as early as possible. The tendency of the professional leagues to draft college athletes prior to graduation only intensified this desire to get student-athletes on the field as soon as possible, before they were lost to the pros.

Today, because of the incompatibility of competitive and academic schedules, we occasionally have the outlandish situation in which some first-year students find themselves in varsity competition before they have even attended their first college class. It is difficult to see how such an experience is in the best interests of the students. In 1991, even the Ivy League caved in and allowed freshmen eligibility in all sports, driven primarily by the need to contain the rising costs of fielding separate freshman teams.

From time to time there are half-hearted attempts to address this situation. In 1999, the NCAA commission concerned with reforming college basketball floated a trial balloon of freshman ineligibility, only to find that 74% of university presidents, coaches, and athletic directors opposed change. In part this was driven by legal concerns about limiting eligibility in basketball, a sport with a disproportionate representation of African-American student-athletes—although this could have been eliminated by simply making all first year students ineligible for varsity competition in all sports. But, in the end, concerns about program cost and athletic competitiveness tended to dominate those of academic success.

A Word about Physical Education

Most universities have long had some less demanding academic programs, where many varsity athletes enroll. In earlier decades, the most common such program was physical education, usually located in a school of education. There was a certain logic to this, since the goal of this program was to produce high school teachers who could teach subjects in physical education and perhaps even coach, the career interests of many athletes. But logic aside, universities found these programs to be convenient holding places for student-athletes with less than sterling academic qualifications.

Historically, Michigan's physical education program served as the academic home for many Michigan athletes in football and basketball. However, during the difficult economic times of the early 1980s, at a time when the School of Education had been targeted for major downsizing, the university separated out the physical education program, restructuring it into a more academically demanding Division of Kinesiology. Over time this division developed highly respectable academic programs at the undergraduate and graduate level in fields such as kinesiology (movement science), physical education, sports management, and athletic training. The quality of students in these programs increased dramatically, to the point today where kinesiology has become one of the most competitive majors in the university for undergraduate admissions. Yet as the program has become more rigorous, it has found it politically difficult to set aside its historical role as the home for athletically talented but academically challenged student-athletes. Each year it is required to admit roughly sixty athletes, with no questions asked. Of these, roughly twenty to thirty fall far below the academic guidelines for admission to the university. While the program continues to provide the counseling and support necessary for these students to receive a meaningful education, it is faced with the growing challenge of accommodating this role within an ever more rigorous and competitive academic major.

Where else can athletes with weak academic skills be accommodated in a university with competitive academic admissions and rigorous academic programs? This, of course, is a question many leading universities face, from Michigan to Berkeley, and Duke to Stanford. Fortunately for the athlete interested only in eligibility, every university has a number of courses taught by faculty members well disposed toward intercollegiate athletics and college athletes. Since these soon become well known to coaches and academic advisors, student-athletes with weaker academic skills are steered toward these safe harbors. Since one can rarely find enough cupcake courses to comprise a true major, some universities have actually created degrees such as a Bachelor of General Studies to facilitate such a strategy.

Isolation of Student–Athletes

Student-athletes too often fall victim to the considerable administrative and cultural separation that exists in many universities between the athletic department and the rest of the university. As I have noted, this gap arises in part because of the ways that intercollegiate athletics is financed and managed as an auxiliary activity. But it also arises at times because of the desire of the athletic director (and occasionally individual coaches) to strengthen their control over programs, students, and staff by isolating them from the mainstream of university life.

The feudal kingdoms created by some czar athletic directors and power coaches can deprive student-athletes of many of the important experiences that should have been part of their education. Their time, their experiences, their friends, and even their studies are dominated by athletics, if not directly by their coaches. Furthermore, many athletic departments are highly compartmentalized so that athletes and coaches from one program have little interaction with those in others.

Since academic progress is critical to athletic eligibility, athletic departments make major investments in providing academic counseling and tracking the academic performance of student-athletes. Yet this approach has an intrinsic conflict of interest, since the athletic department is most concerned with athletic eligibility rather than academic progress. Unfortunately, in many cases the athletics counselors replace the faculty in determining the academic program of athletes. Many student-athletes who enter college with academic interests in areas such as engineering, medicine, or law find themselves channeled instead into less demanding programs such as general studies. The stress is less on academic progress toward meaningful degrees than athletic eligibility.

The intense time demands of competitive athletics prevent many students from exploring other extracurricular activities.

Coaches are limited by NCAA rules in the number of hours per week that they can require students to participate in practice or competition. However, most programs have informal expectations that students will spend many more hours in related activities such as physical training or therapy, study of playbooks, or social events with other team members. During the competitive season, the extensive travel can cause havoc with both academic and extracurricular activities. Of particular concern here are those sports such as basketball, hockey, and baseball that schedule events during the week, seriously disrupting classroom schedules.

Varsity athletes are sometimes isolated from other students by attitudes. While most university students enjoy sports as spectators and even look upon athletes as heroes, they are skeptical about their academic ability or interest. They tend to stereotype student-athletes as dumb jocks, extremely talented as athletes, but certainly not adept as students. There have even been some, particularly among the faculty, who express concerns that universities with nationally ranked athletics programs have an image problem when it comes to academics. In fact, I have even wondered at times whether academic powerhouses such as Ivy League universities sometimes use this argument in recruiting top academic talent away from Michigan. Certainly the image of the Fab Five does not suggest academic prominence.

Yet, over the years, when we conduct surveys about students' admissions decisions or conduct focus groups about their attitudes toward the university, we find something rather interesting. While academic quality is always at the top of the list (with the exception of some Michigan residents who realize that the in-state tuition at Michigan is the best bargain in higher education), ranked somewhere among the next several reasons is athletics. We attract an unusual number of academic superstars who want to attend a university with nationally ranked athletics programs. Surveys indicate that many of these students come to Michigan, in part, to be a part of our athletic tradition. They want to go to a Rose Bowl or a Final Four. They want to be part of the "Go Blue" tradition, even if only as students and spectators.

Sports Injuries

Throughout my years as provost and president, my wife and I always made it a point to attend the end-of-season "Football Bust," a banquet thrown for the football team by the University of Michigan Alumni Club of Detroit. This was always held in a large ballroom at a Detroit hotel, and there were usually several thousand fans in attendance. In addition to the music of the Michigan Marching Band, season film highlights, and a host of athletic celebrities, one of the long-standing traditions was to ask each senior on the team to make a short speech to thank the Alumni Club for the team ring it presented to each team member.

It was not an easy thing for most football players to stand in the spotlight before an audience of several thousand and make even a short speech. A few of the athletes breezed through the speech; others had to be coached. But the most touching speeches of all came from those students who had their athletic career cut short by a serious injury. It was clear that the violent character of college sports had shattered their dreams.

If one looks at the experience of the football players more closely, rare is the case in which an athlete has not experienced a significant injury at some point during his career. Perhaps as important as the coaching staff is the staff of the university's Department of Orthopedic Surgery. It is little wonder that in those rare instances when a football player goes on to medical school, he frequently chooses to specialize in orthopedic surgery. In fact, most graduating student-athletes already know a good deal about sports medicine from personal experience!

While football provides the most extreme case, most other competitive sports have significant injury rates. Student-athletes are pushing the limits of physical strength and endurance, and even in noncontact sports, stress fractures and torn ligaments are common. It is telling that Michigan's Department of Orthopedic Surgery chose to establish a branch clinic right in the center of a new Ann Arbor ice hockey complex. Now hockey players can skate—or rather hobble—right off the ice and onto the examination table. Certainly a clever marketing decision, but also reflective of just how prevalent injuries can be in today's highly competitive sports.

As medicine learns more about sports injuries, there is increasing concern about the risks posed by highly competitive intercollegiate athletics to the student-athlete. New techniques such as MRI and bone scans are now revealing that injuries that were once thought to be correctable through surgery may remain for life. As a result, a significant number of injuries to college athletes, particularly in contact sports such as football, are permanent and could result in premature arthritis or even crippling.

The increasing professionalism of college football has created a faster game with larger and stronger athletes. It is now estimated that a college football player's risk of incurring an injury requiring surgery is over 50 percent. Furthermore, smaller squad sizes result in more practice time and stress for players. With football now a year-round sport for athletes, their bodies simply do not have the chance to recover.

Football is not alone. Basketball has become a contact sport today, placing serious physical stress on athletes. While Olympic sports involve less contact, too many coaches simply assume that by increasing the amount of training, they can increase performance, without taking into account the associated risk of injury.

Women athletes are actually more susceptible to injury in certain sports because of their different muscular structure and tendon flexibility. While gymnastics is probably the most dangerous sport for women, even sports such as crew (rowing) are problematic because of the back injuries that result from the different skeletal structure of women.

The NCAA long ago put into place legislation that obligates the university to continue to provide financial aid to those student-athletes who are unable to complete their college athletic career because of an injury. Yet how many coaches really encourage these students to stay in school, particularly at a time when they are depressed and confused with their injury? After all, some of the best athletes saw college competition as a route into professional athletics rather than an opportunity for an education. All too many drop out of college, their dreams of a professional career shattered, and their academic skills and motivation insufficient to propel them through a degree program.

Universities face the risk of increasing litigation for sports injuries. Already there are numerous cases being filed by student-athletes claiming that they were not adequately warned or protected against injury by their institution. This will become even more serious as more knowledge and evidence becomes available about the dangers of competitive sports.

Clearly universities need to take action now, both to better protect the student-athlete and the institution itself. For example, the growing knowledge base of sports medicine needs to be woven more effectively into the training of coaches. So too, students and parents need better information about the real risks of highly competitive college sports—particularly contact sports such as football. The medical staff treating student-athletes should be independent of the coaching staff and the athletic department, with clear veto power over the participation of players. In no instance should a coach be allowed to overrule or dismiss the team physician. In fact, it may be time for universities to create independent "medical compliance officers," just as they have NCAA rules compliance officers.

Gender Equity

One of the most significant changes that has occurred in intercollegiate athletics in the past two decades has been the emergence of varsity athletics for women. Although gender equity still remains a controversial issue for some of the old guard, it has been accepted as an important and legitimate goal by most major universities. The principal controversy that remains is over how to achieve it.

In the 1970s when women sports leaders first began to use Title IX of the Higher Education Act to push for gender equity, they met strong resistance from the intercollegiate athletics establishment.[8] The demand for equal numbers of varsity opportunities for men and women was the first beachhead for broader parity with respect to expenditures, coaches' compensation, and visibility for women's athletics. Some football coaches and athletic directors saw this as a major threat, and they sought to maintain the status quo.

Early efforts to address these concerns were in the "separate but not so equal" spirit. For example, many universities developed a parallel administrative structure for women's athletics programs, complete with women athletic directors (or, more frequently, women associate athletic directors reporting to the men's athletic director as the top dog) and women faculty representatives. Although women's programs were introduced, these were rarely given the visibility and the financial support of the men's programs. When issues of gender equity were raised at the NCAA meetings, generally the football coaches and athletic directors would find a way to deflect any efforts to achieve real change.[9] In fact the NCAA took over the Association of Intercollegiate Athletics for Women so that they could better control the evolution of women's sports.

But through a series of court rulings and growing pressures from elsewhere on campus, true change began to occur in the 1980s. The number of women's programs expanded greatly; the quality of competition increased dramatically; and the number of women varsity athletes also grew. So too did public interest in women's sports, stimulated by interest in Olympic sports such as gymnastics, soccer, and women's ice hockey; by increasing participation of girls in sports at the K–12 level; and by federal actions pushing for greater gender equity.

The Office of Civil Rights identifies three areas for compliance with Title IX: (1) opportunities for participation, (2) the amount of athletics-based financial aid, and (3) the value of the benefits given to male and female athletes. Today although women comprise 53 percent of the enrollment of Division I institutions, they represent only 40 percent of their varsity athletes (and only 38 percent at schools with major football programs). While women receive 40 percent of athletic scholarships at these institutions, their programs receive only 36 percent of team operating budgets and 28 percent of salary budgets (excluding, of course, other coaching compensation available primarily to men such as broadcasting, licensing, and sports camps).

For many years, the University of Michigan remained an out-lier—or even an outcast—in women's sports. As we noted earlier, one of the early federal investigations of gender discrimination under Title IX aimed at achieving equal opportunity for women in athletics was launched against Michigan.[10] And during the early years of the effort to achieve gender equity in intercollegiate athletics, there was little of which Michigan could be proud.

With a football-dominated athletics culture, Michigan had great difficulty in even understanding much less accepting the importance of varsity athletics opportunities for women. All of the traditional arguments were trotted out to justify Michigan's noninvolvement. Most people feared harming football, the goose that laid the golden eggs. Others said that women students weren't sufficiently interested in sports to justify the expense. Naysayers guessed that attendance would be poor for women's games. During the 1970s and 1980s, the athletic department was pressured to start a few women's sports programs, but these were never given the level of attention or resources men's sports were given.

The university's reluctance to acknowledge the importance of women in intercollegiate athletics could be seen in other ways. Michigan football boosters continued to host stag events until the early 1990s. In fact, the leading booster club in Ann Arbor, the Bob Ufer Quarterback Club, continued to hold its stag dinner to honor several Michigan male athletes until 1993. In that year, one of these athletes asked if he could invite his mother to see him honored. The club refused because of its men-only policy. At this point I hit the ceiling and asked to be put on the speakers' list, which the club was delighted to do. However, I used the opportunity to blast them for their Neanderthal attitudes toward women and told them that the university would no longer allow them to use the Michigan name for such stag events. Apparently my speech must have had some effect, since the next year they invited and honored women athletes as well as men and continue to do so today.

There were many other signs of gender discrimination in the early days. For example, when women were finally allowed to earn letters for varsity competition, they were given smaller Ms than were men. Although the athletic department argued that the normal M would not fit on their smaller letter jackets, women fought this as a matter of equity and eventually won. Michigan continued to have an all-male cheerleader squad until the late 1980s.

Michigan's real progress in women's athletics began with a changing of the guard in the athletic department in 1988 with the Schembechler-Weidenbach athletic director team. Weidenbach had been heavily involved in supporting women's athletics for years, and he was deeply committed to building these programs. Roberson continued this effort to push for gender equity. As a result, during the 1990s, the university made major new commitments to women's sports. It introduced new varsity programs in women's soccer and crew. It built new facilities for women's programs (including new facilities for gymnastics, volleyball, soccer, field hockey, and crew). It substantially increased the financial support of women's programs. And perhaps most significantly, it made a public commitment to achieving true gender equity in the number of varsity opportunities for women, achieving this goal in the late 1990s.

Of course, it is important to acknowledge that when Michigan made the effort during the 1990s to achieve gender equity, it was able to do so in large measure because of the incredible revenue-generating ability of Michigan football. Many other institutions with more limited resources had to face the very real possibility of discontinuing men's sports in order to achieve better gender equity.

To be sure, with the increasing commitment to women's athletics have come many of the concerns characterizing men's programs. For example, there are signs that women's basketball is moving down the same road to excessive commercialism that characterizes the men's program, complete with the March Madness surrounding the NCAA championship. There is increased pressure on admissions offices to admit at-risk female athletes, just as there has been for men. The salaries of women coaches have increased, although they lag very far behind the compensation of celebrity male coaches. Several universities have selected women as athletic directors, although these appointments sometimes encounter strong opposition from the old guard.

In this sense, it would be misleading not to acknowledge the considerable resistance that these efforts faced from the football booster crowd. There are times when it appears that universities take one step forward and then two backward. As we have noted, at Michigan, football has long been and remains king, and women's sports have been viewed by many boosters (although not necessarily most of the coaches and players) as a threat. Michigan continues to invest more in its football program (including Michigan Stadium) than any other university in the nation.

After I stepped down as president, the football crowd took over and once again began to shift priorities away from building the women's programs. Massive new investments were made in Michigan Stadium that depleted the athletic department's financial reserves, critical to women's programs. The compensation of men's football and basketball coaches soared to levels many times larger than the highest salary for any of the coaches of our women's program. It became increasingly apparent that the university was reverting to its old form of a football-dominated program, in which women's sports would be returned to the status of peripheral activities. Sometimes it seems that we never learn.

This on-again, off-again commitment does raise an important issue about the strategy for achieving gender equity. When faced with limited resources, sometimes universities perceive, mistakenly I believe, that their only option is to free up opportunities for women by reducing opportunities for men. In fact, during the period from 1985 to 1997, while the number of women participating in varsity sports increased by 16 percent to 103,252, the number of men athletes declined by 12 percent to 163,636. However, it is clearly wrong to place the burden of eliminating men's sports programs on the back of the women's programs. Rather the burden should be placed squarely where it belongs: on the back of our football programs. After all, it is this absurd practice of tolerating in football a men's athletics program several times as large as any other sport that makes it so hard to achieve gender equity. When the football coaches pushed through the rule changes to allow unlimited substitution in the 1960s and ballooned the size of their sport to involve squad sizes of over one hundred players and dozens of coaches per team, they, in effect, sentenced a number of men's sports programs to extinction. The real question is whether we should continue to accept a football paradigm with so many players, coaches, and expenses at the expense of other sports programs (both men's and women's).

Gender equity is clearly the right goal for higher education. It is not only possible, but imperative if intercollegiate athletics are to play a legitimate role on our campuses, during an era when the enrollment of women students will soon outnumber men by roughly a 60–40 percent margin in American higher education.[11]

Race

One of the most sensitive issues in intercollegiate athletics concerns race.[12] Basketball and increasingly football are dominated by talented black athletes, whose representation in these sports programs far exceeds their presence elsewhere in the university. To be sure, sports provide many minority students with opportunities to attend and benefit from a college education. Furthermore, the importance of teamwork and the common goals of winning can knit together racially diverse teams in ways that few other college experiences achieve.

Yet, on too many campuses, the independence of sports programs from the rest of the university isolates these minority students from broader educational experiences. Many minority athletes eat together, live together, study together, and have little interaction with the white student majority on most campuses. And all too frequently, big-time college sports provides a seductive path that lures talented minority athletes into programs with the elusive goal of a professional sports career rather than a college education.

At a time when colleges and universities are being asked to reassess the role of racial and ethic diversity among their students, faculty, and academic programs, it seems appropriate to challenge higher education as well to examine the issue of diversity in intercollegiate athletics. Here again, the separation that exists between athletic programs and the rest of the university can only harm the educational experiences and opportunities available to minority student-athletes.

The Beginnings of a Solution?

As I noted at the outset of this chapter, most college sports are compatible with academics. To be sure, getting up at 4:00 A.M. for a morning swimming practice and then training again in late afternoon, or running seventy miles a week to train for cross-country, would be extreme for most folks. But student-athletes are a rare breed. They manage to achieve and maintain a competitive edge in academics just as they do in athletics. In fact, there is reason to suspect that many of the same attributes necessary for success in athletics—commitment, dedication, perseverance, hard work—are also important ingredients for success in academics. Yet most student-athletes realize their future will be determined more by their academic experiences than by their athletic experiences while in college.

The notable exceptions are football and basketball, in which the competitive culture is now so distorted that academic progress has often become secondary to athletic performance. Our universities have allowed these two sports to become dominated by the demand for and culture of entertainment. As coaches, athletic directors, trustees, and even university presidents, we seem to have rationalized a system in which these two sports operate outside of academic culture and values of the university, so we can provide quality entertainment for the armchair public—not to mention quality athletes for the pros.

In my view, the damage done to students participating in these programs, not to mention to the university itself, has become simply too great. It is time that we decoupled football and basketball from the world of big-time show business, and reconnected these programs, their coaches, and their student-athletes to the educational mission of the university. If we are unable to conduct these two sports programs as we do our other athletics programs, they are simply not worth continuing. If we are unable to maintain a better balance between the academic and the athletic in football and basketball, it might be far better for our institutions, our students, and our nation if we were to phase them out in favor of flag football and intramural basketball.

Chapter 10   Integrity

Hardly a week goes by without yet another exposé on the sordid nature of intercollegiate athletics. Even as they promote the increasing commercialism of college sports, the sports press is joined by other media in proclaiming that intercollegiate athletics are out of control. They portray coaches and players as dishonest, interested in winning at all costs, boosting their own incomes or chances for a pro contract. They contend that universities turn a blind eye toward dishonest practices so that their programs will continue to win and generate broadcasting dollars and alumni contributors. College sports fans are stereotyped as booster-bubbas, cheering on their favorite teams with their painted faces and lunatic garb, willing to do anything for a winning program. Is college athletics really a den of thieves, a snake pit of dishonest coaches, misbehaving athletes, fat-cat boosters, and greedy universities? Or is something else amiss?

Beyond the occasional booster slipping some cash to an athlete or a coach bending the Byzantine rules of the NCAA, there have indeed been serious incidents involving gambling and point shaving, illegal payments to recruits and players, and academic grade-fixing. On rare occasions, institutions have attempted to build winning programs by methodically cheating, by illegal recruiting, falsifying academic records, and laundering payments to players. Some student-athletes have even blatantly violated the law, committing acts of robbery, vandalism, assault, even rape and murder.

So what is the problem? To be sure, similar incidents happen in other parts of the university and in our society more broadly. Our student-athletes, coaches, and athletic staff's behavior tends to mirror that of other members of the university community and society more generally. While most behave with high integrity and honesty, there are always a few bad apples and some occasional lapses. It is also true that the pressures on college athletes are intense, but then, so too are the pressures intense on other members of the university community. Furthermore, student-athletes are like other students. They are young adults, at a point in their lives when curiosity is encouraged and mistakes should be tolerated as part of the learning experience.

Yet there is one important difference with intercollegiate athletics: its high public visibility. Because of intense media exposure of the revenue sports, football and basketball, the behavior of coaches and athletes is subject to public scrutiny far beyond that of other students, faculty, or staff. The slightest misstep ignites a firestorm in the media, always on the alert for any sign of misbehavior or scandal that might sell more papers or bring in more advertising revenue. This is not to suggest that athletes are always held to higher standards of behavior. In fact, in some cases and some institutions, their misbehavior is tolerated. Cover-ups are common, sometimes even aided and abetted by a friendly sports press. But their flaws, when exposed, certainly receive far greater public attention.

Most coaches and athletes accept that this public exposure goes with the territory. They realize the devastating impact of misbehavior. Student-athletes are told time and time again that they will be viewed, rightly or wrongly, as ambassadors for their university and held accountable for their behavior. Yet the temptations in the show business culture of college football and basketball remain strong.

In this chapter we will consider those issues that impact on the integrity of college sports and the institutions that conduct them. We begin with a discussion of the rules of intercollegiate athletics, as developed and enforced by the NCAA and the conferences. We will then consider the ways in which student-athletes, coaches, and institutions violate these rules, and examine the various policies and procedures aimed at protecting the integrity of sports programs. We will conclude with a brief discussion of the efforts to restructure the complex rules of intercollegiate athletics in ways that align them more clearly with the fundamental purpose of universities.

The Rules of the Game

Rules compliance begins at the Office of the President. The two individuals most directly responsible for the integrity of the university's intercollegiate athletics programs, the athletic director and the faculty athletic representative, report directly to the president. The athletic director, as the chief administrative officer of the athletic department, is responsible for the direct management of intercollegiate athletics. The faculty athletics representative is a university faculty member, appointed by the president and independent of the athletics department, who has institutional authority over the violation reporting process, the submission of petitions to the conference and the NCAA, and representation of the university to the conference and the NCAA. Most universities also have a rules compliance officer, reporting directly to the athletic director and charged with responsibility to promote, evaluate, and direct the athletic department's compliance with university, conference, and NCAA rules.

Each fall, as president of the university, I would receive a large book from the NCAA, several hundred pages long, detailing proposed rule changes that would be voted on at the January NCAA convention. Note that I said rule *changes*. The actual rulebook itself is considerably larger. Each of these rule changes would be associated with a sponsor, sometimes a conference, sometimes a set of institutions or a group of coaches, or sometimes even the presidents themselves. And for months prior to the NCAA convention, I would be lobbied by various constituencies to support or to oppose such rule changes.

While few of the changes were particularly significant for intercollegiate athletics as a whole, each was viewed as vitally important to a particular constituency. Perhaps the wrestling coaches wanted to allow an additional coach to assure the safe training of their athletes. Or swimming coaches wanted an exemption to the twenty-hour-per-week training limit to allow their swimmers to train for the Olympic Games. Or football coaches wanted to allow just a few more contacts with prospective recruits so they could better assess their true abilities. Of course, there were always a few proposed changes clearly designed to tilt the competitive advantage, such as when a group of institutions wanted to relax the rules governing junior college transfers. And there were even blatant examples of commercialism, such as when several institutions sponsored a rule change to allow a lucrative preseason football game in addition to the normal season.

Like most presidents, I delegated the preliminary review of this encyclopedia of proposed changes to the athletic department and to the university's faculty representative. At Michigan, we usually also relied on people with law backgrounds, either on the staff or as our faculty representative, to assist in the compliance function. Additionally, the staff and various committees of the Big Ten Conference helped us make our way through the process of evaluating proposed rules, since the Big Ten universities tried to vote together on most issues (although we sometimes found ourselves split). Usually, major rule changes such as those designed to tighten academic requirements or restructure the governance of intercollegiate athletics received the careful attention of the Big Ten presidents at our December meeting.

It has always struck me as symbolic of college athletics that while the NCAA, in theory at least, has a major responsibility for protecting the welfare of student-athletes, the majority of its rules deal instead with athletic competitiveness.[1] There are pages and pages of rules governing recruiting, student transfers, practice schedules, funding, coaching staff sizes, and such. But only a relatively small number of rules focus on the fundamental welfare of the student-athlete. Perhaps it is inevitable that any rule-making process that flows from coaches, athletic department staff, and conference administrators would tend to focus primarily on what concerns them the most: the relative competitiveness of their institutions in various sports programs.

These examples illustrate an important point. NCAA rules are highly arbitrary, and for the most part designed to maintain a level playing field among institutions, although some would claim they are primarily crafted to benefit some institutions over others. In this sense they are not truly laws of the land. If you break a NCAA rule, you will not go to jail. Rather, the NCAA itself will hand you a penalty, generally a slap on the wrist. Despite the highly artificial nature of these rules, they are given almost cosmic significance by many, including not only coaches and athletic directors, but perhaps even more, the sports press.

Furthermore the strongly political character of the NCAA rulemaking process also extends to its enforcement activities. Usually, the most flagrant rule violations result only in the loss of a few scholarships or recruiting visits or probation for the offending program. The NCAA rarely levies a serious penalty such as restricting broadcasting or postseason competition. While it has the authority to levy the "death sentence" by prohibiting competition for a period of time, this has been done only once, to Southern Methodist University in 1974. Why? Because the financial implications of such sanctions would be too great for other members of the offending institution's conference.

Ironically, while the most serious violations generally go unpunished, many minor violations indirectly result in great harm. Even the suggestion of a NCAA investigation is enough to trigger a feeding frenzy of the sports media, resulting in week after week of sensationalist articles based largely on speculation and rumor. Many institutions—and individuals—have had their reputations seriously damaged by the unsubstantiated exaggeration of media reports during the many months of an institutional or NCAA investigation. Universities have been known to fire coaches simply on the basis of unsubstantiated rumors of rules violations—in a sense, tossing them out as sacrificial lambs to feed the howling wolves of the sports media or appease the gods of the NCAA infractions committees. Even when a thorough investigation turns up a clean bill of health or evidence of only minor violations, the damage to reputation may have already occurred.

In addition to the array of NCAA rules are a set of rules specific to various athletic conferences. In many cases, the conference rules are more relevant and certainly more accepted, since they are usually determined through the interaction of a small set of similar institutions. For example, the Big Ten Conference has rules governing academic standing that are considerably more demanding than the NCAA. And well it should, since the Big Ten is the only athletic conference in the nation in which every one of its member institutions has attained sufficient academic stature to belong to the Association of American Universities, the leading research universities of America. (Even the Ivy League cannot make this claim!)

Beyond this, each institution has its own set of rules, regulations, and operating practices. For example, at Michigan, our regulations governing the level of academic performance necessary for athletic eligibility are traditionally somewhat more stringent than those adopted by the Big Ten Conference.

Violations

Whenever there are rules, there are certain to be violations and violators, as well as sanctions. Here again it is important to understand that most of the rules of the NCAA, the conferences, and the institutions that govern athletics are confined to issues affecting competitiveness rather than the welfare of student-athletes or the institutions where they are enrolled. As such, neither the language nor the enforcement of the rules governing intercollegiate athletics are subject to the long-established principles of jurisprudence that cover civil and criminal violations in our society. Both the judgment on possible violations and the decision on sanctions involve institutional processes at the conference and NCAA level.

The most common forms of rule violation involve relatively innocuous stumblings over complex NCAA rules. Most coaches, students, and athletic department staff try their best to stay within the rules, but the intricacies of the codes and the manner of their enforcement can lead to confusion and mistakes. Over half of all NCAA violations involve recruiting. Most of these are relatively minor. For example, a coach might not know the most recent regulations on the handling of recruiting visits to campus. A student-athlete might not realize that even something as simple as accepting a ride home from a coach could be a violation. Athletic department staff can slip up and fail to file on time the papers certifying the academic eligibility of student-athletes.

To prevent these minor transgressions, most athletic departments have staff specifically charged with keeping an eye on the compliance function in order to keep coaches and players adequately informed on rules. Usually, these minor rules violations are discovered first by the institution and then self-reported to the conference and/or the NCAA. Sometimes the university will levy its own sanctions against the program, such as a temporary ineligibility of the student-athlete or a written reprimand of the coach. It will take steps to make certain that the violations do not recur, and usually the NCAA will accept these self-imposed sanctions as adequate.

The behavior of student-athletes, even when it does not break NCAA rules, can also pose a challenge to institutional integrity. Most incidents involve the same types of misbehavior that arise with any student. The most common behavioral issue with general college students is substance abuse, alcohol in particular. Fortunately, most athletic departments have strong programs for monitoring student behavior involving alcohol or illegal substances such as steroids, marijuana, or cocaine, and they provide counseling help when problems arise. Substance abuse is therefore not usually as serious a problem in athletics as it is in the student body more generally. Other forms of student misbehavior, such as fights, vandalism, or driving violations, can and do occur with student-athletes, just as they do with other students.

Most serious of all are those rare situations in which student-athletes become involved in criminal activities. Assault, theft, sexual assault, and other lawbreaking sometimes involve athletes—just as they do other students. However, relatively minor infractions by high-visibility athletes achieve a notoriety in the media that far exceeds more serious incidents occurring within the general student body. At most universities, such incidents are dealt with either within the disciplinary codes for student behavior, or if serious enough, referred to the criminal court system.

Of course, student-athletes do occasionally violate specific rules governing intercollegiate athletics. Sometimes these violations arise from ignorance, such as when an athlete accepts a ride or a meal (or even a birthday cake, in one high-visibility Michigan case) from a well-intentioned booster. Sometimes the violations are more deliberate, for instance, when student-athletes accept gifts or discounts on athletic apparel from local sports stores. In these cases, all of the machinery of investigation, reporting, and sanctions is activated to protect the integrity of the institution.

Farther up the scale in seriousness are the efforts of boosters or fans or local merchants to become close to the program by providing favors to coaches or to student-athletes. The violations can be quite serious, leading to severe sanctions against the program and the student-athlete. For example, some well-intentioned but misguided boosters may try to buy clothes or meals or even cars for student-athletes. Others may attempt to assist in the recruitment of star athletes. All of these efforts are in clear violation of the rules governing intercollegiate athletics and can be very damaging to the institution. Most coaches and athletic directors go to great lengths to isolate their programs from such dangers, but it is sometimes difficult to control the behavior of young athletes, and trouble can arise.

Considerably more serious are the activities of agents who prowl around the periphery of college sports, attempting to entice star athletes into letting them broker their relationship with professional sports. The astronomical sums associated with contracts in the professional leagues make being a successful agent a very lucrative occupation. And greedy and unscrupulous agents have put the athletic careers of many student-athletes at great risk. Although the activities of these predators is of increasing concern, privacy laws sometimes make it very difficult to monitor these relationships.

Particularly serious is the impact of gambling on the integrity of intercollegiate athletics. Throughout the history of college sports, some of the most serious violations have involved gambling. As Kentucky saw in 1952, Seton Hall in 1983, Boston College in 1995, and Northwestern in 1997, not only does gambling undermine the values of higher education, but it brings with it elements of our society, including organized crime, that can pose great danger to our students and our institutions. Yet, despite this obvious danger, billions of dollars are gambled every weekend on college sports, primarily football and basketball. Every time a newspaper lists the point-spreads for upcoming games, we are reminded of the dollars that are at stake. Our society's increasing tolerance for gambling, whether through state lotteries or casinos or betting on sporting events, is of great concern to college sports. Furthermore, it is estimated that the amount of money illegally wagered on sporting events is several times that wagered legally.

Recent studies suggest that gambling may be far more common among student-athletes than we might expect. Michigan athletic director Joe Roberson sponsored a national survey in 1997 that revealed that 72 percent of student-athletes have gambled at one time or another, with 45 percent of male athletes gambling on sports while attending college. Although only 5 percent of male athletes have provided inside information for gambling purposes or bet on a game in which they participated, even this rate seriously undermines the integrity of college sports.

As gambling becomes more accepted in our society, controlling its impact on college sports will become every more challenging. For example, some universities now offer actual college degrees in gambling (e.g., Central Michigan University and the University of Nevada, Las Vegas). Others tolerate governing board members with casino interests. Both the integrity of our sports programs and our academic institutions will depend on distancing ourselves as far as possible from gambling, whether legal or not. Both the NCAA and Congressionally-appointed commissions have called on the states and the gambling industry to ban gambling on college and amateur sports and to raise the minimum gambling age to 21. But both the industry and the state of Nevada have turned a deaf ear to these pleas. As a result, it is up to university governing boards and presidents, athletic directors and coaches, and conferences and the NCAA to put into place effective mechanisms that shield intercollegiate athletics from this increasingly pervasive and sinister activity in our society.

The organizations responsible for the integrity of college sports, the conferences and the NCAA, believe that the key to integrity lies in the concept of institutional control. Generally, when infractions are discovered, they are eventually traced to a lack of institutional control over the athletics program. It may be a lack of oversight or the inappropriate involvement of boosters or trustees or even the media. Whatever the cause, the result is a breakdown in the system of accountability that eventually ends on the desk of the university president.

Since the principle of institutional control is so important to the integrity of intercollegiate athletics, I will discuss this issue in detail in the next chapter. Suffice it to say at this point that achieving and defending this principle is one of the most difficult tasks of a university president. It requires a level of involvement in intercollegiate athletics that few understand or appreciate.

Playing by the Rules

The University of Michigan has long placed a very high priority on the integrity of our athletics programs. We believe that there is only one way to compete, and that is the right way, by the rules. To be sure, Michigan, like any other large, complex institution, makes mistakes from time to time. Sometimes a young athlete or an overzealous booster does something that embarrasses the university. Occasionally even coaches or staff make mistakes, rarely by intent, but nevertheless in violation of the elaborate rules governing intercollegiate athletics. When mistakes have occurred, the university has accepted full responsibility and taken action to make certain they would not happen again.

Each fall during my presidency, I would schedule a meeting with all of the head coaches of Michigan's various sports programs. I would carefully explain the importance of following the rules to the letter, both for coaches and student-athletes, and make sure they understood that compliance was critical to the integrity of the university.

Although the president is held accountable for the integrity of the athletics program, just as he or she would be for all other university activities, the athletic director, as chief executive officer for the athletic department, must assume the operational responsibility. To be sure, violations at the coaching or student level were sometimes beyond the control or even the knowledge of the athletic director. But in the end, he or she would surely be held accountable. Hence, it was absolutely critical that the athletic director and president develop a relationship of mutual trust, respect, and confidence, since without that open channel of communication, the institution would be at considerable risk.

During my presidency, I was fortunate enough to have athletic directors (Bo Schembechler, Jack Weidenbach, and Joe Roberson) and coaches who were deeply committed to the integrity of intercollegiate athletics at Michigan. Despite this commitment, Michigan, like essentially all major universities, faced occasional challenges. Some of these problems were inherited from earlier times. I have mentioned earlier that shortly after I became president, we discovered that our baseball program had committed a series of violations during the 1980s. These involved the mishandling of university funds, the inappropriate payment of student-athletes, and the inappropriate use of scholarship aid. The moment allegations first became known to Bo Schembechler, who had just taken over as athletic director, he briefed me on the situation and recommended a full-scale investigation, in cooperation with the Big Ten Conference. When it became clear that the alleged violations had indeed occurred, Schembechler moved rapidly to dismiss the baseball coach and imposed a series of self-sanctions on the program, while reporting the full details to both the conference and the NCAA. Even though the violations had occurred during an earlier administration, I thought it was important that we personally accept full responsibility, acknowledge the violations, and take decisive action to make certain they would not happen again. I made just such a statement before the NCAA infractions committee. Largely as a result of the university's thorough investigation and prompt action, the NCAA accepted our self-sanctions of the program while putting the baseball program on probation.

This was the most serious infraction that we dealt with during my presidency, since it involved an intentional violation of NCAA and conference rules by a coach. Other incidents involving student misbehavior raised some concerns but were in most cases typical of the missteps many students make. For example, early in my presidency, a star hockey player got into a fight with his girlfriend and another student, causing not only personal injury but also extensive property damage to her sorority. After an investigation, the vice president for student affairs recommended that I suspend the student for the remainder of the season, even though the team was about to enter the regional championship playoffs. Using my presidential powers, I suspended the player while requiring him to receive counseling before becoming eligible the following year. Although this action disappointed the hockey coach, the circumstances of the case were sufficiently serious that I believed I had to intervene.

What kept us awake at night most were the series of unsubstantiated allegations about impropriety that the local newspapers would launch against us at regular intervals. Generally they would find an anonymous source who would claim a student-athlete or a coach did something wrong, and then we would spend countless hours and dollars trying to track down the truth. Of course, we felt it was important to investigate every one of these allegations, even though we suspected in many cases that the reporters were up to mischief just to sell newspapers.

Life was made even more difficult by the fact that with Michigan's intrusive sunshine laws, which require full disclosure of university records, the newspapers were able to go on fishing expeditions through our records—phone records, expense vouchers, even personnel files—in an effort to put the worst possible face on any accusation. On the other hand, we were also constrained by federal privacy laws in how we could investigate student activities, as well as what we could state publicly during an ongoing investigation. As a result, the press was able to make the most sensational allegations, quoting anonymous sources, without any obligation to back up their claims, and we were constrained to respond by simply say an investigation was under way. There were times when I seriously considered filing a libel suit against one of the newspapers on a particularly flagrant and abusive attack, just to make the point that freedom of the press must be accompanied by some level of accountability and responsibility. Clearly we could never win such a suit. But at least we could use the suit to challenge editors and publishers to hold themselves to a higher level of journalistic standards.

Rules versus Values

It seems clear that the key to integrity in athletic programs lies not in more rules. In fact, the complexity and confusion in the process by which we create and apply rules in intercollegiate athletics is part of the problem. The rules have become so complex, so encumbered with special interests, and, in some cases, so bent out of shape as to be unworkable. Instead, we need first to agree on some fundamental values that should characterize college sports. The Knight Commission made a good start on this effort by proposing the following set of fundamental principles.[2]

1. The educational values, practices, and mission of the institution determine the standards by which intercollegiate athletics are conducted.
2. The responsibility and authority for the administration of the athletic department, including all basic policies, personnel, and finances, are vested in the president.
3. The welfare, health, and safety of student-athletes are primary concerns of athletics administration on campus.
4. Every student-athlete will receive equitable and fair treatment.
5. The admission of student-athletes will be based on their reasonable promise of success in a course of study leading to an academic degree, as determined by the admissions officials.
6. Continuing eligibility will be based on students being able to demonstrate each term that they will graduate within five years of enrolling. Students who do not pass the test will not play.
7. Student-athletes in each sport will be graduated in at least the same proportion as nonathletes who have spent comparable time as full-time students.
8. All funds raised and spent in connection with intercollegiate athletics programs will be channeled through the institution's general financial structure.
9. All athletics-related income from nonuniversity sources for coaches and athletics administrators will be reviewed and approved by the university.

10. Institutions will conduct annual academic and fiscal audits of athletics.

The Knight Commission's work represents a useful first step because the educational welfare of the student-athlete is the cornerstone for most of the principles. Interestingly enough, none of the principles addresses the issue of competitiveness. And it is reassuring to note that nowhere is there a mention of any responsibility of college sports to provide public entertainment.

Concluding Remarks

As obvious as these principles proposed by the Knight Commission are, it is clear that after almost a century of similar efforts, there has been little success in using such values to guide intercollegiate athletics. The reason is simple: there are simply too many inherent conflicts among the objectives and values of the various participants in college sports and the educational values of the university. Although the majority of student-athletes would prefer to prioritize their college education over athletic competition, the grants-in-aid ("pay for play") system and the complex web of NCAA rules tie them tightly to their athletic endeavors. Although coaches profess concern about the welfare of their student-athletes, their own priorities usually lie with competitive advantage and winning. Many if not most universities, and certainly most university presidents, would like to see sports de-emphasized, particularly the big-time sports of football and basketball. Unfortunately, they are seldom able to withstand the pressures from both key constituencies and the public more broadly to provide this form of entertainment. And even the organizations responsible for the integrity of sports, the NCAA and the conferences, are caught in a bind. On the one hand they are charged with the mission of keeping sports clean, yet at the same time, they are expected to generate millions of dollars of broadcasting revenue each year for their member institutions.

Let there be no doubt that the integrity of intercollegiate athletics is a matter of great importance and concern to higher education. College sports subject universities to enormous pressures generated by the interests of alumni and sports fans, the commercial value of college sports in our society, the exploitative and predatory role of the sports press, and the highly competitive cultures of coaches and players. While the unusually high visibility of college sports can sometimes be used to promote the interests of the university, more significantly it places it at considerable risk from flaws, real or perceived, in its programs.

A word of caution, however. In view of the sensationalistic nature of most sports reporting, it is very important to place in perspective the issue of integrity in intercollegiate athletics. One of the great ironies—or perhaps, more accurately, hypocrisies—in college sports is the degree to which those who most aggressively promote and profit from intercollegiate athletics can sometimes be among its most vocal critics. After all, nothing generates more reader interest, circulation, and profits than a scandal, not to mention more fame, awards, and income for those to discover and unveil (or perhaps contrive and exploit) flaws in high-visibility sports programs.

Despite the outlandish significance the press gives to rule violations in intercollegiate athletics, these have implications primarily for the competitiveness of *games* played by students. Hundreds of far more significant events occur every day in the contemporary university through its academic programs, its research, and the services it provides to the public, activities with major implications for our institutions, our nation, and our society. In a pep talk attributed to a Yale coach of modern times, that coach told his team, "Men, you should bear in mind that there are over one billion Chinese today who know nothing about today's game with Harvard, and who could care even less!"

If college athletics programs are to survive and succeed, universities must take steps to protect the integrity of their programs. They must understand and fully comply with NCAA and conference rules, no matter how complex they may become. They must educate coaches, athletes, boosters, and fans about the complex regulations governing recruiting and competition. Universities must put into place and respect a clear system of controls, with the final responsibility resting with the president.

Universities must also recognize that intercollegiate athletics is a peripheral activity of the university. And as such, in the end, the basis for the integrity of intercollegiate athletics is remarkably simple. It is determined by the relationship—and relevance—of college sports to the educational mission of the university and to the education of students.

Chapter 11   Institutional Control

There is no more serious accusation in a rules violations investigation by the NCAA Infractions Committee concerning intercollegiate athletics than a conclusion that the university has lost "institutional control" of its athletics program. But there is also perhaps no accusation more frequently misunderstood by the media, the public, and even the accused institution. To both the coach and the players, institutional control implies that the coach is firmly in control of the program. The athletic director would similarly claim the authority to control the athletic programs. At some level this is both appropriate and understandable, particularly since these would be the first heads to roll in the event of a serious incident.

But institutional control refers to something beyond simply the coach's discipline or the athletic director's authority. It is a process, a system, and a set of values and expectations within the institution. It is very similar to the system of audit controls governing a major corporation. The idea is to make certain that violations do not happen in the first place, rather than to place the blame after the fact. And, as we have noted, the key to this system lies in the recognition that in the end, the president is ultimately responsible for the integrity of college sports. Nevertheless, an array of forces, some structural, some commercial, some adolescent, some obsessed, and some simply foolish, all act to undermine efforts to control intercollegiate athletics.

In this chapter, we will consider several of the powerful forces threatening the university's ability to control intercollegiate athletics: the competitive culture of coaches and athletic directors, the obsession that many members of the public have with college sports, and the influence of professional athletics. Yet a century of failures to control or reform intercollegiate athletics suggests that lack of adequate institutional control of college sports lies within the academy itself, with the abdication by the faculty of its role in governing intercollegiate athletics, the failure of most governing boards to recognize just how damaging big-time college sports can be to their institutions, and the reluctance of most university presidents to risk challenging the ever more commercial and exploitative character of intercollegiate athletics.

An Early Case Study: Steamrolling the President

In his book *Unsportsmanlike Conduct* Walter Byers, director of the NCAA for over thirty years, points to an event that occurred at the University of Michigan shortly after the turn of the century as key in the evolution of college sports.[1] In 1906, the legendary Michigan football coach Fielding Yost managed to defeat the equally legendary Michigan president James Burrill Angell in his efforts to restrain the growth and restore the integrity of college sports. Concerned about the growing professionalism of football, Angell had persuaded several midwestern college presidents to form the Western Athletic Conference, later to become the Big Ten, which would develop and adopt rules to keep football within reasonable bounds. The presidents intended to limit the season to five games, restrict eligibility to three years and to undergraduate students, cap student ticket prices, and prohibit special training tables and training quarters.

The presidents added one additional restriction: the football coach had to be a full-time employee of the university. And it was this condition that triggered Yost's resistance, since he had substantial outside business interests. Although Yost technically reported to President Angell, the founding father of Michigan football executed a perfect end run on these issues and took his complaints instead to the university's board of regents and asked them to withdraw Michigan from the newly formed conference.

Efforts by the Western Conference presidents to accommodate Yost were unsuccessful, the regents voted to overrule Angell and

Michigan football coach Fielding Yost. (Bentley Library.)

withdraw Michigan from the Western Conference, and Coach Yost and his Wolverines were allowed to continue unchecked. Byers writes, "Angell could move a whole conference, but where football was concerned, he could not convince his own coach and his own board. Michigan did not rejoin the Big Ten until November 1917. This act of a coach steamrolling his college president had historic significance although the lesson had to be relearned time and again by succeeding generations of college chief executives." Byers concludes that "this showdown was more significant in charting the course of college athletics than the founding of the NCAA in that same year."[2]

Things have not changed much during the past century. It is not uncommon for powerful coaches and athletic directors, winning-obsessed alumni and fans, or even politicians, to go around or over the president to the governing board concerning an issue in the athletic departments. As tragic as it may seem, there are probably more presidencies in NCAA Division I-A universities that have run aground on the shoals of controversies in sports than any other issue. A modern university president ignores intercollegiate athletics at his or her own peril.

Presidential Responsibility and Authority

Like many other issues in the university, the responsibility and authority for intercollegiate athletics usually ends up on the president's desk in his or her role as chief executive officer of the institution. But the assignment of ultimate responsibility for institutional control in intercollegiate athletics has a more formal character. Under the NCAA constitution, the president has the "ultimate responsibility and final authority for the conduct of the intercollegiate athletics program."[3] For institutional control to exist, this must be clearly understood and accepted by all in the institution, both those from above like the governing board, and those in line-reporting positions such as the athletic director and the coaches.

To some extent, such presidential control can be exerted through the normal chain of command within the university. For example, since coaches report to the athletic director, and the athletic director reports to the president, there are clear lines of authority for presidential control. Failure to respect such presidential authority can, in principle, result in administrative action including dismissal. However, it is also the case that sometimes a celebrity coach or an ambitious athletic director will become sufficiently powerful that he or she can ignore presidential authority and simply execute an end run to alumni, trustees, or even the media to get their way.

The relationship to presidential control of external constituencies such as alumni, fans, and the press is far more complex. These groups generally have little interaction with the university other than through intercollegiate athletics. They understand little about the president's role and respect it even less. To them, the president is primarily a symbolic figure, expected to be in attendance at important athletic events, but viewed as largely inconsequential with respect to the competition on the field or the long-term success of the program—unless, of course, the integrity of the athletic program is called into question, at which point the president can become a convenient scapegoat. However, few among these constituencies take seriously or are even aware of the authority for sports conferred upon the presidents by the NCAA.

Most complex of all are the relationships with those to whom the president reports, the university governing board. Many of the problems in the control of intercollegiate athletics today can be traced directly to the inappropriate involvement of governing boards in the decision-making process about athletics. For the president to fulfill the NCAA-mandated role as final authority, the board must provide its complete and unwavering support.

As Clark Kerr observes, the ideal governing board focuses on major aspects of policy and performance, it selects and supports able presidents, it supports their leadership of the institution, and it concentrates on results.[4] Yet all too frequently some board members become deeply involved in intercollegiate athletics; in many cases, it was their interest in athletics that motivated them to seek a board position in the first place. Many of these trustees become overly close to athletics programs, seeking direct access to coaches, traveling with the team to away games, and developing inappropriate relationships with players. They also sometimes try to intervene in key activities such as recruiting and personnel selection (coaches or athletic directors), thereby seriously undermining the principle of institutional control. Frequently their colleagues on the governing board are either unable or unwilling to address such inappropriate behavior, usually because they are still dependent for support on other issues from the very trustees who are primarily concerned with athletics.

A Personal Vignette: The Search for an Athletic Director

My own experiences involving the search and selection of an athletic director for the University of Michigan help illustrate both the challenges to, and complexity of, presidential authority as the foundation of institutional control. A president is required to recruit and appoint people to fill dozens of important positions in a large university: executive officers, deans, and directors. But no search is more difficult to conduct than one for a new athletic director, at least at a university with big-time sports such as Michigan.

Change was the order of the day in intercollegiate athletics during my years in the presidency. Just prior to my selection as president, a long-standing athletic director, Don Canham, had retired. Although this was no surprise, since Canham had reached the university's mandatory retirement age of seventy, it was nevertheless a difficult moment because of his long tenure, his reluctance to step down, and the problems we faced in selecting a successor. Due to the high level of visibility of the position, stemming in part from Canham's cultivation of the sports press and because of the presence of a celebrity football coach, Bo Schembechler, we recognized at the outset that the search would be very complex.

There were certainly plenty of talented people across the country, and most would have been very interested in the Michigan position. But the process was hindered by the attention focused on the search process not only of those within the university—coaches, faculty, staff—but also of a large group of fans and the sports media. Many folks were convinced that they knew far more than the university administration about who the next athletic director should be, but of course there was no consensus among them. In the end, since only the president would be held accountable for the choice, only the president could make the selection, but his authority on this matter was not left unchallenged.

With this complexity in mind, then president Harold Shapiro wisely asked a former Michigan president, Robben Fleming, to chair a search committee to find a successor to Canham. Not only did Fleming have great credibility within and beyond the university community, but he also had very considerable skills and experience in dealing with complicated political situations. It was truly a thankless task, but Fleming was willing to undertake it to serve the university. Ironically enough, shortly after he began the search, he was also tapped by the board of regents to serve as interim president for a brief period between the time that Shapiro left for Princeton and I was selected as his permanent successor.

The search was complicated by several factors. Although Canham had reached retirement age, he was not particularly happy to step down, and he shared his disappointment with his friends and supporters. Furthermore, football coach Bo Schembechler was at the peak of his popularity, and it was likely that he would have a significant influence on the search. Schembechler had occasionally been at odds with Canham, and it was clear that he wanted an athletic director with whom he could work more comfortably. Finally, there was a certain myth about the importance of the bloodline of the Michigan athletic director. Many of the fans believed that the Michigan AD must be a "Michigan man." After all, Canham had been a former Michigan track coach. Fritz Crisler had been a former Michigan football coach, as had been his successor, Bennie Oosterbaan. Yet, and ironically, very few of Michigan's coaches had been "Michigan men." For example, Yost, Crisler, and Schembechler were all three auslanders, from Chicago, Princeton, and Miami of Ohio, respectively.

Fleming conducted the search with careful attention to both process and integrity. From the beginning it was clear that Schembechler would not only be an important factor, but that he also must be considered as a serious candidate himself. However, the search began with the premise that it would be very difficult for any mortal to hold both the jobs of head football coach and athletic director. The search committee believed that if Schembechler were to become athletic director, he would have to step down as football coach. Yet as the search proceeded, Schembechler made it clear that he was interested in the athletic director job but would not step down as coach. This situation became even more complex when Schembechler had a heart attack in late 1987. For a time there was some doubt as to whether he could even return as coach, much less as both coach and athletic director. But his recovery from surgery was miraculous, and he was back on the field in time for spring practice.

In the meantime, Fleming's committee proceeded to conduct a

thorough search, looking at both internal and external candidates. As the search progressed, there were signs that Schembechler was rethinking his position. Just the football coach's very presence was making it difficult to get many other attractive candidates interested in the position, since Schembechler was far too powerful. Finally, Fleming reached the conclusion that some kind of an arrangement had to be reached with Schembechler.

At that point, Fleming faced his second great challenge: the board of regents. While there was some support for Schembechler on the board, there was also considerable resistance. Some board members were critical of Schembechler's behavior as football coach, particularly during his early and more volatile years. Some expressed skepticism about whether he could do both jobs, particularly in view of his earlier health problems.

In the end, Fleming was able to negotiate an ingenious compromise. A long-serving and well-liked stalwart of the university, Associate Vice President for Business and Finance Jack Weidenbach, was asked to serve as associate athletic director and handle the detailed management of the department while Schembechler was involved in coaching duties. Weidenbach had long served behind the scenes as the link between the university and the athletic department, watching over its physical plant and its finances. Moreover, he had a strong personal interest in athletics. A marathon runner himself, he had long been involved as a volunteer in women's sports. Since he was in his midsixties, such a move would not harm his career. And most important, he had an excellent relationship with Schembechler and the other coaches.

After a bit of negotiation with individual regents, Fleming was able to convince the board that the Schembechler-Weidenbach team solution was the best route for the university, and the dual appointments were approved. This partnership approach worked remarkably well during the brief time it was in place. Schembechler had the experience and public persona to provide strong leadership for the department. His ability to interact with external constituencies such as the press was formidable. In the meantime, Weidenbach focused on the detailed management of the department behind the scenes. Of course, there were times when this part-

Bo Schembechler. (UM Photo Services.)

nership required amusing accommodations, such as when Weidenbach would have to trot out to the huddle during a football practice to get Schembechler's signature on an important document.
But because of the unusual abilities of both Schembechler and
Weidenbach, and their mutual trust and respect for one another,
their team approach worked very well—at least for the brief period
Schembechler served as athletic director.

However, after a year in the position, it became apparent to
Schembechler that carrying two jobs was far more difficult and
stressful than he had imagined. His first year as athletic director
was very successful: a Big Ten football championship, a Rose Bowl
victory over USC, the surprise of the NCAA basketball championship with a substitute coach, Steve Fisher, and a number of Big
Ten championships from other sports such as swimming, track, and
cross-country. There were also downsides, such as the investiga-

tion of serious violations in the baseball program. Schembechler began to realize that, even with Weidenbach as backup, there was simply too much personal stress in handling both jobs. He finally reached the conclusion that it was time to step down. Although we strongly urged him to stay on, he declined, explaining that while he loved coaching, the other demands of the job—long recruiting trips and such—were just too stressful for his health. As we learned later, Schembechler made the decision to step down in part so that he could accept the presidency of the Detroit Tigers, offered to him by his friend and then club owner, Tom Monaghan. Years later, Schembechler acknowledged that this was probably one of the worst decisions of his life. He could have easily continued coaching for several more years, and his brief tenure with the Tigers was not a happy experience. But at the time, he thought it was the right thing to do for himself and his family.

When Schembechler decided that he wanted to step down from the athletic directorship, I faced the challenge of selecting his successor. I was concerned about further unrest among the regents if we had to go through the process again so soon after selecting him. The haste of Schembechler's decision proved a certain advantage, since there was no time to conduct a full-scale search. I asked Jack Weidenbach to serve as interim athletic director, with the support of the board of regents. During the eighteen months of the Schembechler-Weidenbach team, Weidenbach and I had developed a close relationship, and I had full confidence in Weidenbach's leadership of the department. I also believed there were a number of objectives that Weidenbach could accomplish as interim athletic director that might be difficult with a more permanent appointment. For example, there was the enormous task of rebuilding our athletics facilities. As former head of the university plant department, Weidenbach was ideal for this role. We faced another major challenge in establishing the priority and the quality of the women's athletics programs. Weidenbach's deep commitment to women's athletics made this a natural.

While Weidenbach was not a public figure like Bo Schembechler, he was outstanding in managing the department. Furthermore, he had a strong understanding of both the university's and the

Jack Weidenbach. (UM Photo Services.)

department's values and tradition. We worked closely together on a number of critical fronts: renegotiating the distribution of football gate receipt revenue in the Big Ten, opposing major expansion of the Big Ten Conference, building the number and quality of our women's programs, and stressing the importance of our nonrevenue sports. The Weidenbach years were years of both extraordinary success and great progress for Michigan athletics. There is no other five-year period in the history of our athletics programs with more conference championships, bowl wins, Final Four appearances, and All-Americans—both athletic and academic. In addition, the financial structure of Michigan athletics was stabilized, its physical plant was rebuilt, and the coaches and student-athletes were more clearly integrated into the broader life of the campus community.

Unfortunately, Weidenbach was already close to retirement when he agreed to provide leadership for the athletic department, and even though he was a marathon runner (and in good health), he believed it important that he step aside at age seventy. So once again we faced the challenge of selecting a new athletic director. In this case, it seemed appropriate to conduct a thorough national search, consistent with the personnel policies and practices of the university. I asked our vice president and chief financial officer, Farris Womack, to chair a search committee comprised of faculty, students, and staff.

The search committee worked hard and eventually presented us with a slate of several candidates, some regarded as among the top leaders of college sports in America. There was, however, one problem: none of the finalists had credentials as "a Michigan man," someone with an earlier association with the Michigan program. This did not present any difficulties for me or the search committee, since many of our searches end up with a list of final candidates from other institutions. But several boosters, enamored of what they believed were old traditions, began to apply pressure to the regents to force us to look inside the department for a successor.

Although the majority of the regents were supportive of the external candidates, the booster pressure began to get to several board members. It became increasingly clear that the instability among the regents was putting the institution at great risk of embarrassment. We finally concluded that it was simply too dangerous to the university to continue the external search. Instead, with the support of the search committee, I asked an insider, Joe Roberson, director of the fund-raising Campaign for Michigan, to accept an appointment. Roberson's name had been considered early in the search, but his role as the director of the university's billion-dollar fund-raising campaign was felt to be more important.

Roberson's appointment was a surprise to outsiders. He was, however, a former college athlete and professional baseball player. More important, he had served as both dean and interim chancellor of the UM-Flint campus. He was an individual of great integrity, with a strong sense of academic values. Although there was some opposition from one regent, the others supported Roberson's appointment, and the situation was rapidly stabilized. Rober-

Joe Roberson. (UM Photo Services.)

son had served the University of Michigan well in an extraordinary array of assignments, and he was to do the same as our new athletic director.

My participation in the searches for three athletic directors at Michigan was quite an educational experience. It taught me that even the most loyal and thoughtful supporters of the university could come unhinged about athletics. I also learned that the public interest in such high-visibility searches as athletic director or football coach is so intense that when conducted under the constraints of the state's sunshine laws, even a great university like Michigan could be put at considerable risk.

A final anecdote: During one these searches, former athletic director Don Canham was quoted in the local newspaper as observing, "Being an athletic director is not so hard. After all, it's not like being a brain surgeon or a rocket scientist." When I ran into him at a football game, I noted that while it does not take a rocket scientist to be an athletic director, it sure took a rocket scientist to *find* an athletic director, at least at Michigan. I ought to know: once in my early scientific career, I had been involved in a project to develop nuclear rocket engines! There were times when I felt I needed every bit of my rocket and nuclear science to find an athletic director at Michigan.

The Athletic Director

As these elaborate searches would indicate, the athletic director is a key figure in assuring institutional control. As the chief line officer for the athletic department, the athletic director is responsible for its day-to-day management, along with the supervision of its coaches and staff. So too, the athletic director has the direct responsibility for compliance with institutional, conference, and NCAA policies and regulations. However, unlike most other units of the university, the athletic director and the athletic department is usually far removed from the normal reporting, accountability, and policy environment governing academic units. The reporting line is generally to the president or another senior executive officer.

While the athletic director at most universities is delegated considerable authority commensurate with these responsibilities, here too there are complexities. The line-reporting responsibilities for coaches can be a concern in those situations in which a celebrity coach attains a visibility far beyond that of the athletic director, the president, and sometimes even the institution. Since the athletic director must make difficult personnel and resource allocation decisions involving coaches, this can pose a particular challenge. It is clear from this perspective that there is a serious conflict of interest when an athletic director also wears the hat of a head coach. There is little doubt in my mind that the University of Michigan made a serious mistake when it allowed Bo Schembechler to continue as head football coach after he was named athletic director. Not that politics at the time would have allowed any other decision, but this dual appointment clearly undermined the principle of institutional control.

So too, athletic directors are sometimes capable of building their own power bases that allow them to operate outside of normal university control. How could anyone accumulate the power to operate outside of the normal administrative rules, policies, and practices of a university? Answering this question reveals several of the more significant challenges to intercollegiate athletics.

The first issue involves the influence of athletic boosters, who not only take great interest in an athletic program, but also become so emotionally involved that they are willing to go to almost any length to ensure the success of the program. Knowing how to identify and cultivate such fanatic loyalty is one of the most important tools of both athletic directors and celebrity coaches in acquiring power. Sometimes these boosters are alumni; sometimes they are local businessmen (always men, never women); sometimes they are even trustees or regents of the university. It is easy to spot this crowd: they generally hang around the press box during games; they invariably have the best seats in the stadium; and they frequently show up as sponsors listed on the closing credits of coaches' television programs.

A second issue involves the behavior of the sports press. It is a fact of life that the public perception of intercollegiate athletics in America is controlled to an alarming extent by perhaps one hundred or fewer sportswriters and commentators. The regional perceptions of a university like Michigan are determined by perhaps no more than a dozen sportswriters with the major papers, along with a handful of broadcasters. It doesn't take a marketing genius to target these individuals, cultivate them, wine and dine them, and keep them happy. In years past, our athletic department would throw a party for the media the evening before every football game. Sportswriters were also always given special attention in the press box and showered with the personal attention of the athletic director throughout the year. And the payoff, both in terms of Michigan's visibility and the athletic director's reputation and power, was apparent.

Today things are far different. Beyond superficial differences such as the alcohol-free nature of university functions associated with athletic events—a far cry from the free-flowing booze of earlier times—there is a significant difference in the nature of the sports press. Most of the younger sportswriters tend more toward the investigative style of journalism more common in the past two decades than the promotional nostalgia of a Grantland Rice. They realize their fame and fortune will not come from making heroes of coaches or athletic directors. Rather, they will make their names through hard-nosed investigative stories, exposing the sordid underside of intercollegiate athletics (even as they contribute to the commercialization and professionalization of college sports by hyping it even further). To be sure, there is still an aging group of writers and broadcasters of the old school, easily manipulated by coaches and athletic directors. But this is a vanishing breed, largely ignored by their younger colleagues.

Fortunately, the dictatorial athletic director (a.k.a. czar) has also vanished from the college sports scene. The management of a modern intercollegiate athletics program involves a broad range of skills: leadership, fiscal management, personnel relations, public relations, and, perhaps most important, a deep understanding and acceptance of academic values that are pre-eminent in a university. Few university presidents lament the disappearance of the czar athletic director, and presidents are instead seeking people with far broader management experience and who also appreciate the educational mission of a university. Many also seek leadership committed to better integrating intercollegiate athletics with the other activities of the university rather than building independent empires.

During my presidency at Michigan I had the opportunity to work with three quite different individuals in this role. Bo Schembechler came out of the coaching ranks as one of the nation's leading football coaches. His understanding of the competitive nature of intercollegiate athletics and the management of the public relations interface with the sports media was unparalleled. Jack Weidenbach, although an athlete himself, came from a background in business, finance, and management. He provided the athletic department with leadership that recognized clearly the organizational, financial, and management complexities of major athletics programs. Finally, Joe Roberson brought his experience as a former professional athlete, a fund-raiser, a university administrator, and most important, as an educator.

Although each of our athletic directors had an important impact on our programs, increasingly I have come to believe that today university presidents should look first to the ranks of educators for such leadership. That doesn't mean that every athletic director should come from the ranks of the tenured faculty or have a background as an academic administrator. But I have concluded that in these times in which intercollegiate athletics has been pulled so far away from the educational mission and academic values of the university by the entertainment industry, it is more important than ever that those leading our athletics programs have some experience as educators. After all, most of the participants in these programs are students, not fledgling professional athletes. And the primary concern should be the academic welfare of these students, not national ranking or commercial value.

The Coaches

Where do coaches stand in the hierarchy of institutional control? Certainly coaches are closest to their programs and their athletes, to fans and the sports press, and to the temptations and pressures that can lead to problems. Certainly too, most coaches are insistent upon if not obsessed with control, over their players, their assistants, and their programs. In fact, many coaches would have you believe that many of the problems in college sports today arise from the interference and layer after layer of complex rules that are forced upon their programs by presidents and others who simply do not understand the nature of intercollegiate athletics.

While most coaches attempt to comply with the myriad rules and regulations governing intercollegiate athletics, there are always a few who view these less as constraints and more as challenges, to be shaped, bent, and possibly even broken in the effort to build winning programs.

The Faculty

As we have noted, the ultimate responsibility for the educational mission and the academic integrity of the university rests with the faculty. Hence, it is logical to expect some involvement by faculty in the control of intercollegiate athletics. In reality, while many faculty members have some interest in sports as spectators, and some have educational responsibilities as teachers of student-athletes, relatively few have a direct involvement with intercollegiate athletics. Usually these few include those faculty members appointed to key committees such as the faculty boards in control of intercollegiate athletics or faculty athletic representatives to the conference or NCAA.

But there have been many problems with this traditional organization. First, over the years, many faculty athletics boards have been watered down with the addition of alumni and university administrators, sometimes even selected by the athletic director. Second, faculty board members are easily co-opted by the perquisites showered upon them by the athletic department: complimentary tickets, preferential seating, travel to postseason bowls and tournaments, and so forth. Even more dangerous to institutional control are those boards that possess a degree of autonomy from the normal university decision process. The athletic director can sometimes use these boards to shield the department from standard university policies and practices in areas such as finance, personnel, and facilities. This only widens the gap between athletics and the rest of the university.

Perhaps more significant than the faculty athletic boards are the faculty athletics representatives to major athletic associations such as the NCAA or the conferences. These individuals not only actively participate in the governance of these organizations, but they also serve as an interface with the institution on issues of rule violations and sanctions. Universities generally appoint some of their stronger and more distinguished faculty to serve in these important roles. For example, during the 1960s when the Pacific Coast Conference was experiencing a rash of violations, the University of California at Berkeley appointed a Nobel laureate chemist, Glenn Seaborg, as their faculty representative for athletics.

Of course, faculty representatives like Seaborg are the exception. It is interesting to note how many of the faculty members appointed to athletics boards or as faculty representatives come from professional school backgrounds, particularly from law. This is not altogether surprising, since understanding and coping with the complex rule and governance structure of the NCAA does benefit from a legal background. Yet few faculty members from professional schools have any direct experience in the education and counseling of undergraduate students, those who comprise intercollegiate athletics. This may be one of the reasons why most NCAA and conference activities tend to lean more toward rules, regulations, and governance rather than the welfare of student-athletes.

A Missing Constituency

In considering the various internal and external constituencies either determining or threatening institutional control of intercollegiate athletics, there is one group conspicuously absent from most discussions: students. To be sure, the behavior of student-athletes is critical in determining the integrity of college sports, but we all too frequently approach this as a top-down control or discipline issue, by administrators, faculty, or coaches.

Yet universities learned decades ago that most students are serious and responsible. They want to be involved in major decisions that affect their educational experience. Student involvement in the development of key policies and activities affecting the university has long been an important principle. Students are represented on major university committees, including those bodies conducting search for key positions such as the university president. Students are even members of the governing boards of some institutions.

Student involvement in either policy development or governance of intercollegiate athletics, however, is strangely absent or weak at best. While students are sometimes allowed to serve on the board in control of athletics, these are rarely student-athletes but rather others chosen from student government. How many coaches or athletic directors have advisory bodies of student-athletes to represent the interests of athletes? And while the conferences and the NCAA have formed advisory groups of student-athletes in recent years, rarely is their voice loud on key policy matters or decisions.

The Role of Alumni and Fans

Alumni, fans, and boosters also play very key roles in attempts to maintain institutional control. Most rule violations can be traced, at one point or another, to the inappropriate activities of such external constituencies. Usually such violations involve inappropriate favors provided to recruits or student-athletes, sometimes with a coach's knowledge, but in most cases without the knowledge of anyone in the institution.

Every recruit, athlete, and coach is required to sign a statement each year that they have complied fully with NCAA rules. In contrast, alumni and fans are not bound by such a pact and can sometimes break through this veil to seriously damage the institution. Strong coaches and athletic directors will quickly identify possible problems and take swift action to isolate such people from players and programs. But it is not always easy. The challenges in dealing with those alumni and fans who intensely identify with college sports are formidable.

Alumni can also become so obsessed with athletics programs that they undermine their governance and hence integrity by putting excessive pressure on coaches, athletic directors, and even university presidents. Through their financial contributions or political influence, they attempt to influence important decisions such as the selection of coaches or athletic directors. They can interfere with university governance by putting direct pressure on governing boards. In some cases, such alumni boosters actually manage to get themselves appointed or elected to institutional governing boards with the intent of directly influencing the athletic department. In fact, in the 1940s, a former Michigan football coach Harry Kipke actually became a member of the university's board of regents.

One of the most extraordinary aspects of college sports is the way in which normally sane and rational people suddenly lose touch with reality and become obsessed with athletics. Although we usually think of the obsessed—or perhaps "possessed"—as old alumni, returning to the campus every fall to cheer on the team and relive old memories, today's intensely promoted, big-time showbiz form of football and basketball has created new levels of obsession in a wide spectrum of people. Just watch the behavior of a crowd at any major college sporting event, or listen to the conversations before or after a big game. Even the most rational people can suddenly become fanatics over college sports.

My concern here is not with general public interest in college sports, which has been a normal feature in American society for a

The football tailgate crowd

century, but rather those fans who have an exaggerated attachment to an athletic program. For these people, college sports have become one of the most important aspects of their lives. They count among the most important moments in their lives a major win or an outstanding season. They not only become depressed after a loss, but they may even become angry, demanding retribution from the coach or the institution. This fascination, almost fixation, with college sports can become almost pathological. Playing to this obsession has become a favorite tactic of the sports media—and to some coaches and athletic directors—always trying to portray college football and basketball as far more than a game, as one of the cosmic events of our age.

Of particular concern are those sports fans who have no attachment to the university except through its athletics programs. As I used to walk through tailgate crowds on my way to a Michigan football game, I used to marvel at just how few of these fans had any connection whatsoever to the university. The tailgate crowd was similar to those one would find at NFL games, primarily attracted to the university by the success of our football program. These fans have attached themselves to the teams much as they would to a professional franchise. They frequently have little understanding or concern about the more fundamental educational purpose of the institution. Their conduct often is more boorish and outlandish than alumni or students because they care little about the embarrassment or damage to the university that can result from their inappropriate behavior.

But what about the behavior of students? Certainly many students do love college sports. But less than 25 percent of the spectators at Big Ten football and basketball games are students.[5] In fact, most students do not attend athletic events on a regular basis. Ironically enough, students are perhaps the one constituency that takes sports in the right spirit. Sure some love to go to games and cheer loudly. They are proud when Michigan wins. But they also have a certain detachment, far removed from the obsession of their elders. Michigan is ahead? Great! Michigan is behind? So what. Let's start the wave or throw some marshmallows and enjoy ourselves. After all, it's only a game, isn't it?

This raises an interesting point. Clearly, varsity sports are no longer designed to provide extracurricular opportunities for students. Furthermore, most faculty and staff, while perhaps interested, regard intercollegiate athletics as only a peripheral activity of their university. There is even evidence to suggest that most alumni do not care that strongly either, except for a small group of loud and occasionally influential alumni who want winning programs. Hence, if the games are not for the players, the faculty, the students, or the alumni, we must conclude that they are really designed today primarily for public entertainment.

The Pros

Many of the most serious conflicts between athletic and academic priorities occur in those sports where collegiate participation serves, for a very talented few, as a training ground for professional careers. It is certainly the case that professional football and basketball rely on intercollegiate athletics much as professional baseball and hockey rely on their own farm clubs.

If there is sufficient separation between college and professional sports, then who can deny the opportunities that the latter provides to athletes of exceptional ability? Only a small number of college athletes have the skills to make it to the professional leagues (e.g., only 0.5 percent of all Division I basketball players make it to the NBA). Unfortunately, in recent years, professional sports have become a far more intrusive and negative influence. The feeding frenzy of professional agents seeking out college athletes has led to the serious abuse of academic and athletic standards. Professional teams take a "meat market" approach to the professional draft. College athletes are expected to drop their academic activities to participate in tryout camps designed to measure their physical abilities, and the lure of professional riches distorts the academic priorities of student-athletes.

Perhaps the most serious threat is the increasing tendency for professional sports to entice college athletes into professional careers—or, at least into the professional draft—long before they have had an opportunity to complete their academic degrees. This trend represents professional teams and agents' cynical and abusive attitude toward the well-being of student-athletes. It frequently leads to the most tragic of circumstances in which students are encouraged to drop out of college to pursue the will-of-the-wisp of a short-lived career in professional sports. Furthermore, it leads to a vicious cycle, in which the quality of the college game deteriorates sufficiently that many players who have little chance of a professional career follow their more talented teammates and also leave college early to go into the draft.

Unfortunately, despite the importance of college athletics to their future, the leaders of professional sports have yet to demonstrate either the interest or the sense of responsibility to develop guidelines that will protect the best long-term interests of student-athletes. Instead they—and many members of the media—call for even fewer limitations on the interaction between college and professional sports, such as allowing student-athletes to test the water by participating in the professional draft without jeopardizing their college eligibility. Few professional leagues seem to realize that they are harming not only the college game but also their own future by drafting college students before they have finished their education.

In my more cynical moments, I sometimes wonder if weakening college sports by prematurely drafting underclass athletes may be precisely what the professional leagues wish to accomplish. After all, college football and basketball are strong competitors for spectator interest, television market share, and advertising dollars. What professional sporting event, aside from the Super Bowl or World Series, can compete with the NCAA Final Four or the football Bowl Championship Series? No professional football franchise can approach the fan interest or loyalty of major football powers such as Michigan, Notre Dame, Penn State, or Ohio State. Perhaps, buried deep within the corporate offices of the professional leagues or among the owners, there is a sinister plot to degrade the quality of college sports—and hence the competitive commercial value of its events—by luring its talent prematurely into the professional draft.

Reform Efforts

Periodically, the concerns about college athletics will reach a crescendo (or more accurately, a cacophony) sufficient to trigger a reform movement. As we noted in chapter 4, almost a century ago concerns about professionalism and brutality in college football led to the formation of athletic conferences and the NCAA. Two decades later in 1929, the Carnegie Foundation for the Advancement of Teaching issued a scathing report calling for major reforms, noting the following list of concerns.[6]

> The materialistic impulse transmitted through the university by the erection of an opulent athletic power structure.
>
> The commercial extension of the student-athlete program into the domain of advertising and public relations.
>
> The reluctance of university leadership to take unpopular stands and bring athletics into a sincere relation to the academic purposes of the institution.
>
> The sordid system of subsidized recruitment, in which alumni often take part, "the most disgraceful phase of recent intercollegiate athletics."
>
> The professional nature of the student-athlete's duty ("it is work, not play") and the extreme difficulty of balancing the time and energy requisite to that duty against academic responsibilities.
>
> The unfortunate message sent to secondary schools of the exaggerated place of athletics in higher education.
>
> The growth both within and without the university of a cynical and tainted environment in which the efforts of a "demoralizing and corrupt system" proceed "alike for the boy who takes the money and for the agent who arranges it, and for the whole group of college and secondary school boys who know about it."

Sound familiar? Such a report could have been written in almost any decade of the twentieth century, since most of these issues have withstood effort after effort to reform college sports.

The NCAA tried again to reign in football with the proposed Sanity Code of 1948,[7] which addressed many of the issues raised by the Carnegie report: recruiting, the amateur status of athletes, scholarships, and specific academic requirements. The Sanity Code was designed to rein in the "full-ride" practice of awarding grants-in-aid based on how well the player competed and move instead to need-based financial aid for student-athletes, administered through normal university channels. More specifically, the NCAA proposed that student-athletes receive financial support only if they could demonstrate financial need and meet the university's normal entrance requirements, consistent with need-based financial aid policies available to all students. If student-athletes ranked in the top 25 percent of their high school graduating class, they could also receive scholarship support regardless of need—that is, an academic rather than an athletic scholarship. In either case, the university could not withdraw support from students if they were unable to or decided not to compete.

Yet once again, the power coaches and athletic directors mounted an effective resistance, and instead of reforming football, the NCAA established the current system of grants-in-aid, dependent only upon athletic eligibility. As television stimulated the growth in popularity of college football as public entertainment, the coaches continued to push successfully for further professionalization: traveling squad limits were junked, limits on the size of coaching staffs were relaxed, grants were restricted to one year at a time, unlimited substitution was implemented, freshmen were made eligible to compete at the varsity level, the season was lengthened, the preseason and postseason games were increased, and on and on.

In the early 1980s, a group of major university presidents tried once again to deal with these issues. In essence, the group concluded that the problems with college sports were bred so deeply into our large universities and our national culture more generally that there was little chance for substantive reform through traditional mechanisms. Further, they concluded that the NCAA was serving primarily as a trade association representing the interests of coaches and athletic directors rather than their institutions and therefore represented many of the problems rather than the solutions. Hence, they sought to introduce presidential control of the NCAA through a presidential governing board so that they could pursue reforms such as eliminating freshman eligibility, prohibiting spring football practice, and limiting seasons of play for various sports. Of course all of these actions would have been very threatening to both the coaches and the status quo, and the presidential governing board was defeated by last-minute parliamentary maneuvers.

However, this effort did lead to the formation of the NCAA Presidents' Commission in the mid-1980s. This commission was charged with exerting stronger presidential leadership in controlling and maintaining proper compatibility between college sports and higher education. Aided by the Knight Commission effort of the late 1980s,[8] the Presidents' Commission has taken a number of steps to strengthen academic standards for recruiting and eligibility, Proposition 48 being an example. It has also restructured the NCAA itself, putting into place a new governance organization that recognizes the great diversity of institutions by transforming the NCAA from an association into a federation of groups of similar institutions. The presidents also ensured that they would have the final authority in the new federation.

However, even these recent efforts by the Presidents' Commission tend to deal more at the margin than with the core issues that drive the commercialization and professionalism of college sports. The fundamental character of intercollegiate athletics continues to thwart true reform. The NCAA and the conferences remain more committed to promoting and defending the commercialism of college sports than making certain that they are aligned with the educational mission of the university. The coaches and athletic directors, needless to say, resist any efforts to de-emphasize and reform that might challenge their income and lifestyles. And in many cases it has been the presidents themselves who have driven intercollegiate athletics with their desire for more revenue from events such as the NCAA basketball tournament or postseason play in football. Like the others associated with intercollegiate athletics, the presidents all too frequently give priority to competitive issues or revenue generation rather than to the welfare of student-athletes or the alignment of sports with the educational mission of the university.

Presidential Politics

Intercollegiate athletics has long posed an interesting challenge to university presidents. Both they and their institutions are always at some risk from sports, given the potential damage to their reputation brought on by any serious violations in their sports programs. They are also subject to great pressures exerted by the athletics enterprise itself—from coaches, the sports media, and the legion of loyal alumni and sports boosters. Although President Angell of the University of Michigan may have been one of the most determined and courageous of the early leaders in his efforts to contain football, he was also one of the most embarrassed when Coach Yost went over his head to the regents.

This pattern has been repeated again and again throughout the years. While there have been a few successful efforts by university presidents to rein in sports on their campuses—Chicago's president Robert Maynard Hutchens being perhaps the most extreme example when he pulled his university out of big-time athletics—there have been far more defeats of university presidents at the hands of powerful coaches, athletic directors, or alumni boosters.

One could well make the point, however, that it has been the occasional efforts of university presidents to exercise their authority over intercollegiate athletics outside of the normal university management channels that has caused many of the problems in college sports today. As we have noted, university presidents are themselves driven to become directly involved in the management of intercollegiate athletics, by internal pressures from sources such as governing boards or external pressures exerted by boosters, politicians, the media, or the public are large. They take part in personnel decisions such as the selection of coaches or in financial matters or even in competitive strategies. In fact, some presidents have attempted to use the springboard provided by the visibility of college sports to lift their institutions to higher recognition in other arenas.

Just up the road from Ann Arbor is one of the best examples: President John Hannah's use of college football in the 1950s to transform Michigan Agricultural College into Michigan State University, a member of the Big Ten Conference and of the prestigious Association of American Universities.[9] In the late 1940s, Hannah lobbied hard to have Michigan State fill the vacancy left in the Big Ten Conference by the University of Chicago's withdrawal. Although he was strongly opposed in this effort by the University of Michigan, which sought to maintain its status as the state's only major university, Hannah's political skills, both within the conference and the Michigan State Legislature, largely neutralized Michigan's opposition. Using contributions from local businessmen, Hannah recruited top players and built Michigan State's prowess as a football school long before it achieved academic quality. His philosophy was simple: to advance Michigan State, it was necessary to beat the University of Michigan on the football field in the fall and then again in the legislature in the spring. He believed that success on the field translated into national publicity, enlarged financial support, and growth. And he was right.

Other institutions have since followed the athletic route to eventual academic recognition: the University of Houston, Florida State University, North Carolina State University, and perhaps most notably, UCLA, which used its high visibility for athletic success to transform a city college into one of the great academic institutions in the world! Largely as a result of this success, every year there are more and more colleges and universities that set their sights on developing successful athletics programs and moving into Division I-A. At last count, some 106 universities are committed to Division I-A football and 301 to Division I basketball.

Perhaps the ineffectiveness of university presidents in reforming or even controlling intercollegiate athletics is understandable in view of this yin-yang duality of college sports as both a threat and an opportunity. As a result, presidents suffer from a classic approach-avoidance syndrome. In the end, it is probably a wiser course for their personal survival, if not for the welfare of their institution, for them to pass rule after rule while decrying the ills of college sports, yet always avoiding a real challenge to the athletics establishment. Most university presidents are not around long enough to sustain any true reform agenda. And when life is short, it is always easier to go with the flow and allow market share, revenue opportunities, and publicity to determine the direction of college sports. Yet as with all other matters involving the university, the buck eventually ends up on the president's desk. The reform of intercollegiate athletics is clearly the presidents' responsibility. Yet few appear to be up to the challenge.

Conclusion

The NCAA places great emphasis on the principle of institutional control as the key to the integrity of intercollegiate athletics. Yet it is clear that very few of the universities engaged in big-time sports enjoy the same degree of control over these activities as they do over the academic programs of the institution. Powerful external forces arising from fan and alumni pressure, commercial interests, the sports press, and the entertainment industry have long since eroded true institutional control. Although some university presidents have taken strong verbal positions in support of reform agendas, in reality few have chosen to ride into battle against these formidable foes. The challenge is simply too risky and too intractable.

Today, as in earlier decades, big-time college football and basketball threaten the educational values of higher education with the commercial values of the entertainment industry because few really want to change the structure or the rules of the enterprise. In fact, one might well conclude that true reform of intercollegiate athletics cannot be driven from within the enterprise, since the pressures to maintain the status quo are simply too strong. Instead, it may require action from beyond the campus and the current college sports establishment.

PART IV
Tilting at
Windmills

Chapter 12   **Back to Basics**

For just as long as intercollegiate athletics have been a part of American higher education, concerns have been raised about their integrity and appropriateness within the university. Generation after generation has taken on the challenge of reforming college sports, and all have essentially failed. Before we join what has become a long tradition of proposing a set of remedies to cure the ills of college sports, I want first to take a somewhat different approach and address three fundamental questions. First, why should universities conduct intercollegiate athletics in the first place? After all, most universities around the world do not regard competitive sports as a significant component of their activities. Why have college sports become so important in the United States?

Second, what are the key sources of the problems that have arisen over the years with college sports? What so distorts them from the amateur ideal, driving them toward commercialism and professionalization? What are the real risks posed by college sports to higher education?

Third, we need to understand better why we have had so much difficulty in getting intercollegiate athletics under control. For over a century, college sports have faced problems of professionalism, commercialism, and misbehavior. Despite many efforts both within and external to higher education over this period, we still are unable to correct its deficiencies. Why?

Finally, with this background, we are prepared to turn to the most difficult question: What can we do about it? How can we address the concerns about college sports?

The Fundamental Questions

Fundamental Question 1: Why should universities conduct intercollegiate athletics in the first place?

Answer: First and foremost, we should regard athletics as but one component of the opportunities for learning we provide our students. We should embrace the ideal of a scholar-athlete and its objective of educating the whole person, even if we realize this ideal is rarely achievable. We should also recognize the role of athletics as a spectator activity that unites our campuses and those who identify with our institutions, but this should always be a secondary priority. While it is true that intercollegiate athletics has become a major form of entertainment for the public at large, it is my belief that the university has no obligation to support or embrace this particular function.

Fundamental Question 2: What causes the distortion of intercollegiate athletics? What generates the pressure?

Answer: The entertainment industry, the broadcasting networks and sports media, have recognized the commercial value of college football and basketball. With the all-too-willing cooperation of higher education, they have transformed them into big-time show business, driven by the commercial objectives and values of the entertainment industry. As a result, today football and basketball have little in common with other campus activities. They are conducted much as professional franchises, driven by goals such as national rankings, commercial appeal, market share, and coaching compensation. Concern about the welfare of student-athletes or the educational role of varsity competition has largely dropped off the radar screen of those responsible for the leadership and integrity of these activities, of coaches, athletic directors, governing boards, conferences, the NCAA, and, unfortunately, all too many college presidents.

Fundamental Question 3: Why do universities have so much difficulty getting athletics under university control?

Answer: The institutions and organizations responsible for controlling intercollegiate athletics—our universities, athletic conferences, and the NCAA itself—are unable to reconcile their conflicting objectives of maintaining the integrity of college sports and exploiting their great popularity in our society. They are unable or unwilling to acknowledge or cope with the pressures of the entertainment industry, which has captured college athletics and transformed athletic events into commercial products. The very organizations we depend upon to regulate intercollegiate athletics have frequently been co-opted by this commercial aspect since their activities are funded primarily by revenues from broadcasting contracts. Furthermore, these organizations have been given strong marching orders from their member universities to maximize revenues, even at the expense of educational values.

Fundamental Question 4: What can we do about it?

What can we do to tame the beast, to prevent intercollegiate athletics from threatening or undermining the character, mission, and reputation of our colleges and universities? How can we realign sports with the educational values and priorities of universities? While I think the television moratorium idea I proposed in chapter 8 would make a great two-by-four to get the college-sports mule's attention, in this and the remaining chapters I will analyze several more pragmatic approaches.

Facing Up to Reality

We need to begin by facing up to reality. We need to understand that in their current form, big-time sports have the capacity to cause great harm both to their participants and their host academic institutions. We need to understand that the abuses that occur in sports, the violations of NCAA or conference rules, the inappropriate behavior of coaches or student-athletes, are symptoms of more fundamental problems. One could even argue that the presence of gamesmanship, commercialism, and professionalization in college sports is less the cause of concerns and more the result of even deeper issues, such as the abandonment of the educational role for intercollegiate athletics and its independence from the rest of the university.

The key flaw in intercollegiate athletics as we conduct it today is its independence from and irrelevance to the educational mission and academic values of our universities. Big-time football and basketball are, in reality, commercial entertainment enterprises that have absolutely nothing whatsoever to do with the educational mission of universities. Although we like to pretend intercollegiate athletics is an amateur enterprise, in reality at the most competitive level, these two sports have never been amateur activities. They have always involved professional coaches and athletes who attend college to compete rather than pursue an education.[1] Far from games designed to provide students with recreational or educational experiences, big-time football and basketball are designed primarily to entertain the public and to generate income.

We allow our athletic departments to run these programs as largely independent businesses, recruiting talented athletes primarily to be performers in these commercial activities rather than students in our universities. We ignore university policies and rules governing other staff and allow our coaches to market the reputation of the university for their personal gain. And although our athletic directors boast of the profits generated by their successful programs, in reality these big-time college sports programs are heavily subsidized through hidden institutional expenses and tax-exempt status.

But far more serious than the inconsistency and hypocrisy has been the damage such commercial activities have caused our institutions. In a sense, we have allowed a foreign culture to invade our institutions and infect college sports, a culture of false values and misguided goals that may be natural for the entertainment industry but has no place within the university. This culture not only drives but sometimes even sanctions a disregard for educational values in those involved in college sports—coaches, players, fans, the media, and the press. The university is not only unable to control this culture; it is frequently corrupted by it.

In conducting big-time sports programs, we have not only tolerated but promoted an activity that exploits young people, recruiting them to our institutions first and foremost as athletes to fuel our entertainment businesses, and largely ignoring their intellectual development or educational goals. In so doing, we have undermined the very foundation of our role as educational institutions and created a spirit of cynicism both within our student body and through society more broadly that has seriously damaged the reputation of higher education in America.

We have allowed those who profit from big-time college sports—celebrity coaches, athletic directors, the sports press, the entertainment industry—to exploit strong and occasionally obsessive public interest to pressure and manipulate the university to their own ends. Far too much of the time and attention of university leaders, from presidents to governing boards to faculty leaders, are consumed by the ever-present demands of intercollegiate athletics, to the serious detriment of more important priorities of the university such as teaching and scholarship. Far too many university leaders have been distracted, damaged, or even destroyed by the scandals created by winning obsessed coaches, ambitious athletic directors, or demanding fans. Far too few universities are able to truly control the enterprise, to keep the beast of big-time college sports in the cage.

The university's inability to control sports is nothing new. It is a challenge that has been apparent, yet met unsuccessfully, for almost a century. At times we seem almost resigned to our continued failure to reform the enterprise. Yet the mere fact that in the past higher education has been unable to align intercollegiate athletics in an acceptable manner with the educational mission and values of the university is no reason that we should not continue to try to do so. Indeed, perhaps if we begin our efforts by admitting that big-time sports have nothing to do with the educational mission of our universities, we can at least set aside the hypocrisy and pretension that have inhibited past efforts at reform and de-emphasis.

The Fundamental Principles

The first step in realigning intercollegiate athletics with academic priorities is to reestablish the fundamental reasons why an institution wishes to conduct competitive athletics programs. These reasons will then determine the philosophy and fundamental principles that govern these activities. My earlier discussion of the evolution of sports suggested the following reasons for conducting these activities: The primary purpose of sports is to provide an educational opportunity for students beyond the classroom, much like other university-sponsored extracurricular activities. A secondary benefit, at least for major spectator sports, lies in their role in serving as events that unify the campus community and those who identify with the institution such as alumni.

That's it. Just these two reasons. There are no other valid reasons for conducting intercollegiate athletics that are consistent with the fundamental mission and academic values of the university.

But what about the role that intercollegiate athletics play in providing entertainment for the public at large? It is my belief that the university has no responsibility to shape or sustain sports to play this role. True, the university provides entertainment in many forms, from art exhibitions to music concerts to theatrical productions. But in these other instances, these activities evolve directly from academic programs and involve students and faculty. And in none of these cases is public entertainment a determining priority. Nor should it be for athletic events.

Yet intercollegiate athletics—at least football and basketball—have been allowed to evolve into a form of mass entertainment divorced from the academic enterprise. And as they have done so, the culture of college sports has moved farther and farther from the values characterizing an educational institution. While these reasons make a good starting point, some issues need further consideration.

The Welfare of Student-Athletes

Athletic programs should always be guided by concern for what is best for the student. For example, in deciding on the admission of a student-athlete, one must always ask whether or not the prospective student has the capacity to benefit from an undergraduate education at the institution. Is the university confident that, with sufficient academic support, the student has the ability to pursue meaningful studies and to graduate? Only those students who have a high probability of graduating should be admitted.

In this regard, it is important to recognize that the underlying principle of admissions policies at most selective institutions is to achieve a student body of distinction and depth. Most institutions are aware that excellence is a multidimensional characteristic. It comes in many forms—in academic ability, artistic ability, and even athletic ability. For that reason, few institutions today insist on blind, one-dimensional standards for all students (test scores or grade point average). Rather, they seek diversity in their student bodies, and it is this search for diversity that in many ways justifies the commitment to building successful intercollegiate athletics programs.

The admission of student-athletes must occur within the normal academic structure. In most academic institutions, the chief academic officer, usually the provost or vice president for academic affairs, has the ultimate responsibility for the quality, standards, and success of the academic programs of the institution. These responsibilities include admissions, academic counseling, and academic eligibility. The final decision on admissions and academic standing of student-athletes should rest with the provost and his or her designees. Following admission, there should be careful monitoring of the student's progress toward a degree by academic officers, and not simply monitoring by staff in the department of intercollegiate athletics. It should also include the provision of sufficient academic support services in light of the unusual pressures and time commitments of student-athletes. However, in no instance should athletics staff influence the academic objectives of student-athletes, for instance by steering them toward less demanding courses or majors. Universities should make certain that student-athletes are completing course requirements and advancing toward real degrees. There should also be a commitment of adequate financial aid and support until students graduate—not just until they complete their athletic eligibility.

Of equal importance is a commitment to fairness. During the 1970s and 1980s, a major effort was made to provide women students with opportunities equal to those of men. To the degree that intercollegiate athletics is justified for its value in character building and in education, it seems clear that women should be given the same access as men to such programs. In those institutions that have stressed spectator athletics, high priority should be given to introducing a series of athletics programs designed primarily for student participation. Broad participation should be encouraged for all students, not just those involved in competitive or varsity athletics.

The Treatment of Coaches

Coaches should be treated first and foremost as teachers, not as managers of athletic programs. They should be evaluated and rewarded not simply on the competitive success of their teams, but more significantly on the development and academic success of the young men and women in their programs. If this philosophy were adopted more generally, it would lead to extended commitments by institutions to coaches, as well as more consistent methods of compensation from universities, thereby avoiding the need for unusual compensation derived from sources such as shoe contracts, broadcasting income, and sports camps.

More specifically, coaches should also be subject to the same personnel policies that govern other university employees. They should not be allowed to profit from endorsements or independent consulting or broadcasting contracts that exploit the university's reputation. They should be subject to the same conflict-of-interest regulations that govern other university staff. And their compensation levels should be in line with those of university faculty and staff with similar responsibilities.

Financing

A serious imbalance exists between the competitive pressure to generate revenues, expenditure control, and cost containment. Far too many intercollegiate athletics programs are allowed to operate without sufficient university supervision. Such programs must come under the general scrutiny and operational structures characterizing other university units. During periods in which higher education is being asked to assess its efficiency carefully in an effort to reduce costs, intercollegiate athletics must be looked at from a similar perspective. In the next chapter, I will outline several specific proposals for mainstreaming the financing of intercollegiate athletics.

Integrity

There is only one way to play, and that is by the rules. But here, merely the good intention to comply with the complex and sometimes illogical rules promulgated by the college sports bureaucracy is not sufficient. To honor our commitment to student-athletes and to our academic programs, we must implement adequate institutional control to insure that our programs, our coaches, and our players respect and adhere both to the rules governing intercollegiate athletic competition and those values underpinning the educational mission of the university. Yet it is important that those bodies charged with the formulation and enforcement of rules, the athletic conferences and the NCAA, achieve a more appropriate balance between the driving concerns of athletic competitiveness and the welfare of student-athletes. Furthermore, we have to acknowledge and accept the importance of presidential control. Efforts to undermine such institutional control, whether by ambitious coaches or athletic directors, meddlesome trustees, or enthusiastic alumni and fans, must be resisted and eliminated.

Winning

How does one evaluate successful athletic programs? Won-lost records? Revenue (gate receipts)? Graduation rates of student-athletes? The number of athletes who go on to national recognition and professional careers? In most institutions we aspire to excellence in intercollegiate athletics in the same ways we do in every other endeavor. Just as we seek to have the leading programs in the nation in psychology or classical studies or engineering or law, we also aspire to leadership in football or swimming or softball. But, as important as winning is, it must not become the dominant goal. Winning must not come at the expense of other more important objectives, such as the integrity of our programs and the academic success of our student-athletes.

A Possible Philosophy

Most colleges and universities are certainly not reticent about their efforts to achieve excellence in academics. They boast about their national standing on the various ranking scales in academic disciplines. What is wrong, then, about also aspiring to excellence, to leadership, in intercollegiate athletics? Nothing, if these aspirations are driven by a concern for the opportunities offered to students rather than primarily for the reputation of the institution or for the financial bottom line.

I am among those who truly believe that athletic competition can play an important role in a university's central mission of education. If one were to listen to the talks given to our teams in the locker room, one would hear words such as pride, sacrifice, dedication, courage, confidence, leadership, integrity, honor, and honesty. It is clear that intercollegiate athletics has the capacity to provide students with an important opportunity to develop these qualities so essential in later life, particularly when led by inspiring and committed coaches.

These programs can also do more, because they can provide models not simply for the university community, but for others throughout society. Many of us, adults and children alike, identify with these teams, sharing their thrill in victory and suffering with them in defeat. While college sports are games, they also provide in many ways a remarkable model of life. And those factors that lead to a program's long-term success are also the factors that prepare young men and women for life itself. We must always place primary emphasis on the first word in the term *student-athlete*. But it is also important that we acknowledge that the lessons that our coaches teach student-athletes are some of the most important lessons of life—lessons as important as those we teach in the classroom, the library, and the laboratory.

It is certainly understandable why some would propose spinning off college sports, at least big-time football and basketball, from our universities, conducting them as professional franchises with compensated athletes who, at most, participate in remedial educational programs. A century of frustration in controlling intercollegiate athletics in the face of ever growing public interest and ever increasing commercial value can lead educators to simply give up, to conclude that these activities no longer have a place in an institution committed to education and scholarship.

Yet, to abandon hope and call for the professionalization of football and basketball is to throw out the baby with the bathwater. It is my belief that intercollegiate athletics, including these two high-visibility sports, is sufficiently valuable as an educational opportunity for students that we should continue efforts to reform rather than reject. To this end, then, let me turn to several specific proposals designed to realign college sports with the mission, values, and character of the university.

Chapter 13　Roads to Reform

　　　　　　　　　　While the track record of efforts to reform intercollegiate athletics is not encouraging, it nevertheless is vitally important that educators continue to strive to control varsity sports and align them more appropriately with the educational values of their host institutions.

In this spirit, then, and recognizing that I may be tilting with windmills, let me offer for consideration an array of proposals aimed at reforming intercollegiate athletics. A word of warning at the outset: Many of these proposals have been chosen and worded to be provocative, both to those involved in higher education and to those constituencies that have pulled intercollegiate athletics further and further from the educational mission of the university. The intent clearly is to force both our thinking and our public debate "out of the box."

Let me begin with several important premises.

1. Although it is clearly only an ideal, the most important role of intercollegiate athletics should be to provide educational and recreational opportunities for students that extend beyond the classroom.
2. Most issues and concerns about sports today derive from the fact that the culture and values of intercollegiate athletics have drifted far away from the academic principles of their host universities. They have been driven away by the powerful forces that see college sports primarily in terms of their commercial value as a form of mass entertainment.
3. The key to reform and restructuring is simple in concept at least: to sever or at least weaken the linkages between intercollegiate athletics and the entertainment industry, particularly the

broadcasting media and the press, and to build strong ties to the academic enterprise of the university.

4. Finally, the majority of the problems arising in intercollegiate athletics occur in two sports: football and men's basketball. Hence, most reform efforts should focus on these two activities.

In the previous chapters we considered a variety of the issues and concerns in the world of modern college sports. These provide a framework for the areas where action is needed. Yet before we turn to proposals addressing each of these concerns, it is useful to consider several of the more dramatic—indeed, draconian—proposals occasionally floated by frustrated university leaders, naive sportswriters, and greedy network executives alike.

Draconian Proposals

Let us first consider a series of extreme proposals that are occasionally suggested but usually discarded as unrealistic.

1. To create a separate category of students who would train for professional sports careers.
2. To complete the professionalization of college sports by paying salaries to athletes (pay for play).
3. To spin off big-time sports from higher education—most particularly, football and basketball—and make them independent professional franchises.

Proposal 1: Tolerating Remedial Academic Programs

One approach would simply acknowledge that some student-athletes enter college primarily to compete in athletics in the hopes of a professional athletic career with little interest in an education. They are recruited as talented performers to sustain the commercial entertainment franchises that our big-time athletics programs have become. Why should we demand that they meet the full academic requirements imposed on other students? Instead, we should simply do our best to provide them with some remedial educational opportunities for the brief time they are on campus, before they are drafted into the professional leagues.

After all, we enroll other students in our universities based on unusual skills or talents, for example as musicians or artists. Yet even though these students may seek professional careers in the performing or visual arts, we nevertheless expect them to meet the same academic requirements faced by other students. In fact, these students come to our universities rather than enrolling in music conservatories or art schools because they recognize the importance of a strong undergraduate education. Why should student-athletes be treated differently? One could go further and suggest that such a remedial approach would not only erode the academic integrity of the university, but also do a major disservice to those student-athletes who do desire a college education.

As demeaning as remedial programs for athletes may sound, this is the route taken by a great many institutions. They certainly never acknowledge that their approach to competitive athletics is to create a remedial educational program for "student-athletes" as opposed to "student-students." But that is precisely what they do. Even some of those institutions that boast most loudly about high graduation rates for their varsity programs too frequently provide the blue-chip athletes with a remedial education only, culminating in a meaningless degree.

Proposal 1 sounds like a cop-out, doesn't it?

Proposal 2: Pay for Play

What about keeping varsity football and basketball as university activities, but simply allowing these sports to operate in a more professional manner by paying student-athletes? We allow celebrity coaches to benefit from compensation levels more comparable to those in professional sports or in the entertainment industry than in the academy. Why not allow the athletes who sustain these revenue sports to share in the spoils? After all, universities conduct many other commercial activities, like health care, broadcasting, theatrical performance, and investment management (although students are not paid in these activities). Why shouldn't they also consider operating professional athletic franchises?

Late in his three-decade-long tenure as executive director of the NCAA, Walter Byers created quite a controversy by suggesting that student-athletes be allowed to endorse products, with the income going into a trust available to them when they graduated or completed their eligibility. He argued that since colleges and coaches were exploiting their talent for income, athletes deserved the same access to the free market as coaches enjoyed.[1] As Byers noted, colleges are already paying their athletes through the current grants-in-aid system, providing them with more generous financial support than other students, without the attendant need or academic performance requirements. Since these "athletic scholarships" are contingent upon athletic performance, they already represent a major step toward pay-for-play.

Perhaps the pay-for-play approach would make sense if the primary reason that student-athletes enrolled in the university was to participate in sports. But, at least for most of these individuals, the purpose of enrolling is to get a college education, not to compete in varsity athletics. To be sure, at some institutions a few exceptional athletes will have the opportunity to play professional sports, but this is certainly not a sufficient number to support a proposal to pay all student-athletes, even in the revenue sports. Rather, for all but these few, the principal reward for athletic competition will be a college education, a commodity of far greater value to most than any possible pay-for-play compensation.

If there is a disparity between the treatment of coaches and players, then it seems far more appropriate to deal with the real problem: the inconsistency of compensating coaches at professional/entertainment rates in a university where all others are rewarded as educators. Those who insist on pay-for-play might instead consider another feature of the compensation pattern followed in professional athletics: that no coach makes more than the top athletes do on his or her team!

Proposal 3: Spin-Off

One could well argue that big-time college football and basketball have become so dominated by the entertainment industry, so far removed from the educational values of the university, and so difficult to control, that it would be best to push them even further away from the university. Athletic directors indeed boast that they run self-supporting businesses. Perhaps we should take them up on this, and build true financial firewalls that eliminate all institutional subsidies, such as the use of student fees to finance capital facilities or administrative support or assistance in fund-raising or licensing. Indeed, one might go even further at the national level and stop pretending that these commercial entertainment enterprises deserve their tax-exempt status as "educational" activities. Minus institutional subsidies or favorable tax status, our athletic departments would quickly learn the discipline of cost containment. If they were forced to run as truly self-supporting businesses, they would probably be forced to bring compensation patterns under control, since they would have to employ coaches at real market prices, not at the inflated deals now dictated by their celebrity status. And who knows, they might even decide it was in their best interest to actually deprofessionalize certain elements of their programs. In fact, much of the hypocrisy and financial chicanery associated with college sports might disappear if we simply stopped pretending that big-time athletics had any relationship whatsoever to the educational mission of the university and instead restructured and relabeled them as commercial entertainment businesses.

There are some who suggest a still more draconian strategy of completely spinning off big-time college football and basketball. These two sports could then be reconfigured along the same lines as the minor league teams of professional baseball, associated with the communities in which they compete, but not with educational institutions. The massive facilities at universities—football stadiums, basketball arenas, training facilities—would also need to be transferred to these professional franchises or the sponsoring communities, but this should not pose a serious problem.

Several years ago, Rick Telander, a former sportswriter for *Sports Illustrated,* came up with an interesting proposal that illustrates the possibilities of a spin-off strategy,[2] by proposing that we restructure the major football programs as franchises in a new professional football league for players ages eighteen to twenty-two, similar to the junior leagues in professional hockey. The players in this age group would have to be high school graduates, but not necessarily college students. They would be paid at rates comparable to other minor league franchises, complete with bonuses and other incentives. Coaches would continue to be paid at the level of the professional marketplace. Since these junior professional leagues would develop players for the National Football League, some level of NFL subsidy would be appropriate, since for a league with $17 billion of television contracts, some support would not seem too much of a burden.

Those universities currently conducting Division I-A programs would be faced with a decision. They could retain big-time football programs by owning and operating franchises in this new professional league, using school facilities, emblems, and mascots. If so, they would have to operate these franchises as true commercial enterprises, much as the owners of professional NFL teams. Although the primary functions of these junior professional teams would be to develop young football players for the NFL, to entertain the public, and perhaps to turn a profit, universities could also commit to providing players with educational benefits, provided they met admission standards.

If universities did not desire affiliation with this professional league, they could retain football but only as an amateur university activity, with true students as participants and teaching staff as coaches. There would be no athletic scholarships, no redshirting, no freshman eligibility or spring practice, no commercial endorsements or media patronizing, and no drafting of players until their eligibility was completed or they decided to turn pro. In fact, these "college football programs" would be a part of the university like any other extracurricular activity.

Of course this action would pose a significant challenge to the other athletic programs of the university, since they would no longer be subsidized by the revenues generated by these big-time football and basketball programs. But if college sports are truly to be a part of the educational enterprise of the university, then support from other revenue sources such as student tuition and fees seems altogether appropriate. For many institutions, this would not even be a significant budget issue, since most of the revenue generated by football and basketball goes to support only those two programs. For example, covering the $15 million per year cost of the "nonrevenue" varsity sports at Michigan would correspond to only a 3 percent increase in student tuition.

Note that this bifurcation of college football into professional and amateur programs solves many of the existing problems. The players in the professional leagues would be employees and hence receive the government-mandated employment protection and benefits. There would be no more hypocrisy from the coaches in these leagues; they would not have to think about education at all. Fans of big-time college football could still root for the professional teams, since they would probably still be affiliated with universities, except in attitude and compensation.

On the other hand, coaches of the amateur programs would no longer be celebrities, but career college teachers who could afford to be concerned about their players' education. Students might become much more interested in their college football teams once they see that players really were students like themselves. Furthermore, the low-key "amateur" model of competitive sports is far more consistent with the objective of providing an extracurricular and hopefully educational activity for students.

As Telander admits, there would be many opponents. Big-time coaches, athletic directors, and boosters would probably be outraged at the loss of jobs and power. High school players would be faced with the decision of going pro and trying to make the big time or becoming real college students. And the NFL would complain because it would have to pay for what it has always gotten for free, a steady supply of talent.

Clearly, the arguments against spinning off the revenue sports—or, to use medical terms, amputating those programs most badly infected by the gangrene of the entertainment industry—cannot be based on forgone revenue or even forgone opportunities for student participation in these sports. There are already extensive club sport and intramural activities in football and basketball on most campuses, which involve many times more students as participants than the varsity programs.

The real argument against spin-off is a political one. Could universities withstand the great pressure from the media, not to mention the alumni and fans, if these long-standing traditions were jettisoned? Probably so. After all, they have withstood far worse over history: plague, war, the Dark Ages, the Inquisition, the McCarthy era, and even the invasion of Nike. The more serious question is whether the presidents and the governing boards could withstand this onslaught. Probably not. Most university leaders would be reluctant ever to make such a decision, since their own survival is at stake.

The sad fact is that the American public has become addicted to college sports. It has become so ingrained in our culture, that major efforts to de-emphasize intercollegiate athletics inevitably encounter formidable resistance.

Mainstreaming College Sports

The first step in reconnecting college sports to the academic enterprise is to stop treating our athletic departments, coaches, and student-athletes as special members of the university community, subject to different rules and procedures, policies and practices than the rest of university. We need to mainstream our athletics programs and their participants.

We need to first make certain that our athletics programs are not allowed to ignore or undermine academic principles or priorities. For example, clearly the admission of student-athletes, their academic standing, and their eligibility for athletic competition must be controlled by the faculty. While there are formal policies and procedures to achieve this through faculty bodies such as boards in control of intercollegiate athletes or faculty athletic representatives, we have noted that all too often these are manipulated by athletic directors and coaches or subverted by a central administration under pressure to achieve winning programs. The faculty should also have firm control of both the competitive and training calendar of student-athletes to make certain they have adequate time and opportunity to meet academic requirements. Furthermore, faculty counselors rather than athletic department staff should play the key role in academic advising, to make certain that student-athletes are not pressured by coaches into enrolling in less demanding courses and programs.

In a similar spirit, medical staff providing care for student-athletes should be independent of the athletic department and provided with a clear veto power over the participation of athletes in either training or competition. In all cases, the health of the student-athlete should take priority over the competitive needs of a program.

The athletic departments of universities should be subject to the same financial controls as other university units. Their financial operations should be reported through the usual channels to the university's chief financial officer and should be subject to the same rigorous internal and external audit requirements. Independent financial organizations such as foundations or booster clubs should be eliminated or discouraged or at least rigorously controlled by the university. Sports camps for school-age athletes should be operated by the university, not as independent businesses of coaches.

Yet these steps may not be sufficient to provide adequate financial controls, when we demand that our athletic departments become financially self-supporting, that is, generate sufficient revenue to cover all of their operating expenditures. In fact, I have reached the conclusion that one of the best ways to control intercollegiate athletics is for university to intentionally support at least a part of the athletic department budget from general academic resources, albeit accompanied by a counterflow of athletic department revenue into general university accounts to lessen financial impact on academic programs.

There is a fundamental rationale for such a linkage. If we really believe that college sports are justified in part because of their educational value to students, then it is altogether appropriate to support them from academic resources. These firm financial linkages between the athletic and academic budget would make this relationship far clearer. It would represent an important step toward the goal of better aligning sports with the educational mission of our universities.

Having universities subsidize their athletic department budget would link athletics more strongly with the rest of the university, thereby providing more leverage for the administration to insist on both wise financial management and expenditure controls common in the academic enterprise. Perhaps the best way to drive this home would be to place the salaries of all coaches and athletics staff directly on the academic budget. For more affluent athletics programs, one could compensate this by "taxing" athletics revenue for the support of general university functions such as libraries so that the burden on the academic enterprise was minimized.

In the case of Michigan, roughly one-third of the $45 million budget of the athletics department is for personnel. In my proposal, this $15 million part of the budget would be transferred to the Office of the Provost, which oversees the General and Education Budget of the university. In return, the athletic department would be taxed at least this amount, so that one-third of its revenue flowed back into the General and Education Budget for use in the educational enterprise. In this model, the university's central administration, more specifically, the provost and the chief financial officer, would have control over all personnel expenditure policies in the athletic department, thereby significantly tightening financial controls over the entire enterprise.

The specific proposal to link athletics more tightly to the rest of the university by supporting all staff and coaching salaries with funds from the General and Education Budget, with a corresponding transfer of comparable athletic department revenue into the discretionary resource pools of the provost, is just one of many possibilities. However, the principle is clear: to establish a clear budget control line from the academic part of the university, thereby allowing academic values and objectives to have some influence over intercollegiate athletics. Furthermore, the athletic department should not be absolved from the financial pressures or responsibilities felt by the rest of the institution. For example, rigorous cost containment and total quality management programs are just as important in athletics as they are elsewhere in the institution, and they should be insisted upon by the chief budget officer of the university.

The athletic department should also be subject to the same personnel and management policies and practices enforced elsewhere in the university. Personnel searches, hiring decisions and negotiations, and appointments should be similar to those for other university staff. For example, equal opportunity principles should clearly be applied. Hiring decisions should be made through the usual processes, without undue interference from the president or trustees, but also with a broader, more consultative process than that used by most athletic directors. As I mentioned in the previous chapter, the compensation of coaches should be constrained to levels more comparable to those of faculty and staff with similar responsibilities. They should be restricted in the amount of outside activity and income they can earn, just like other employees. Coaches should be also subject to the same conflict-of-interest regulations that govern other university staff. And the influence of both power coaches and ambitious athletic directors with external constituencies that threaten institutional control should be tightly controlled.

While it is critically important to make certain that athletics activities are subject to the same independent internal and external financial audits as the rest of the university, they should also be subject to regular independent audits of their compliance with NCAA, conference, and institutional rules governing intercollegiate athletics. Most universities already have some degree of oversight, provided both by internal compliance functions within the athletic department, by their boards in control of athletics, and by the faculty representative who reports directly to the president. Yet something more is needed: a regular external audit conducted by an independent organization such as a major accounting firm, reporting jointly to the athletic director, the president, and the governing board. In a sense, this is analogous to the audits in major federal contractors for compliance with federal ethics regulations.

In terms of presidential control, the chief executive officer of the university clearly must have both the ultimate authority and accept the final responsibility for intercollegiate athletics, as with every other activity of the institution. But, just as clearly, this authority must be exercised through delegation to the athletic director, just as one would delegate authority to the dean of an academic school or the director of the university hospital. The president must select strong leadership in the athletic director, and then require him or her to operate within the standard framework of policies, procedures, and practices of the university. It is essential that presidential involvement in university sports move through normal administrative channels and not through special devices.

Severing the Ties That Bind

Earlier in this book, I described a provocative proposal I once made to the Big Ten presidents to consider a moratorium on the televising of all conference athletic events. While this was never intended nor was it taken as a serious proposal, it does address the right goal: Somehow we must loosen the grip that the entertainment industry has on intercollegiate athletics so that we can better align these programs with the educational mission of our institutions. Incidentally, I include members of the sports press within the entertainment industry, since these days they clearly are driven more by entertainment values and bottom-line priorities than journalistic values. Like the broadcasting media, their primary goals are circulation and advertising revenue, rather than truth and objectivity.

Driving the Money-Changers from the Temple

It is both surprising and disturbing to recognize just how far universities have gone to accommodate the intrusive interests of the sports media. To be sure, the high visibility of a program can occasionally attract the interest of potential recruits. It can also enhance the negotiating power of institutions for broadcasting contracts and increase the market value of celebrity coaches.

But inviting the press onto the practice field or into the locker room is a classic example of the prey inviting the predator to dinner. To sell advertising, whether for a newspaper or a network, one needs to create an entertainment product with commercial appeal. The more sensationalism, the more controversy, the better, even if in the process one destroys a player, a coach, or even a program. Not only do we tolerate these predators, we actually cultivate and patronize them—granted, with little respect for their motives or their craft.

Perhaps the first step in freeing intercollegiate athletics from the stranglehold of the entertainment industry is to recognize that most members of the sports press have a vested interest in promoting the commercial character of college sports. They have a totally different set of values and expectations from those of the university. Hence they should be treated as foreign agents, with little interest in the welfare of the university as an educational institution.

While we certainly should not attempt to hide from the press, universities are already painfully exposed by the sunshine laws that exist in many states. There is no reason why we should further pander to the press, inviting them into our locker rooms or requiring our student-athletes to appear before the klieg lights in press conferences. If coaches want to play the media game, that is their business, as long as they do not market the reputation of the university.

Recognize That Money Isn't Everything

As a next step, we need to stop this nonsense of negotiating every broadcasting contract or championship event as if money were the only priority. Those representing higher education—and here I include university presidents as well as athletic directors, conference commissioners, and NCAA officials—too often seem to toss academic values or institutional reputation aside in favor of the top dollar. You want our teams to play on Sunday afternoon or at midnight? No problem. You want our players available for press conferences at all hours of the day and night? Right on. Beer commercials throughout the broadcast? Nike swooshes plastered on anything in television camera range? Sure, for the right price.

As the famous football broadcaster Keith Jackson used to put it, "Whoa, Nellie!" Let's first draw out some lines in the sand to protect fundamental educational values. At the top of the list must be the academic welfare of our students and the image of our institution. Let's make these non-negotiable preconditions that we will not abandon. In fact, perhaps we should include an educator at the table in each of these negotiations with veto power should academic values and priorities be threatened. Sure we would lose a bit of money, but we might save our academic soul in the process.

And while we are at it, let us admit that it is long past time that we reined in the influence of the sports apparel manufacturers. Their distortion of college sports, through bribing coaches with shoe contracts to use and promote their equipment, sponsoring summer basketball camps for high school basketball players for the convenience of coaches and agents, and plastering their insignia over every visible surface in our sporting events (including our players) is, quite frankly, obscene. It is time to call a halt, perhaps by refusing to allow our coaches, our players, our institutions, and our values to be bought by these companies. As I acknowledged earlier, I believe that Michigan and other universities are ill advised to enter into contractual arrangements with sports apparel companies, or anyone else who intends to exploit the university's reputation. It is a bargain with the devil, and it can only cause harm to the institution.

Ending the Celebrity Treatment of Coaches

Of particular importance in the reform process is a willingness on the part of the university to break the culture of celebrity coaches and require both employment policies and compensation arrangements that are more consistent with the rest of the university. Of course, since one university would have difficulty in going it alone, there would have to be a more general agreement in higher education that coaches would be subject to the same personnel policies and compensation parameters as other university faculty and staff.

Clearly the same conflict-of-interest policies that apply elsewhere in the university should apply to coaches as well. No longer should coaches be allowed to profit personally from the university's reputation or visibility. If there is a market for their lucrative sideline activities, these should be developed and conducted by the university itself with income flowing to the institution for general purposes (including academic priorities). The involvement of coaches in these activities should be included as a component of their base compensation agreement, which, in turn, should be comparable to that of faculty rather than independent celebrity entrepreneurs. In fact, coaches on full-time appointments should be held to the same constraints on outside activity and income as other employees. Reining in the astronomical compensation of coaches will, without a doubt, encounter strong resistance not only from coaches but also from the sports media. At the University of Michigan, for example, although the local newspapers berate the institution for the salaries of senior administrators and exceptional faculty, seeing any salary that rises above $200,000 as exorbitant, they laud the athletic department for long-term coaching contracts paying the head football and men's basketball coaches many times this amount. After all, in the entertainment industry, market share is usually determined more by star appeal than by program content.

Requiring coaches to adhere to normal university conflict-of-interest policies is certain to chase some of the more highly compensated celebrity coaches off the campuses and into the professional leagues, though perhaps this is not such a bad outcome. Is Indiana University really well served by having its image determined by Bobby Knight, or Florida by Steve Spurrier, or even Penn State by Joe Paterno? While these are, to be sure, very successful coaches, there are hundreds of distinguished faculty members and alumni of these important universities who are far more appropriate as symbols of the institution. Furthermore, one has to question whether it is in the best interests of a university to have its most visible, well compensated, and powerful employees associated with the athletic department rather than the academic enterprise.

While some claim that extraordinary compensation is necessary to attract the best coaches, it seems more likely that cutting back compensation would simply cull out those coaches more suited to professional athletics. Those who are interested in the broader mission and values of the university would be asked to accept a more reasonable compensation model, as do faculty.

This wouldn't necessarily degrade the quality of coaching in intercollegiate athletics either. There are thousands of talented coaches who would be all too willing to jump at the opportunity of a head-coaching position at the more modest compensation rates of faculty. Indeed, by redirecting the celebrity revenue away from head coaches and into the university, it would be possible to pay assistant coaches reasonable salaries. In fact, one might make a strong case that if athletic directors were required to operate their athletic departments as truly self-supporting activities, with no subsidies or year-end bailouts, they would be far less tolerant of the astronomical compensation of celebrity coaches, since this would come out of the department's bottom line.

Recognizing Diversity

Part of the challenge of reforming athletics is simply recognizing the great diversity, not only among various sports programs but also among institutions. Although we tend to think of college athletics in terms of one-dimensional comparisons of marquee sports such as football or basketball, in reality there is a complex diversity to the institutions and the sports programs they sponsor.

Institutional Diversity

The NCAA is comprised of 983 institutions, ranging from vast, comprehensive research universities, such as the University of Michigan and the University of California, to comprehensive four-year institutions, such as Eastern Michigan University or Cal State–Long Beach, to small liberal arts colleges, such as Kalamazoo College and Occidental College. Clearly these institutions are quite different in scope, character, mission, and goals from an academic perspective, and the same is true for their perspectives on and objectives for college sports. Just as it would make no sense to have small liberal arts colleges set academic priorities for major research universities, it makes no sense for the fifty or so major AAU-class institutions to have their athletics programs controlled by the majority vote of the NCAA. Even within conferences, it is important to recognize the profound differences among institutions. Within the Big Ten, large institutions, such as Michigan,

Ohio State, and Penn State, will clearly have different missions and objectives for their intercollegiate athletics programs than more focused institutions such as Purdue, Northwestern, and Indiana, just as they have significantly different academic missions and objectives.

It is essential to recognize and respect this diversity among academic institutions, even as we seek a common ground for athletic competition. It is unlikely that the present NCAA will ever have the capacity to do this. In many ways, the intense desire of the nine-hundred-plus Division I, II, and III institutions to achieve the public visibility and financial success of the fifty "AAU class" institutions in athletics, perhaps as a surrogate for similar parity in academics, currently drives much of the abuse in college sports today. The massive dollars generated by the major institutions through events such as the national championship basketball tournament have fueled a massive bureaucracy within the NCAA, which not only is incapable of controlling abuse, but actually contributes to it through staggering inefficiency and red tape.

In early 1996, the NCAA took a major step toward restructuring itself to be able to recognize institutional diversity while facilitating presidential control. By a 90 percent vote of all the member institutions, it transformed itself from an "association," governed by the tyranny of one institution–one vote, into a "federation" of three divisions (I, II, and III), each with sufficient autonomy to control its own destiny and recognize institutional diversity. The total NCAA federation is now being controlled by a small executive committee of university presidents, the majority of whom come from the larger institutions in Division I, which have the most at stake in sports. While athletic administrators, coaches, and faculty will have important roles and input in divisions, this new structure is consistent with the Knight Commission's view that, in the end, the integrity of college sports depends on presidential control.

Similar steps probably should occur within conferences to recognize the diversity of members. For example, within the Big Ten, some universities no longer have the desire or financial resources to field nationally competitive programs across the full spectrum of sports. Such differences in institutional priorities should be tolerated and encouraged. Several Big Ten schools, Penn State, Michigan, and Ohio State, are generally able to compete at the national level year after year in football. Rather than seeking to pull these programs down to the competitive level of programs at institutions that have chosen not to compete at a very high level, one should, instead, accept the fact that some institutions will, and should, build nationally competitive programs in this sport, just as others will in hockey or women's basketball or soccer. Why should a conference seek to make every institution competitive in any particular sport? It should be an institutional decision.

Program Diversity

At the present time, there are twenty-three varsity sports at Michigan, ten for men and thirteen for women. All seek national competitiveness; all offer full grants-in-aid; all are supported by revenue sports (football, men's basketball, and hockey). Yet, these twenty-three sports provide opportunities for participation in intercollegiate athletics to only about seven hundred students out of an undergraduate student body of twenty-two thousand. The only alternative opportunities are first, club sports that receive financial support only from contributors with volunteer coaches, poor equipment and facilities, or second, intramural athletics, supported by student fees. The Michigan model stands in sharp contrast to the model at most Ivy League schools, in which universities maintain thirty to forty varsity sports in an effort to provide broad opportunities for student participation. Since none of these sports are able to generate substantial revenue, they are supported primarily by student fees.

It is becoming increasingly clear that our objectives of cost containment and gender equity will require some differentiation among sports, a so-called core sports, or tiering, approach, in which some sports are maintained at nationally competitive levels, while others aim at achieving only regional or conference competitiveness. It might also be appropriate to consider a broader set of sports tiering in an effort to provide a significant increase in opportunities for student participation. One such model might be a hybrid of the Michigan and Ivy League models.

At the highest tier would be programs that aim at national competitiveness. These would be characterized by full grants-in-aid, high-quality coaching staffs, facilities, and support. They would be supported by athletic department revenue and would include many of our present programs: men's football, men's and women's basketball, men's and women's swimming, hockey, softball and baseball, et cetera. At the next level would be regionally or conference-level competitive sports, characterized by high-quality coaching, facilities, and support, but only by limited (perhaps, only need-based) grants-in-aid. Again, these would be supported by athletic department revenue.

At the third level would be a number of varsity sports programs with professional coaches but more limited facilities and support and no grants-in-aid. These programs, designed to increase opportunities for student participation, would be supported entirely from student fees. While such programs, which might include crew, lacrosse, and skiing, would generally compete on a regional basis, they might from time to time achieve national prominence. Below these would be a variety of what might be called "super" club sports, similar to our present club sports, but subsidized to some degree by student fees. Included in this latter group might be junior varsity opportunities in nationally competitive sports, such as baseball, basketball, and hockey. Finally, there would be a broad array of intramural sports opportunities and informal athletics programs, as there are today.

While such a tiering approach might appear to be a bold departure from tradition at institutions like Michigan, it has proven to be a very successful approach at other institutions that manage to combine nationally competitive programs with broad opportunities for student participation, Stanford and Penn State being two notable examples. The positive impact on the educational experience provided to undergraduates through varsity competition has been vividly demonstrated by the Ivy League for decades.

This raises an important issue: if varsity competition can have a positive impact on a student's educational experience, then why do we limit this opportunity to only a tiny fraction of the study body? At Michigan, only about 3 percent of our entire student body participate in varsity athletics. Put another way, our semi-professional approach to sports is depriving countless numbers of students of the educational opportunities afforded by competitive athletics. Perhaps one of the most compelling reasons for de-emphasizing and broadening varsity sports is simply to provide more of our students with the educational opportunities associated with athletic participation.

Deregulation

In his provocative book, *Unsportsmanlike Conduct: Exploiting College Athletes*, former NCAA executive director Walter Byers stated his strong conviction that it was time to set free, to deregulate, college sports.[3] He had concluded that after a century of so-called reform, intercollegiate athletics and the organizations responsible for its regulation had become more bureaucratic, more rule-bound and more ponderous than ever, yet still vulnerable to the same concerns about integrity and student welfare. To maintain the amateurism of the student-athletes, the NCAA (or rather its member institutions) proposed more and more rules, more and more compliance regulations, and established a large, centralized bureaucracy to administer the entire apparatus. But as student-athletes became more and more enmeshed in regulation, coaches remained free to exploit for vast personal gain the popularity of college sports as public entertainment. Driven by the greed of institutions, of coaches, and of the entertainment industry, and by the insatiable appetite of armchair America, college sports have become more commercialized and professionalized than ever.

Byers accepted this history, and noted that reform movements in college athletics have never been able to reform much of anything because they "seemed to be constantly chasing the horse after it had escaped from the barn." He maintained that we should forget about returning today's flourishing big-time college sports industry to a more idyllic amateur activity, coexisting comfortably with the academic side of campus life. Byers advocated that we free the athlete. Colleges should end their grant-in-aid (pay-for-play) system and evenhandedly treat athletes like other students. We should award them financial aid on the same terms and conditions and through the same processes as those established for other undergraduates. And we should allow student-athletes to access the marketplace, just as other students exploit their own special talents. More specifically, Byers recommended the following steps toward deregulating college athletics:

1. Repeal the role of the NCAA as national arbiter of the term, value, and conditions of an athlete's scholarship and as controller of an athlete's outside income during his or her collegiate tenure. Instead, colleges should award financial assistance to athletes on the same basis and through the same agency that makes financial aid decisions for all students. Furthermore, repeal the one-year limit on grants because it is simply an artificial ceiling held in place for the purpose of shuffling player personnel and allocating money elsewhere. By removing the artificial salary cap set by grants-in-aid, colleges or their benefactors would be free to provide financial assistance to athletes to attend college before or after their period of eligibility.
2. End the NCAA ban that prevents players from holding a job during the school year.
3. Repeal the transfer rule, which unreasonably binds athletes to their current colleges.
4. Force the NCAA to allow players to consult agents in making sports career choices. (After all, Byers notes, even coaches now have agents!)
5. Ask state legislatures to amend workmen's compensation laws to require that colleges provide coverage for varsity athletes and other students engaged in auxiliary enterprises.

There might actually be a great deal of enthusiasm for such a deregulated approach. Clearly those students with exceptional athletic talent would benefit greatly. Furthermore, the vast appetite of the American public for college sports would continue to be satisfied. And this approach might even be more acceptable to government bodies such as state legislatures, Congress, and the courts, since it would explicitly recognize student-athletes as "employees" in a university's athletic department.

The fundamental flaw in Byers's approach is that it has nothing to do with the educational mission of the university. It would certainly provide a training ground for those very few athletes destined for brief careers as professional athletes or other roles in athletics such as coaches or sports broadcasters. But for 90 percent of today's student-athletes, the "set them free" approach would push them even further from the educational activities of the university.

In my view, the deregulation approach has merit only if after deregulating sports, the host universities then decide which of their many sports programs continue to have any relevance to the educational mission of the university. These would then be absorbed as club sports: no grants-in-aid, no celebrity coaches, no television, et cetera. The remainder of the enterprise would be spun off as professional athletics programs, perhaps as the minor league franchises of professional teams.

Governance

We have noted throughout this book the great difficulty in governing intercollegiate athletics, in maintaining both its integrity and its relevance to the academic enterprise of the university. Who is at fault? No one, and at the same time, everyone.

Coaches and athletic directors are simply responding to their marching orders—and the incentive systems and opportunities—as dictated by their institutions, boosters, and the sports media as they try to build winning and profitable programs. Sportswriters and broadcasters are in the entertainment business, and, the fundamental goal of a business is to make a profit, not to promote truth, justice, and the American way.

This is an important point. Much of the force driving the evolution of college sports has come from those who have serious financial interests in the commercialization of the enterprise. Clearly coaches, who benefit personally from shoe contracts, coaching camps and clinics, television appearances, and the lecture circuit have a strong interest in making sure that college sports are good show business. But many of those in higher leadership positions also have monetary interests. Some of the most powerful athletic directors have had major commercial interests on the side, and even those selected for the leadership of athletic associations such as the NCAA or conferences sometimes come from the ranks of coaches, athletic directors, or even sportswriters! The infiltration of the leadership structure of colleges sports by those with past or current commercial interests is a serious matter that is all too frequently ignored by administrators of higher education.

And what about the presidents? Certainly most presidents do understand the limited importance of sports in the broader scheme of their universities as well as the very substantial risks they pose to their institutions. Yet few are willing to step up to the challenge of reforming big-time sports. All too frequently university presidents take the easy way out, focusing on short-term tactics of building winning, profitable programs rather than on longer-term, strategic, and far more politically difficult issues such as realigning sports with the educational mission and values of the university.

Perhaps it is time to try something quite different. There are two key constituencies that have been seriously underrepresented in the real power structure of intercollegiate athletics for some time: educators and students. Note here I say *educators,* not faculty. As I mentioned earlier, the common practice has been to select the faculty athletic representatives from professional schools such as law and medicine rather than from faculty members who actually teach undergraduates. Perhaps it is time to require that any faculty members serving on faculty boards for control of intercollegiate athletics or as faculty athletic representatives have extensive experience in teaching, counseling, and working with undergraduate students. Perhaps we should insist that they come from fields such as history or math or even chemistry, like Nobel laureate Glenn Seaborg, who served as faculty representative for the University of California.

Or, even more to the point, perhaps we should insist that beyond the requirements for management, leadership, and athletic experience that we establish in our searches for athletic directors, we give an even higher priority to experience as an educator. We have at least one example at Michigan: Joe Roberson, our athletic director in the mid-1990s. While Joe was a former college and professional athlete as well as a proven administrator and fundraiser, he was first and foremost an educator, with extensive experience in teaching and counseling undergraduates. What better way to empower the educator in the governance of intercollegiate athletics than to insist that all athletic directors come from the faculty?

Finally, it may be time for us to empower student-athletes by giving them a place at the table in the governance of intercollegiate athletics. After the student activism of the 1960s, we now find students involved in essentially all of the major functions of the university, from search committees to select the president to student representation on the governing board of the institution. Yet, aside from an occasional advisory committee or token role, we rarely find student-athletes represented in any positions of power in intercollegiate athletics. Even the student members on athletic boards of control are generally drawn from the spectator ranks, from athletic wanna-bes, rather than from the varsity teams.

If we are going to consider proposals to set the student-athlete free, we should first consider empowering them to participate in a meaningful way in the governance of intercollegiate athletics.

Some More Specific and More Controversial Proposals

Eliminating First-Year Eligibility in Revenue Sports

The practice of allowing first-year students to compete at the varsity level in such big-time sports as football, basketball, and hockey must be challenged and eliminated. The transition to college is difficult enough for most students without adding the additional pressure of varsity competition in media-intensive sports.

On the surface, the issue seems quite simple. Student-athletes, especially those in highly commercial, high-pressure sports, have great difficulty balancing the intense demand of their athletics activities with the academic requirements of their first year. It is difficult enough to adjust to the academic and social pace of a modern university without the additional burdens of athletic competition. Beyond academic demands, the social and intellectual development of students in their early college experience can be critical not only to their future education but to their later life as well.

The Big Ten Conference has long supported the elimination of first-year eligibility, but other conferences, particularly those involving smaller institutions that depend on first-year students to sustain programs, have long resisted this change because it would reduce their competitiveness. However, this is one of those issues in which the concern for student welfare should dominate. Yet one conference cannot act alone.

The elimination of first-year eligibility would also be consistent with prohibiting transfer students (including junior college transfers) from competing immediately after arriving on campus.

Restructuring the NCAA Basketball Tournament

Here is another heretical suggestion: it is time that we intentionally downgraded the NCAA basketball tournament! As I have noted on several occasions, this event is the most extreme example of commercialism in college sports and seriously tarnishes the image of higher education in America. It also provides a source of funding that not only sustains but also distorts the bureaucracy of organized college sports. It is hard to accept that the dollars generated by the tournament glue together the hundreds of diverse institutions comprising the NCAA. Rather, the obsession with these funds, the ever-present arguments over their distribution, and the bureaucracy and commercial culture they sustain have done great damage to intercollegiate athletics.

My proposal is simple: Let us return to the NCAA tournament format of three decades ago: a two-week tournament, with sixteen teams comprised of conference champions only, with a few at-large teams representing only the very best of the smaller institutions. No conference tournaments at the end of the season to select yet another conference representative. No teams with mediocre records. No conferences with more than one team in the draw. This format would once again emphasize the importance of the season-

long gauntlet a team must navigate to win a conference championship. And for most teams in the nation, players would put away
their uniforms several weeks early and return to classes and get
ready for exams.

But we couldn't afford to lose all of these dollars, opponents
could argue. Nonsense. The average income from the NCAA Tournament today is roughly $1 million per participating institution,
about 5 percent of the athletics budget of a typical Division I-A
institution. It seems a small price to pay to take the image of
higher education as framed by basketball broadcasters off the air,
doesn't it?

Returning to Single-Platoon Football

When confronting the excessive escalation of costs and the
demand to move toward greater gender equity, both athletic
departments and the sports press always try to exempt football
from these discussions. To play football, they rationalize, requires
large squads and coaching staffs, expensive facilities, and significant investment. Since this is the sports program that generates
most of the revenue in intercollegiate athletics, they argue that we
should set it apart, thereby protecting the goose that lays the
golden eggs. Indeed, there have even been lobbying efforts aimed
at Congress to exempt football from the same set of rules that
apply to other sports programs (e.g., to make football exempt from
legislation that requires gender equity).

As I have noted, over the years, college football coaches have
driven the professionalization of the sport, demanding unlimited
substitution, first-year eligibility, specialized training facilities and
residences, and first-class treatment in all aspects of football.
Throughout its early years, college football was regarded as a two-
way sport, with participants playing both on offense and defense,
just like soccer or basketball. Although there was a brief flirtation
with two-platoon football during the war years, the game returned
to single-platoon in the 1950s and early 1960s. However, under
pressures from coaches, unlimited substitution was gradually
introduced in the 1960s, making college football more similar to
professional competition. The size of teams, coaching staffs, and

budgets expanded rapidly. Moving to unlimited substitution not only enlarged programs, coaching staffs, and budgets, it transformed the head football coach into a chief executive officer—perhaps better, a general—with greater power and prestige, while their participation in actual coaching receded.

An obvious technical fix that would solve many of the problems presented by the current paradigm of college football would be to return to the limited substitution rules in place prior to the 1960s in which football players were expected to play both ways, offense and defense. This would effectively cut in half the parameters of football teams: the number of players (from over 100 to 50), the number of coaches, and, very significantly, the costs (grants-in-aid, coaching salaries, equipment and travel expenses).

Such a change could even improve the quality of the game since requiring athletes to play more diverse roles would place a higher premium on recruiting outstanding all-around athletes rather than finely-honed specialists. Injuries might go down, since smaller, more athletic players would not generate the same level of physical trauma. It would trigger a significant restructuring of high school football, once again dramatically reducing costs and placing a premium on developing the complete athlete. And, while this change would decouple college football from the highly specialized needs of the professional leagues, many believe this would not be an altogether bad prospect, allowing more student-athletes to stay in school until they complete their degrees.

Controlling the Length of Sports Seasons

One of the more flagrant examples of how out of control intercollegiate athletics has become is provided by the length and intensity of competitive seasons for many sports. While football is intense, at least it is confined to a weekly event. Of course, some of the more successful teams will find themselves in a holiday bowl that will prolong the season by a month or so. Athletic directors continue to pressure their institutions and the NCAA to add additional games early in the season in an effort to generate more revenue. And if the NCAA and the presidents lose their resolve to insist on academic priorities and resist the temptation for a national football championship playoff, some teams might even find themselves in a playoff series that runs for additional few weeks. Yet, while the competitive season may last only a term, major college football programs have extensive spring practice. Furthermore, many coaches use a postseason bowl game as an excuse for extensive practice sessions, more designed to prepare for the next season than the bowl game itself. Furthermore, football players are expected to train year-round, stressing both conditioning and skill development.

Basketball and ice hockey provide examples of sports that are played far too long and far too frequently. Both now begin in early November and continue through early April, thereby clobbering the better part of two academic terms. Furthermore, both have two or even three games scheduled every week, with extensive travel schedules that seriously undermine the opportunity for study. Basketball has effectively sold its competitive calendar to the television broadcasting networks, ready and willing to play anytime, anyplace for the right price, regardless of the inconvenience to players or spectators. However, at least these athletic programs compete on campus. In many of the spring sports, the teams from northern institutions must spend much of their time traveling to warmer climates for competition. Their seasons start while it is still winter in the north and continue until well after spring commencement.

A call for a bit of sanity, please! If those responsible for intercollegiate athletics were truly concerned with the educational welfare of student-athletes, they would accept scheduling constraints. The competitive seasons for all sports programs would be confined to a single academic term: some in the fall (football, cross-country, soccer, field hockey, volleyball); some in the winter term (basketball, ice hockey, swimming, gymnastics, wrestling); and some beginning in spring (March or later) and continuing through summer for northern institutions (baseball, softball, tennis, golf, track and field). Spring football practice should be finally recognized as the excess it has become and eliminated entirely. Off-season training should be truly voluntary, without the intense involvement of coaches and professional trainers that we see today. The intention would be to provide opportunities for student-athletes to have one complete term in each calendar year to enroll in class without regard to training, practice, or competition commitments. Unfortunately, it is doubtful that the athletics establishment would do this on its own. Hence, this is one place where the faculty itself should step up and demand compliance with the academic calendar.

Decoupling from the Pros

Although it is customary for academic administrators to dream wistfully of the amateur ideal of college sports, in reality modern intercollegiate athletics is closer to professional athletics than ever. College players are not compensated at the level of the pros, although there are times when we wonder as a star player drives an expensive new car into the parking lot. But college coaches are clearly compensated at professional levels. Football and basketball games are approached as commercial products, and the revenue from many college programs far exceeds that of their local professional team. Clearly the Michigan Wolverines are a bigger business than the Detroit Lions or the Detroit Pistons.

Little wonder that sportswriters tend to lump together their coverage of college and professional sports, assuming that the same values and standards apply to both—at least until a violation of the voluminous NCAA rulebook occurs or a young student-athlete misbehaves. And the pros tend to view colleges as their farm teams, feeling free to lure away a talented college player at any time, long before they have finished their education and without regard to the impact of their loss on the college program.

If college sports are to remain relevant and valuable to higher education, we must break them free not only from the sports media but from professional sports as well. It is time to call a summit meeting of the presidents of universities with major athletics programs and the owners of professional franchises and have a candid discussion about the dangers professional sports pose to college sports. If owners are unwilling to demonstrate more of a sense of social responsibility toward the educational welfare of the student-athlete, perhaps we can appeal to their self-interest. While raiding athletically precocious undergraduates from the college ranks may be an attractive short-term strategy, over the longer term it erodes the talent base of the professional leagues, as the declining popularity of professional baseball and basketball clearly indicates. If higher education really went on the offensive against the intrusion of professional sports, it could cause great havoc in the professional leagues, since it could dry up their principal source of talent. Perhaps such action is necessary to bring the professional club owners to the table for serious discussions with higher education.

In the spirit of tilting at windmills, let me offer a proposal that might enable professional sports to step up to their responsibility both to the athlete and to the institutions that have assisted in developing their athletic talent. The idea is quite simple: whenever a professional team recruits student-athletes prior to the completion of their academic degree, the professional club would be required to place in escrow with the university an amount sufficient to fund the students' eventual completion of their degrees when they return, during or after their professional careers. This would accomplish several objectives. First, it would provide an insurance policy for the students that would allow them to complete their degrees. Second, it would also provide an incentive for professional teams to allow students to finish their studies before playing professionally, thereby avoiding the expense of the escrow account. Finally, in the event that the student did not return to complete his or her education, the reversion of the funds to the university would compensate it, to some degree, for the investment it had made in developing the athletic ability of the student through its own grants-in-aid.

Here it should be noted that sometimes athletes do negotiate a clause in their professional contracts to finance their return to finish their education, but most do not, and hence the rationale for this proposal. A simple enough concept, but probably unrealistic without a sea change in the attitude of the owners of professional franchises.

Concluding Observations

Put any group of university leaders in a room, close the door, lower the blinds, and ask them to discuss what really needs to be done to reform college sports. Their candid discussion will not only contain most of the proposals mentioned in this chapter along with many other creative and provocative suggestions but will also reinforce the sense of just how far college football and basketball have drifted from the educational mission of the university. Most will also acknowledge that sports are a major thorn in the side of the university, subjecting their institutions to inappropriate pressures from alumni, the press, and the entertainment industry; destabilizing their governing boards; and occasionally infuriating their faculties.

Yet most presidents also seem resigned to the status quo. They tend to agree with Robert Atwell, former president of the American Council on Education, when he concluded, "I'm not sure this beast can be put back in the cage. The public attachment to big-time intercollegiate football and basketball is so insane that I don't know if it can be done. That's not the NCAA's fault. That's the public's fault."[4]

Can we blame the presidents for their reluctance to beard the lion? The contemporary university presidency is plagued by a serious imbalance between responsibility and authority. Most presidents suffer from a serious overload of activities, responsibilities, and action. Their political capital is very limited. Since in the general scheme of university priorities, intercollegiate athletics today has such a low relevance to the rest of university life, and its problems seem so intractable, few presidents choose to fight a battle where the personal risks are so large and the chances of success seem so remote.

Yet, I believe that if university presidents would take a stand together and call for the de-emphasis of big-time college sports, they would likely be successful. However, I also suspect it will take a major stimulus, a cosmic event, to galvanize such a united front. As college sports career out of control toward the edge of the cliff, perhaps such opportunities will arise in the not-too-distant future.

Chapter 14   Reform or Extinction?

A century of experience does not leave one with great confidence that we can constrain the commercialization and professionalization of college sports. The insatiable interests of the American public in college sports, the vested interests of celebrity coaches and ambitious athletic directors, the powerful commercial forces of the sports media, the entertainment industry, the sports apparel companies, and the professional leagues all appear formidable. Few university leaders, whether presidents or governing boards or faculty leaders, are willing to challenge the status quo by questioning why an educational institution should manage such a commercial entertainment business as big-time college sports in the first place. To be sure, we commission study after study and pass rule after rule in efforts to appear concerned about the abuse and corruption in big-time sports. But we do so within organizations such as the NCAA that are designed primarily to promote and defend big-time sports against reform and de-emphasis. Little wonder that the commercial evolution of the college sports entertainment industry continues. Millionaire coaches, the Final Four, a Division I-A football championship playoff, "Just Do It!" and not-to-worry.

Millions of years ago, the dinosaurs were also thought to be irresistible, rulers of the earth, unchallenged and dominant. Yet we now know that a cosmic event occurred, the impact of a meteor or a comet, that so changed the environment of the planet that within a short time, all of the dinosaurs had disappeared. They became extinct. Is there any possibility for the cosmic extinction of intercollegiate athletics?

Perhaps the Michigan Band has a premonition concerning the future of big-time college football.

Roads to Extinction

A Major Gambling Scandal

College basketball was seriously damaged in the early 1950s by a series of gambling scandals, most notably that at the University of Kentucky. This stimulated, in part, a major effort by the American Council on Education to de-emphasize college sports. Only a concerted effort by the sports press, which had largely ignored the gambling scandals, and a skillful public relations effort by the NCAA were able to head off this reform effort.[1]

Today, things are different. Legalized gambling through state lotteries and casinos has increased enormously, and hence the risks to college athletics. Even the majority of college athletes have been found to gamble on occasion. While many in the sports press would probably continue to downplay the seriousness of gambling, their investigative reporters and editors would certainly go on the attack, as evidenced by the modest gambling scandal at Northwestern in 1997. A major scandal, for instance, one involving several major institutions or fixing a major sporting event such as the NCAA Final Four, would not only trigger an overwhelming reaction by the media but also, in all likelihood, calls for federal legislation to change the very nature of college sports.

The seeds for such corruption are all about us. The rapid growth of state lotteries, the spread of casinos, and the staggering magnitude of the illegal gambling on college sports all raise serious concerns.

An Uprising of the Proletariat Faculty against the Celebrity Coaches

It has always been a wonder to me that college faculties, long concerned and outspoken about their own salaries relative to those of academic administrators, remain relatively passive in the face of the exorbitant compensation of coaches. Today's celebrity football or basketball coach makes several times as much as the highest-paid professor on the campus, and most have a lifestyle to flaunt it. This is sometimes usually portrayed by the coaches and sports press as simply a consequence of their commercial value. Yet, in reality, it reflects the marketing of their sports program and their host institution in a manner that would be quite illegal for faculty and staff because of conflict-of-interest regulations and restrictions on outside activity and compensation.

Perhaps many faculty members are simply not aware of the true compensation levels of coaches, disguised by complex financial reporting arrangements or hidden by the sports press. Few faculty members recognize that in most institutions, where intercollegiate athletics operates at a loss requiring institutional subsidy from tuition revenue or state support, this excessive compensation in effect comes directly out of the salaries of faculty and the financial aid available to students. But the new financial reporting requirements of the NCAA, combined with the ever-increasing use of sunshine laws to pry loose such information from public institutions, make it likely that the excessive compensation and extravagant lifestyles of celebrity coaches will become more commonly known. Sooner or later, the faculty will pick up their hoes and pitchforks and march to the administration building—the *athletics* administration building, that is—to demand "Off with their heads!" in a classical revolution of the proletariat against the elites. Guillotine, guillotine, guillotine!

See You in Court

The courts may some day rule that the NCAA regulations violate the Sherman Antitrust Act of 1890. "The NCAA has gotten away for decades without being scrutinized under the law because the courts have said that college sports is as much about amateurism and education as it is about commercialism. But the more you commercialize what you do, the more you make judges think that the antitrust laws should apply to you."[2]

In 1984 the Supreme Court found that some of the NCAA rules were essential to the conduct of intercollegiate athletics, but that restricting the number of television appearances was not. In 1998, the U.S. court of appeals upheld an antitrust verdict in a class-action suit brought by assistant coaches whose annual wages had been limited to $16,000 (the restricted-earnings coaches). In that case, *Law vs. NCAA*, a U.S. district court ruled that the restriction constituted price-fixing. Later a jury awarded at least nineteen hundred coaches $67 million in damages, which was later settled by the NCAA for an amount of $54.5 million (not including legal costs).[3]

Some note that while the courts have been tolerant of NCAA restrictions on athletes, even the standards on eligibility and amateurism may rest on shaky legal foundations.[4] Those advocating paying student-athletes a stipend usually fail to recognize the substantial legal risk this would entail. Paid student-athletes would likely be entitled to workers' compensation and collective bargaining opportunities if the courts classified them as university employees. The Supreme Court will have plenty of opportunities to take up these issues, because plaintiffs will continue to file suits. The NCAA has so many rules that it provides a fertile field for lawyers to plow for profitable litigation.

Furthermore, college athletics programs continue to be classified as not-for-profit for tax purposes, even though they are involved in commercial activities (in competition with for-profit companies) that generate hundreds of millions of dollars in income each year. Most athletic departments continue to allow expenditures to increase faster than income so that they rarely generate a positive bottom line. But each of their many activities, from football gate receipts to parking revenue to licensing, does operate, in effect, as a for-profit activity. Furthermore, because of their not-for-profit character, contributions to the departments, not simply as gifts but to purchase the rights to premium seats at athletic events, are also tax deductible.

Intercollegiate athletics has long been able to parlay its fundamental principle of amateur competition into special treatment by government. For example, when the current grants-in-aid system was put into place in the 1950s, there was concern that government might classify athletes as employees and make them eligible for protection under laws such as those governing workers' compensation. Universities were able to dodge this by crafting language such as *athletic scholarships, student-athletes,* and *college teams* (rather than the term *clubs* used in the professional leagues).[5] Suppose, however, that intercollegiate athletics drifts so far from the university's educational mission that student-athletes become recognized for what they are: employees of the university's athletic department.

Since higher education has come under increasing pressure from the federal government about the taxation of "unrelated business income," it would not be surprising if there were a gradual erosion of the long-standing protection of intercollegiate athletics as a nonprofit activity. And, in today's increasingly litigious society, sooner or later some student-athlete is going to win a court case to establish his or her status as a university employee—at least as long as athletes are "paid to play" through the current grants-in-aid system—and be granted rights to the full range of employment protections. This would be a major shock to the college athletics enterprise that could well undermine its already fragile financial viability.

Most vulnerable of all is the NCAA's status as a nonprofit educational association (and ditto for many major athletic conferences). Universities have long argued that athletics programs are educational endeavors, and that the donations they receive should be treated with the same tax-exempt status of its academic programs. Thus far, these arguments have been accepted by the courts.

Yet today, with billions of dollars flowing into our athletics programs from television broadcasting, advertising, and merchandising, the tax-exempt status of college sports seems increasingly questionable. How can any commercial sports business that pays its coaches million-dollar salaries, that negotiates agreements with sports apparel companies that require its athletes to wear their equipment, that plasters advertising on every square inch of its stadiums, arenas, and player uniforms, and that licenses and markets its emblems on every product from T-shirts to toilet seats, possibly pretend to be an educational activity? How can boosters claim that the huge sums they pay athletic departments just to have a right to purchase a ticket for premium seat or lease a skybox should be tax-deductible? It shouldn't be, and soon it probably won't be.

Beyond the tax-exempt status of the athletics programs conducted by individual universities, one must also question the similar status given to athletic conferences and the NCAA. After all, the NCAA generates over $270 million a year through aggressively negotiated and highly commercialized broadcasting contracts. It operates with a management culture of corporate-level compensation (currently $690,000 per year for its director) and perquisites (country club memberships, first-class air travel, lucrative housing allowances, and golden parachutes).[6] It even admits to behaving like heavy-hitting business donors and corporate sponsors so that it can relate to them. In reality, the NCAA currently functions not as an educational association but as a professional sports organization like the National Football League or the National Basketball Association, with similar values and objectives, and with a very decidedly for-profit character!

The Pros Devour All of Their Seed Corn

There are few better examples of the shortsighted and irresponsible mind-set of professional sports than the practice in recent years of drafting college athletes long before they have an opportunity to complete their education. To be sure, college athletes have every right to respond to the incredible financial opportunities that professional teams dangle before them. And many college athletes are physically talented enough to contribute to these teams, although they may be very young and emotionally immature. Indeed, in some sports, even high school athletes can be competitive on the field or court.

The luring of underclass athletes prematurely into professional careers is obviously a very short-range strategy both for the students and the professional teams. Few student-athletes have either the emotional or competitive maturity to adapt easily to the professional lifestyle. Although they certainly can earn substantial income and even contribute their athletic talents to professional teams, it is likely that they will have sacrificed not only their educational opportunities but also their professional longevity by leaving college prematurely.

From the viewpoint of professional sports, there are serious financial implications for drafting college players. Professional sports are show business, pure and simple. Profit is determined by star attractions, name players like Michael Jordan or John Elway or Mark McGwire. Yet, increasingly, professional teams are drafting college undergraduates before they have the opportunity to establish name recognition, thereby slowly eroding the market power of the professional enterprise. In a very real sense, professional teams are devouring their seed corn, the next generation of talented athletes, which they need to sustain fan interest and profits.

Baseball provides an excellent case study. College baseball, while providing an enjoyable experience for student-athletes, attracts little fan interest because the professional leagues tend to draft most of the more talented players quite early in their college careers, decimating college teams. Some colleges even try to outguess the pros by recruiting players they believe will contribute but not become so visible that they are lured off by the professional leagues. Ironically, few of the players lured away by the professional draft go immediately into the major leagues. Rather, they are farmed out to minor league teams, which, from a competitive development perspective, are little different from the college teams but, of course, don't provide the opportunity for a college education.

So what is the cosmic extinction scenario? Perhaps the professional leagues will devour so much college talent that they will decimate college sports as a source of talented, market-attractive athletes and destroy their own market appeal or profitability in the process. Surely the owners, managers, coaches, and commissioners couldn't be this shortsighted, and greedy, could they? Remember the buffalo, the abalone, and the whale . . .

Shifting Athletic Interests in the Schools

When I was growing up in a small farm town in central Missouri, we had a choice of only one sport for each season: football for the fall, basketball for the winter, track for the spring, and baseball for the summer. Nothing else. If you wanted to participate in a sport, you played football in the fall, basketball in the winter, track in the spring, and baseball in the summer. Girls were confined to the sideline as cheerleaders or members of the pep squad.

Today the choices are far more varied, and the participation of school-age athletes far more diverse. One finds that the most popular sports for student participation have become the Olympic sports, such as soccer, swimming, and hockey, reflecting world popularity. The uniquely American sports such as football and baseball are declining rapidly in popularity at the grade school level. Just walk around school playgrounds or high school athletic facilities and count the number of boys and girls involved in world sports such as soccer. Or go any weekend to public parks and see what games are being played.

Why is this happening? Beyond global popularity, the world sports are also those that do not require unusual physical attributes beyond athletic ability. Rather, they require speed, stamina, athletic ability, and intelligence—attributes that seem more broadly distributed among the populace than the physical characteristics of an offensive tackle or a power forward.

There is a real possibility that the source of talented athletes for King Football may be drying up. Just imagine a world in the year 2020 when the nation's college football stadiums are reconfigured to accommodate sell-out crowds for soccer—both men's and women's! And football is relegated to a club sport played on the soccer practice field, usually following the weekly rugby match. Impossible, say the ghosts of Fielding Yost and Fritz Crisler. No. Just consider the fate of an earlier king: Tyrannosaurus rex!

Rollerball

Perhaps you remember a science fiction motion picture from years ago, *Rollerball*, starring James Caan, that painted a stark picture of the future of competitive sports. In the dark, *1984*-like future portrayed in this film, international corporations use sports as an opiate for the masses. Competitive sports have evolved into a form, rollerball, that combines aspects of basketball, football, professional wrestling, and roller derby. During the course of the film, the rules are continually changed to make the sport more and more violent and hence more entertaining to the masses. Eventually, the entire enterprise topples under its own weight.

The same could well happen to college sports, or at least to big-time football and basketball. Each year we see new steps taken to enhance the commercial appeal of events, changing rules, reorganizing conferences, creating new playoff schemes such as divisional playoffs or end-of-season tournaments, lengthening seasons and rearranging schedules for the convenience of broadcasters, and so on. Football stadiums and basketball arenas are plastered with more and more advertising and reconfigured for the benefit of the television audience rather than the spectator. And student-athletes are placed under more and more pressure, pulled farther and farther away from their academic programs, and forced to accommodate media demands and compete in excessively long and inconvenient schedules. Just as in *Rollerball*, we seem headed for collapse.

Imagine a future in which commercial interests have been allowed to totally dominate college sports. In their efforts to hype their products, our football stadiums and basketball arenas have become circuslike. They are decorated with garish imitations of university symbols—perhaps the school's fight song ringing the stadium in ten-foot-high letters or gigantic statues of the school mascot—designed to appeal to fan loyalty. The stadium venue is surrounded by vendors hawking every conceivable product, all licensed by and generating profits for the athletic department. Inside the stadium or arena, huge electronic scoreboards loom over the spectators, deluging them with commercial advertising, even as other signage rotates from commercial message to commercial message, all placed at strategic locations to capture the eye of the television cameras, of course.

In this bizarre future, players are required to wear advertising on their uniforms and use only approved equipment from participating sports apparel companies. Even coaches join in the advertising blitz, using their status as million-dollar celebrities to market their own line of sideline fashions. Every game is not only televised, but also narrowcast over the Internet using sophisticated multimedia technology—for a subscription price, of course. Virtual reality Internet sites provide the viewer with the ability to control the viewing experience. And the athletic department maintains a large staff of expensive public relations, media, and technology professionals to make certain this commercial entertainment business has high visibility and market share.

An extreme vision of the brave new world faced by college sports, to be sure. Yet the efforts to commercialize and professionalize intercollegiate athletics have become so blatant and extreme that a *Rollerball* future seems increasingly certain. In fact, some would maintain it has already arrived!

Put another way, the greed and corruption characterizing college sports may soon create an enterprise so revolting in its crass commercialism that the universities come to their senses and cast it aside.

A Call to Sanity

Intercollegiate athletics should be and, indeed, are an important part of higher education. College sports provide an important educational opportunity to student participants. They are important as a unifying force for university communities, on campus and beyond. However, higher education has no obligation to conduct sports in a manner responsive or subservient to armchair America or the minions of sportswriters, entertainment promoters, or athletics apparel executives, particularly if doing so conflicts with the fundamental educational missions of our institutions.

Yet, for over a century, big-time sports (that is, football and

Brave, New World

basketball) have been conducted by universities largely as independent, commercial entertainment enterprises. Many within higher education are aware of the tenuous connection of this particular form of intercollegiate athletics to the educational mission of the university. Many recognize the serious damage that has been caused to higher education not simply by its occasional scandal and corruption, but its very culture of commercialism and hypocrisy. Many have tried over the years to reform big-time college sports, or at least limit its growth and negative impact on the academic mission of colleges and universities.

But the insatiable appetite of the American public for the entertainment provided by college sports, whetted by the self-serving, promotional role of the sports media, have thwarted attempts at reform and de-emphasis. The pervasive influence and commercial opportunity afforded by modern media, from television to the Internet, has driven the expansion and evolution of college sports into a national entertainment industry. And university leaders, presidents and trustees alike, have largely acquiesced, preferring to join in the commercial arms race rather than risk the wrath of the press or the public by attempting true reform.

Yet today higher education is entering an era of extraordinary change. Even the very survival of the university as a social institution is being called into question because of its increasing difficulty in meeting the needs of a knowledge-driven society. This time of great change, of shifting paradigms, provides a context and a rationale for once again examining the proper role and character of all university activities, including intercollegiate athletics.

We are obliged to ask the difficult question of whether it makes sense for the twenty-first-century university to conduct commercial activities at the current level of big-time football and basketball. Is there any logical reason for an academic institution, with the fundamental mission of teaching and scholarship, to mount and sustain a professional and commercial enterprise simply to satisfy the public desire for entertainment, and the commercial goals of the marketplace? Why should the university squander its resources, distract its leadership, and erode its most fundamental values and integrity with these commercial activities, particularly at a time when it will face so many other challenges in responding to the changing educational needs of our society?

The answers are obvious. We have no business being in the entertainment business. We must either reform and restructure intercollegiate athletics on terms congruent with the educational purpose of our institutions, or spin big-time football and basketball off as independent, professional, and commercial enterprises no longer related to higher education.

Clearly my first preference would be to restructure, de-emphasize, and retain intercollegiate athletics on our terms. We need to decouple college sports from the entertainment industry and reconnect it with the educational mission of our institutions. In this regard, we must bear in mind that the focus of our reform efforts should be on those two sports where most of the problems arise—and, ironically, the two sports that were originally spawned on our campuses—football and basketball. While the many other varsity sports conducted by our universities face challenges, they pale in comparison with the two highly visible "revenue" sports that have been taken over by those who pander to armchair America.

Here, the key to the control of intercollegiate athletics and to proper alignment with the academic values and priorities of the institution will be the effort of universities to resist the pressures to transform college sports into an entertainment industry. The academy simply must recapture control of college sports from those who promote them for their own financial gain: the media, the entertainment industry, and even the coaches and athletic directors themselves.

Clearly this will not be easy, as a century of ill-fated efforts to de-emphasize and reform college sports so clearly indicates. Those who benefit most from big-time college sports as an entertainment industry, the celebrity coaches and athletic directors, the sport media and the networks, the sports apparel industry and the advertisers, will defend the status quo to the hilt. So too will those millions of fans and boosters resist change who see the American university only as a source of entertainment on Saturday afternoons in the fall. But the forces of change in our society are powerful, and they are reshaping all of our institutions—our corporations, our governments, our universities, even our nation-states. This unique period of change for higher education may provide an unusual opportunity to reform college sports, to reconnect it with our mission as educators.

If we are unable to do this, we must then insist that society respect our roles as educational institutions and allow us to spin off big-time college sports to more appropriate venues. Minor league baseball and hockey franchises have long provided opportunities for young, aspiring athletes to develop their skills while entertaining the public. There is no reason why similar leagues could not be created in football and basketball, allowing those athletes and coaches interested in participating in professional athletics to do so, and allowing our campuses to reintroduce de-emphasized versions of these sports back into our existing portfolios of intercollegiate sports programs. Certainly there would be some cost associated with spinning off these programs, particularly in the sense that the revenue from big-time football and basketball would no longer be available to subsidize our other varsity programs. But these costs are a small price to pay to refocus our attention on our core mission of education and restore our integrity as academic institutions.

As we enter a new century of intercollegiate athletics in America, it is essential for universities to establish their own priorities, objectives, and principles for college sports. Higher education must then commit itself to holding fast to these objectives in the face of the enormous pressure exerted by the media and the public at large. In the end, college athletics must reflect the fundamental academic values of the university. There is no acceptable alternative if we are to retain our academic values and integrity while serving the very real and rapidly growing educational needs of our society.

Notes

Chapter 1

1. Rick Telander, *The Hundred-Yard Lie: The Corruption of College Football and What We Can Do to Stop It* (New York: Simon and Schuster, 1989), 24.
2. William C. Friday and Theodore M. Hesburgh, *Report of the Knight Foundation Commission on Intercollegiate Athletics, March 1991–March 1993* (Miami: John S. and James L. Knight Foundation, 1993), 8.
3. Murray Sperber, *College Sports, Inc.* (New York: Henry Holt, 1990).

Chapter 2

1. This was also when my wife and I first arrived in Ann Arbor.
2. The strategy of using special student fees to finance athletic facilities that the students would later have to purchase tickets to attend is a time-honored practice in intercollegiate athletics. It is but one example of the sleight of hand used to disguise the institutional subsidy of varsity sports.
3. Many others simply observed that only at Michigan would a basketball arena be named after a former football coach, Fritz Crisler. In fact, the hockey arena is also named after a Michigan football coach, Fielding Yost.
4. Bo Schembechler and Mitch Albom, *Bo* (New York: Warner Books, 1989).
5. Murray Sperber, *College Sports, Inc.* (New York: Henry Holt, 1990).
6. Mitch Albom, *Fab Five* (New York: Warner Books, 1993).
7. Someday Michigan hopes to do the same for men, but the accounting system used to measure gender participation will not allow it as long as king football continues to suit up one hundred players a game. But more on this in a later chapter.

Chapter 4

1. Murray Sperber, *Onward to Victory: The Crises That Shaped College Sports* (New York: Henry Holt, 1998).
2. Andrew D. White, in Ronald A. Smith, *Sports and Freedom: The Rise of Big-Time College Athletics* (New York: Oxford University Press, 1990), 74.
3. Quoted in Walter Byers with Charles Hammer, *Unsportsmanlike Conduct:*

Exploiting College Athletes (Ann Arbor: University of Michigan Press, 1995), 40.

4. Murray, Sperber, "In Praise of Student Athletes: The NCAA Is Haunted by Its Past," *Chronicle of Higher Education,* January 8, 1999, p. A76.
5. Carnegie Foundation report, in Sperber, *Onward to Victory,* 30.
6. Robert Hutchens, in Sperber, *Onward to Victory,* 37.
7. American Council on Education and Sanity Code, in Sperber, *Onward to Victory,* 363–68.
8. Murray Sperber, *Shake Down the Thunder: The Creation of Notre Dame Football* (New York: Henry Holt, 1993).
9. Murray Sperber, *College Sports, Inc.* (New York: Henry Holt, 1990), xi.
10. The site devoted to Michigan athletics is <http://www.mgoblue.com>.

Chapter 5

1. John Henry Newman, *The Idea of a University* (New Haven: Yale University Press, 1996); Jacques Barzun, *The American University* (Chicago: University of Chicago Press, 1968).
2. John Immerwahr, *The Price of Admission: The Growing Importance of Higher Education* (Washington, D.C.: National Center for Public Policy and Higher Education, spring 1998).
3. Joseph L. Dionne and Thomas Kean, *Breaking the Social Contract: The Fiscal Crisis in Higher Education,* Report of the Commission on National Investment in Higher Education (New York: Council for Aid to Education, 1997).
4. David W. Breneman, Joni E. Finney, and Brian M. Roherty, *Shaping the Future: Higher Education Finance in the 1990s* (California Higher Education Policy Center, April 1997).
5. Cyril O. Houle, *Governing Boards* (San Francisco: Jossey-Bass, 1989).
6. Clark Kerr and Marian L. Grade, *The Guardians: Boards of Trustees of American Colleges and Universities: What They Do and How Well They Do It* (Washington, D.C.: Association of Governing Boards, 1989).
7. Clark Kerr and Marian L. Grade, *The Guardians.*
8. Donald Kennedy, "Another Century's End, Another Revolution for Higher Education," *Change,* May/June (1995), 8–15.
9. "Renewing the Academic Presidency: Stronger Leadership for Tougher Times," *Report of the Commission on the Academic Presidency* (Washington, D.C.: Association of Governing Boards of Universities and Colleges, 1996), 9.
10. William C. Friday and Theodore M. Hesburgh, *Report of the Knight Foundation Commission on Intercollegiate Athletics, March 1991–March 1993* (Miami: John S. and James L. Knight Foundation, 1993), 5.

Chapter 6

1. Walter Byers with Charles Hammer, *Unsportsmanlike Conduct: Exploiting College Athletes* (Ann Arbor: University of Michigan Press, 1995).
2. Big Ten BICIA, in Murray Sperber, *Onward to Victory: The Crises That Shaped College Sports* (New York: Henry Holt, 1998).
3. Sperber, *Onward to Victory,* 174.
4. Mike McGraw, Steven Rock, and Karen Dillon, "Money Games: Inside the NCAA," *Kansas City Star,* October 5–10, 1997.
5. Byers, *Unsportsmanlike Conduct,* 2.
6. Peter T. Flawn, *A Primer for University Presidents: Managing the Modern University* (Austin: University of Texas Press, 1990), 157.

Chapter 7

1. Murray Sperber, *College Sports, Inc.* (New York: Henry Holt, 1990).
2. Walter Byers with Charles Hammer, *Unsportsmanlike Conduct: Exploiting College Athletes* (Ann Arbor: University of Michigan Press, 1995).
3. Welch Suggs, "Graduation Rates Hit Lowest Levels in Seven Years for Athletes in Football and Basketball," *Chronicle of Higher Education,* September 10, 1999, A57–A62.
4. William C. Dowling, "To Cleanse Colleges of Sports Corruption, End Recruiting Based on Physical Skills" *Chronicle of Higher Education,* July 9, 1999, B9.
5. Richard G. Sheehan, *Keeping Score: The Economics of Big Time Sports* (New York: Diamond Communications, 1996), chaps. 11, 12.
6. Mike McGraw, Steven Rock, and Karen Dillon, "Money Games: Inside the NCAA," *Kansas City Star,* October 5, 1997.
7. Barnet D. Wolf, "OSU Sports Get Down to Business," *Columbus Dispatch,* December 10, 1998.
8. Athletic Operations Survey, 1993–94, Big Ten Conference, Chicago, 1994.
9. Sperber, *College Sports, Inc.*
10. One of the editors of this manuscript made an interesting observation about these numbers. Since only about 100 of the 700 varsity athletes receiving financial aid at Michigan are associated with the football and basketball programs, these revenue sports are providing roughly $6 million per year to provide financial aid for the 600 student-athletes in non-revenue sports such as swimming, golf, and tennis. While this generosity is laudable from one perspective, the fact that athletic scholarships are physical-skill-based rather than need-based raises another issue. Sports like tennis, gymnastics, swimming, and field hockey are primarily played by white, relatively affluent athletes, while football and basketball involve predominantly low-income black athletes. The current system of

skill-based rather than need-based financial aid in intercollegiate athletics has the perverse effect of asking those who are economically less fortunate to support the education of those student-athletes whose affluent backgrounds have enabled them to excel in the "country club" sports.

Chapter 8

1. Harvey Araton, "BizBall," *New York Times Sunday Magazine,* October 18, 1998, 59–64.
2. Ted Gup, "Losses Surpass Victories, by Far, in Big-Time College Sports," *Chronicle of Higher Education,* December 18, 1998, A57.
3. Murray Sperber, *College Sports, Inc.* (New York: Henry Holt, 1990).
4. The University of Michigan states quite specifically that its conflict-of-interest policy "does not apply to Athletic Department coaches and staff," but then goes on to explain that "it does provide guidelines to aid in evaluating and approving outside employment for Department personnel." But of course, no other faculty and staff have the benefit of such "guidelines."
5. William C. Friday and Theodore M. Hesburgh, *Report of the Knight Foundation Commission on Intercollegiate Athletics, March 1991–March 1993* (Miami: John S. and James L. Knight Foundation, 1993), 6.
6. NCAA Committee on Coaches Compensation, in Sperber, *College Sports, Inc.,* 380.
7. Mike McGraw, Steven Rock, and Karen Dillon, "Money Games: Inside the NCAA," *Kansas City Star,* October 6, 1997.
8. Richard G. Sheehan, *Keeping Score,* chap. 11.
9. I told our athletics director that there was no way I would ever let the team go to the Poulon Weedeater Bowl, just on general principles!
10. Murray Sperber, *Onward to Victory: The Crises That Shaped College Sports* (New York: Henry Holt, 1998).
11. Kim Clarke, News and Information Office, University of Michigan, November, 1988.
12. The one exception here is the "color commentator," the old coach or former player, who milks a bit more out of his fame on the field by joining a broadcasting team.
13. John Underwood, "Student-Athletes: The Sham, The Shame," *Sports Illustrated,* May 19, 1980, 36–72; Jerry Kirshenbaum, "An American Disgrace," February 27, 1989.
14. Mike McGraw, Steven Rock, and Karen Dillon, "Money Games: Inside the NCAA," *Kansas City Star,* October 5–10, 1997.
15. Sperber, *Onward to Victory.*
16. McGraw, Rock, and Dillon, "Money Games," October 5, 1997.
17. Mitch Albom, *Fab Five* (New York: Warner Books, 1993).

Chapter 9

1. Murray Sperber, "In Praise of 'Student-Athletes': The NCAA Is Haunted by Its Past," *Chronicle of Higher Education,* January 8, 1999, A76.
2. David Goldfield, "Weaker NCAA Standards Won't Help Black Athletes," *Chronicle of Higher Education,* April 9, 1999, A64.
3. Goldfield, "Weaker NCAA Standards," A64.
4. Here we need to be careful about leaping to conclusions about the role a particular program plays as a home for at-risk athletes. For example, Michigan has a very large and diverse student body (twenty-two thousand undergraduates), and Admissions can use a number of measures to determine eligibility. The Department of Kinesiology, which evolved out of the old physical education program in the School of Education into an independent unit of the university, used to admit many academically at-risk athletes. As I will discuss later in this chapter, Kinesiology is now among the more competitive units to gain admission to—significantly more difficult than engineering for nonrecruited student-athletes. Furthermore, admissions problems are not unique to athletics. The university has a top-ranked music school that depends on recruiting very talented musicians who may not always have comparable academic skills. It is not unusual for music faculty and staff, just like coaches, to lobby for the admission of highly talented, yet academically at-risk musicians.
5. Grants-in-aid, in Walter Byers with Charles Hammer, *Unsportsmanlike Conduct: Exploiting College Athletes* (Ann Arbor: University of Michigan Press, 1995).
6. Karla Haworth, "Graduation Rates for Athletes Fall," *Chronicle of Higher Education,* November 20, 1998, A41.
7. *Chronicle of Higher Education,* July 25, 1997, A43–A44. Welch Suggs, "Graduation Rates Hit Lowest Levels in Seven Years for Athletes in Football and Basketball," *Chronicle of Higher Education,* September 10, 1999, A57–A62.
8. Welch Suggs, "More Women Participate in Intercollegiate Athletics," *Chronicle of Higher Education,* May 21, 1999.
9. Murray Sperber, *Onward to Victory: The Crises That Shaped College Sports* (New York: Henry Holt, 1998).
10. Matina Horner, "Sex Differences in Achievement Motivation and Performance in Competitive and Non-Competitive Situations," Ph.D. diss., University of Michigan, 1968.
11. 1999–2000 Almanac, *Chronicle of Higher Education,* Ben Gose, "College Officials Gather to Discuss a Species in Decline: the Male Student," September, 1999; *Chronicle of Higher Education,* November 18, 1999.

12. Ted Gup, "Losses Surpass Victories, by Far, in Big-Time College Sports," *Chronicle of Higher Education,* December 18, 1998, A52.

Chapter 10

1. Murray Sperber, "In Praise of 'Student-Athletes": The NCAA Is Haunted by Its Past," *Chronicle of Higher Education,* January 8, 1999, A76.
2. William C. Friday and Theodore M. Hesburgh, *Report of the Knight Foundation Commission on Intercollegiate Athletics, March 1991–March 1993* (Miami: John S. and James L. Knight Foundation, 1993), 30–32.

Chapter 11

1. Walter Byers with Charles Hammer, *Unsportsmanlike Conduct: Exploiting College Athletes* (Ann Arbor: University of Michigan Press, 1995).
2. Byers, *Unsportsmanlike Conduct,* 37–38.
3. William C. Friday and Theodore M. Hesburgh, *Report of the Knight Foundation Commission on Intercollegiate Athletics, March 1991–March 1993* (Maine: John S. And James L. Knight Foundation, 1993), 12–14.
4. Clark Kerr and Marian L. Grade, *The Guardians: Boards of Trustees of American Colleges and Universities* (Washington, D.C.: Association of Governing Boards of Universities and Colleges, 1989).
5. Barnet D. Wolf, "OSU Sports Get Down to Business," *Columbus Dispatch,* December 10, 1998.
6. Murray Sperber, *Onward to Victory: The Crises That Shaped College Sports* (New York: Henry Holt, 1998), 30.
7. Sperber, *Onward to Victory.*
8. William C. Friday and Theodore M. Hesburgh, *Report of the Knight Foundation Commission on Intercollegiate Athletics, March 1991–March 1993* (Miami: John S. and James L. Knight Foundation, 1993).
9. Sperber, *Onward to Victory;* Byers, *Unsportsmanlike Conduct.*

Chapter 12

1. Murray Sperber, *Onward to Victory; The Crises That Shaped College Sports* (New York: Henry Holt, 1998).

Chapter 13

1. Walter Byers, with Charles Hammer, *Unsportsmanlike Conduct: Exploiting College Athletes* (Ann Arbor: University of Michigan Press, 1995).
2. Rick Telander, *The Hundred Yard Lie: The Corruption of College Football and What We Can Do to Stop It* (New York: Simon and Schuster, 1989).
3. Proposal in Byers, *Unsportsmanlike Conduct.*
4. Mike McGraw, Steven Rock, and Karen Dillon, "Money Games: Inside the NCAA," *Kansas City Star,* October 5, 1997.

Chapter 14

1. Murray Sperber, *Onward to Victory; The Crises That Shaped College Sports* (New York: Henry Holt, 1998).
2. Jim Naughton, "Antitrust Suits Could Poke Holes in NCAA's Rule Book, Some Predict," *Chronicle of Higher Education,* June 19, 1998, A45.
3. Naughton, "Antitrust Suits," A45.
4. Murray Sperber, "In Praise of 'Student-Athletes': The NCAA Is Haunted by Its Past," *Chronicle of Higher Education,* January 8, 1999, A76.
5. Murray Sperber, *College Sports, Inc.* (New York: Henry Holt, 1990).
6. Mike McGraw, Steven Rock, and Karen Dillon, "Money Games: Inside the NCAA" *Kansas City Star,* 1997, October 5–10, 1997.

Index